Clockwise beginning upper right:

1 - The Lighthouse in Alexandria, Egypt,
one of the seven wonders of the ancient world.

2 - The Statue of Liberty, New York, New York.

3 - Salvo Palace in the Plaza Independencia,
the most important plaza in Montevideo, Uruguay.

4 - The Coliseum in Rome, Italy.

# TWO LIVES
## ON FOUR CONTINENTS
A DOUBLE MEMOIR

*For Nahrim,*
*With much admiration*
*Mary Tonetti Dorra*

# TWO LIVES
## ON FOUR CONTINENTS
### A DOUBLE MEMOIR

Mary Tonetti Dorra

For Sylvie McKee and Henry Lawrence Casher,
my grandchildren, so that they will understand a little more
about those who came before them.

"…no treasure-house of Atreus was ever as rich
as a well-stored memory."

—EDITH WHARTON

Clement Dorra with Henri.

# I
# Alexandria, Egypt
## THE GOOD LIFE OF MY EARLY YEARS

"CLEMENT," HE SAID *with a smile, looking me in the eye as he settled into the comfortable chair behind his desk. I could see the pillows softening behind him when his back reached the chair.*

*"My wife, Emilie, and I are planning to give a first rate hospital to the city of Alexandria and we need a good surgeon to be in charge. We both think you are the one for the job." His voice was soft, but authoritative, and I, like everyone else who came in contact with him, respected that self-confidence. I not only admired him but also liked him. The picture behind his desk was a Corot landscape I happened to notice.*

*Struggling to catch my breath, I could hardly keep from smiling when I finally answered him. "Of course, that would be a great honor, Mr. Castro, and I thank you for considering me."*

*He hesitated before continuing. "Although we are Jews we do not want our hospital, which will be named the Hotel Israelite, to be exclusively for the Sephardic Jews in Alexandria. It will be a hospital for all people, including those of us in the foreign community of Alexandria. Do you understand me?" His slim fingers curled around his small, neatly trimmed moustache as he spoke. "It will be primarily for our 'International Community' here in Alexandria but anyone —including the Muslims can come if they so desire."*

*"Yes, Sir." I began, but before I could continue he interrupted.*

*"There is one hitch, as they say in England." He cleared his throat and began in a lowered voice. "That is…if you marry our daughter Aimée. She is 17 now, and we know that you two are in the same circle of friends and share many interests."*

*"We are, and I think it would be an honor to be Aimée's husband and to be the head surgeon of your clinic…" I was bursting with pride and pleasure and could hardly wait to see Aimée.*

Later, when I was about to begin a new career in New York, this conversation—between my father, Clement Dorra, and his soon-to-be father-in-law, would be quoted to me verbatim. My father remembered it in every detail. He apparently felt he had to explain their "arranged marriage situation," and I saw his difficulty in beginning what was clearly hard for him to say. "I respected your mother and even, I suppose, loved her in a certain way although it was not in the way that most people think of love as we know it today." He continued, "You should know, my son, that Egypt was a very different place in those days. We had a very different, highly charged, energetic, way of living."

My memories of that good life in Alexandria often came unexpectedly: the boardwalk and the many promenades my father and I had together along the beach with its beautiful golden sand and the sailboats in the distance. He always took me for a walk on the beach when he had something serious to say. But now, as my father delivered the news to me about his arranged marriage, there was no sandy beach, no playful boxing of my ears and no lightening of tone with gentle laughter as he usually did when I was a boy. We were sitting at the dimly lit bar of the Algonquin Hotel in 1946 on a rainy gray day in New York, which appropriately matched the sadness that crept over me as he began what he called, his "explanation." His dour expression was an anomaly to me and his everpresent smile had disappeared.

The news shouldn't have been a shock or even a surprise to me given their estrangement over the years. As he spoke, I remembered the wave of sadness that would suddenly cover Maman's face, replacing her otherwise lively expression, and I couldn't help noticing at those times that her responses to my father were rather distant. It was as if she had no interest in what he was explaining and that whatever he said didn't matter to her. On numerous occasions, those close to her in the household observed her palpable impatience with him, which she made no effort to hide.

Yet I knew they enjoyed each other's company when they went out together in the evening. Despite that, my father was more of a social creature than my mother. He believed in hard work but also insisted on having a good time in the evenings, even if it meant going out alone and explaining Maman's absence with a headache or some other malaise. He was often "away on business."

Consequently, due to these frequent absences it was my mother who lit up my life. She and Grandmother Castro insisted, "nothing was too good for 'le petit.' "Why shouldn't he have another pain de chocolat if he wants." I smiled when I remembered how she indulged my every whim. Sometimes Maman and Papa were both away and my asthma attacks seemed to have no end, with each breath becoming tighter, shorter, and more painful. Often, these would arrive during the full-moon, with whirling dervishes—members of a primitivist Muslim sect—would practice their art before delirious audiences. They would turn like tops to the rhythms of tom-toms so as to induce a frenzy intended to bring about holy exaltation, all the while egged on by the screams of the spectators. It went on for hours, ever louder, ever more threatening. For every one of my labored breaths, there were six, then seven, eight…tom-tom beats. The rhythm of my breathing and that of the drumming intertwined, creating an infernal music inside and around me. The twirling and the drumbeats, mother had said, were nothing but an expression of superstition, of the forces of darkness, of anger, of resentment against progress and enlightenment, of hatred also, for the "impure" such as we Jews were. The drumbeats seemed to threaten our future just as the asthma was challenging my breathing. I wondered later in life whether children had made similar associations unconsciously linking personal suffering and hostile social forces, and possibly cause Jews and others like them to look a little sad much of the time. But then, I also realized such irrational associations are the recipes of superstition.

Our daily luncheon table in Alexandria, whether Papa was there or not, was always a treat for me. I enjoyed not only the delicacies of our French chef who had come straight from Paris but also the conversations of the adults, which were always lively. I sat quietly listening to whatever was said by those family members and occasional guests, all of whom had strong opinions and who enjoyed expressing themselves. Everyone, that is, except me. I sat quietly as I was instructed to do, and at times the adults seemed to have forgotten that I was there. I heard everything, like the scandals at the Houseboat—their very exclusive club where their Bloomsbury-like crowd gathered for gossip— as long as it was only mildly malicious. Things told in confidence remained secret; others, meant to be disseminated, were rapidly broadcast around town. And when scandal hit one of them, as it did when Madame X was found to be sleeping with her husband's boss, the others made a common front to deflect or overcome it as best they could. It was, in other words, an ideal association of friends, loyal and affectionate towards one another and dedicated to the enjoyment of each other's company. Until things soured, which they inevitably did, that is. I must admit that those stories of the Houseboat crowd interested me as much as their conversations about Voltaire, and the endless pros and cons of being a citizen of the world as opposed to being a Christian or a Jew.

When Papa explained to me that day in New York what marriage meant to both of them, unconventional as it seemed, I began to understand them both for the first time. I thought back on the wonderful times the three of us spent together when everyone was happy. Once, as a joyous surprise, they came to pick me up at my school in Switzerland, and finally happy arriving in France we drove along the Riviera and on to Paris, stopping for a memorable meal at Avalon. Strong memories of Paris came back of their taking me, an eleven year old, to the Louvre to introduce me to their favorite paintings, the times when they took me for an evening boat ride on the Seine, a climb up the towers of Notre Dame in honor of Victor Hugo's Hunchback, and a descent into the Paris sewers in honor of Jean Valjean. Maman's enthusiasm for Chopin was so contagious that the sounds of those piano concerts devoted to Chopin will always be with me. I was even taken along to the Parisian couturiers for mother's biannual shopping sprees. I loved seeing those beautiful gowns by Worth and Poiret which she would wear in Alexandria at the most important balls and dinners. When I didn't understand the simplicity of Chanel's elegant little black dress she explained that often the most beautiful things in life were also the simplest. I have treasured those fragments of my childhood memories particularly when I worked dismally during the war at the factory in Rugby and was at the same time studying for my degree in Engineering at night school.

Looking out from the Algonquin bar at the rainy streets of New York, the waiter appeared to ask if we would like another aperitif or a whisky. We had already had two each, so Papa waved him away and continued, "Marriage for both of us was sacred, and while love was not essential, affection and sustained mutual respect were. Your mother and her friends in Alexandria all believed that there must be an almost absolute guarantee of one's spouse's privacy. And she loved her own privacy above all else, I believe."

"And she gave you freedom along with your privacy, didn't she?" I ventured to say as I took the last sip of my Cinzano.

He looked at me with his eyebrows raised in a quizzical manner, wondering, I supposed, how I knew that, and where that question would take the conversation.

"Yes. She did, and it wasn't until lately that I realized how much she gave me and how much I valued her, even loved her in a very unique way. There was always respect but love, as the poets describe it, was something we didn't consider."

"You didn't consider?"

"In those days we all believed in total amorous freedom short of causing a scandal which was to be avoided at all costs. Indeed, the fear of scandal ranked higher than any other moral or religious consideration, you know."

Years earlier, when Maman and I were in England during the war and

Father was already in New York I remarked, in one of our many reminiscing conversations, that they had been separated so much of their married life. She replied "Yes. Your father and I believe we are both happier when we are apart, and yet, divorce is unthinkable. But there are worldly ways of coping with incompatibility."

After insistent questioning on my part, I remember her referring to a happily married couple I knew that lived in separate, but adjoining, quarters. She seemed to want to close the conversation by adding, "For the children, two welcoming homes are better than none!"

I understood what she meant, although at the time the comparison to our own lives did not seem relevant. Whenever Father appeared it was a joyful occasion for us both, but as far as my young life was concerned, I didn't have a second welcoming home, and I felt very much his absence.

Father looked at his watch and we both realized it was time to meet Maman at the Plaza for lunch. He touched my elbow and concluded the conversation with his usual cheery tone; "Perhaps it is living in the new world that has caused us to understand how differently we feel about each other today. We seem to have left those old views behind us in Egypt and in France." His smile reappeared, and it had suddenly stopped raining.

I LOVED IT WHEN MAMAN asked me to come and chat with her before she went out in the evening. I can still smell the *Vol de Nuit* perfume she wore, a scent I have always identified with the good life of Alexandria. The glorious parties with superb French food that Maman designed for their friends was only one example of that good life shared by the international set in Alexandria in those days. Full orchestras played at the balls and all the ladies wore stunning French clothes purchased for the big galas. They all traveled to Paris and the Riviera during the stunning summer heat waves. The Egyptian servants took pride in the way they took care of the family and our every need.

But there were ominous political rumblings in the backdrop of the good life in Alexandria, which I occasionally saw manifested in the street riots from my window. I had to stay indoors when they occurred, but there was one every few weeks. They would start as huge student-led processions screaming their way through the city's main arteries. From time to time, there were clashes with the police, and deaths. The rioters were asking for the departure of foreigners—meaning primarily the British troops stationed at various points in the country, and occasionally for that of the TurcoAlbanian ruling family. There were also calls for the expulsion of foreign "leeches." We Dorras were among "the leeches." Mother would tell even casual acquaintances that she was much happier in Paris than in Egypt. She would not mind, she explained, living quite simply there, as long as she could become a concert pianist and go to concerts and theatre every night.

My schooling had been a little chaotic. I had started out in a kindergarten run by Italian nuns, was then sent to the *Lycée Francais*, then to the *Lycée de l'Union Juive*, which had recently been founded under the aegis of the Jewish Community by friends and relatives who believed that a school that would be independent from Christian religious orders and the French Mission should be open to all qualified students. It provided classes all the way to the French baccalaureate. Except for the inevitable bitter one, my teachers, mostly women, were entertaining, voluble, and enormously serious when it came to conveying knowledge. I loved my studies.

These were interrupted late in 1932, when I was eight, at a time when my asthma had become unbearable. Professor Vallery-Radot-Pasteur was consulted that summer. I had to leave the city and breathe good air, he determined. I immediately saw the sun-lit beaches of Juan-les-Pins in my inner eye, and made a plea for the seashore, but Pasteur's grandson frowned, stared at me, and said with finality, "For the chest, we recommend mountain air."

I was sent to a home for less-than-healthy children at Villars-de-Lans in the French Alps. However, mountain flowers, it has since been established, release particularly noxious allergens, and I was mostly ill there.

The home was a large chalet; there were around thirty pupils. We would be taken on long walks twice a day, except in the thick of winter when we skied and skated. We had three hours of classes a day, under the recently retired schoolmistress who was a lady with sculpted wrinkles who taught long division and the rules of spelling, made us memorize irregular verbs and explained the subtleties of the conditional and the subjunctive—all with skill and enthusiasm. During my stints in the infirmary, I usually shared a room with a mostly older student who was only too pleased to have a companion and would talk to me for hours on end. And I was often considered safe enough to share a room with girls, who confided in me as if I were a long-lost friend.

The following year was spent at a much bigger, more luxurious and more expensive children's home which was supposed to offer a much better educational program, at Villars-sur-Ollon in Switzerland. The regimen was about the same, but my various classes were taught by the same cadaveric, sad-eyed, ever-haughty, greying man wearing rimless glasses and sporting a crew-cut, who solemnly reeled off rules without any concern for his listeners. We would pass notes covered with crude drawings as well as chocolate bars and nougat from bench to bench to while away the time. Even my stays in the infirmary were disappointing, as the patients had single rooms for the sake of hygiene. My only joy there was hearing the soundtracks of movies being screened in the adjoining auditorium. There were excellent sports facilities, and on my good days, I played soccer and ice hockey and in the winter skied and skated—all sports I came to love.

And on many good days, I trudged along on our daily walk, behind my classmates and the sad teacher, short of breath and with blistered feet. We would first follow the main road, then climb along mountain paths towards some bleak, rock-strewn pasture above the tree-line, and then trudge back. I was longingly dreaming all the while of a black Opel convertible with a red stripe and a red leather interior that Mother once said she would buy, in which I would sink comfortably as she would drive me away for good, mildly inebriated by a whiff of *Vol de Nuit*. The instructor, I learned later, succumbed to a platonic love and hung himself a couple of years later.

Back in Egypt, in the fall of 1934, I returned to the *Lycée de l'Union Juive*, glad to find my old friends and its lively classes. On one occasion, Monsieur Petitot, the headmaster, entered the classroom accompanied by two assistants who carried a phonograph and a record album. There was to be a lesson of music appreciation—the first ever at the school, and the last. He played Beethoven's Pastoral Symphony, briefly interrupting the performance now and then to point out the programmatic elements: birds, the rustling of a stream, a rustic dance, a storm, serene nature after the storm. It was the best a literary man with little ear for music could do, I later learned. I liked the music, and was delighted by the descriptions, and that evening I enthusiastically reported the event to Maman who was in the petit salon having a drink with her ever-kindly but somewhat hermetic cousin Victor. They burst out laughing. It was all the idea of Marthe Naggar, their relative, the mother of my classmate and friend Simon and a member of the Community's School Board, they exclaimed. Marthe had been preaching newfangled ideas on education, and particularly the teaching of the arts in the schools. Under her purview, however, it was nothing but a blue-stocking, and she had gone too far, they said. As for that poor Petitot, he was a wonderful headmaster, but all he understood about music was the program in programmatic pieces.

Maman and Victor, in a bid to outdo Marthe and Petitot, took charge of my own music education. Almost every evening for a few weeks the three of us listened to recordings of chamber music, starting with Beethoven's Kreutzer Sonata. I had to recognize the various movements, and within them the principal and secondary themes and their variants, and be able to whistle them all. Whenever I succeeded, Victor's flabby, sun-reddened cheeks would tremble slightly, his usually sad blue eyes would twinkle with joy, and a baritone laugh would shake his ample paunch. I also had to specify when the violin and when the piano led and when they had equal weight. And I learned to distinguish various harmonies and rhythmic patterns.

I also had to articulate the feelings the music aroused in me. Never mind the birds, streams, storms and peasant dances. I was to avoid references to material imagery; music existed in an abstract realm, and I was to remain in that realm. Words, even in song, only reinforced in their own way, the feelings expressed by the music- and this, Maman added, applied to literature. One can do only so much with words and descriptions. They serve an intellectual purpose, yet are but supports for the poetic meaning, which is communicated indirectly by sounds and rhythms. Indeed, Maman and Victor had been thoroughly molded by the aesthetics of the Symbolist movement in their youth and beyond, developing my taste for music, they unknowingly gave me a baptism in the theories of that movement in literature and the plastic arts—a movement to the study of which I was to devote many years of my professional life. Even more importantly, I now realize Victor was conveying to me in those few and brief moments of intimacy the warmth and attention Father was only able to give me much later.

In order to make up for lost study time, a private tutor, Mademoiselle Ben-Amon, came to the house for two hours every weekday evening. And, since I had never had any course in Arabic, another tutor, Monsieur They Saidenberg, came for one hour a day for an intensive program in that language, also throwing in a little Hebrew. They were products of the *Lycée de l'Union* and the *Lycée Francais* respectively, and both owed much to the social philosophy of the French educational establishment.

In 1935 there was a shift in the tiller in my education. On the one hand, the level of performance of the Egyptian public schools and universities was rapidly rising. On the other, Muslim families were becoming increasingly active and powerful in government, business, finance, the law and medicine. One day, Father and Mother came to my room with a new plan. From now on, I would have to blend into the Egyptian landscape; that meant learning to speak Arabic perfectly, being well-versed in Islamic culture, making Egyptian friends and obtaining professional degrees that would qualify me for both an Egyptian and a European career. In order to be in every way the equal of future Egyptian colleagues, I would have to attend Egyptian schools, and study at the same time with tutors at home to prepare for the French baccalaureate. It would be strenuous work but I trusted that whatever they decided was for the best. Putting me immediately into an Egyptian public school might have turned out to be too harsh, so therefore my parents decided to send me to a private school run by another minority group, The Christian Copts. They had resisted conversion to Islam over some thirteen centuries. Often mistreated by Muslim rulers and the people, they had nevertheless maintained dedication to education which in some ways paralleled the Jews. As a group they tended to be sophisticated and benevolent.

From then on, Monsieur Saidenberg would continue to teach me the necessary mathematics and science to keep up with the French system. Mademoiselle Ben-Amon was to be in charge of French, literature, history and geography as well as to promote her firm belief in hard work and strict discipline as the only way to succeed in life. A native, Wahib Effendi, helped me perfect my Arabic. An old Rabbi, furthermore, came every Sunday morning to prepare me to read prayers in Hebrew for the Tefelim (Sephardic equivalent for Bar-Mitzvah), for Father believed I should go through the religious rites of passage in case I should ever want to become a devout Jew. I was able to persuade the Rabbi to dictate the Hebrew prayers and I wrote them down phonetically in French on sheets I pinned over the book's pages for the ceremony. When Father discovered my stratagem he ushered the Rabbi to the door. "As for you," he told me, "don't you ever try to cheat God! Either you read the prayers in Hebrew or there will be no Tefelim."

"No Tefelim," I answered with assurance and relief.

Perhaps because the pressure of two courses of study was excessive, ill health put an end to my academic endeavors. It looked as if the year would be wasted; but it was not. There was another shift of the tiller; a powerful one. One day as I was recovering from asthma, Father and Mother came again to my room to inform me of another plan. "I was wrong when I urged you to blend into the Egyptian landscape," Father said. "Things are changing too fast; you will never succeed here, and the political situation of the Jews is worsening by the day. Britain and Egypt have just signed a treaty stipulating that the British would close their bases within ten years and we might well find ourselves facing once again something like the Arab revolt of 1882 and there will be no one to protect us." He said I would continue my studies in France and that I might never come back to Egypt. He would help me financially as long as he could, but he had no idea what the future had in store, and I should certainly not count on him to help me in my career. I received this news with surprise and was made aware for the first time of some financial limitations in the Dorra household. Up to that time I thought everything was possible because we could afford it. Seeing Papa looking so grave was frightening.

But there was a ray of hope, however. If I did well at school I would stand a good chance to enter one of the professional *Grandes Ecoles*. Once in,

I would have a minimum of financial worries, as my studies and upkeep would be paid for by the government. Moreover, once I graduated I would easily become French, and with my credentials would be more or less assured of a job for life—unless, of course, I did something very foolish.

"The French are very paternalistic once you are in the system," he added with a smile. "You might become prime minister, or a humble artillery officer, but you would survive. Besides, you seem to be in better health in Paris than here."

I would immediately have to prepare myself to reach the level of the appropriate grade in a French *Lycée*, but I was still too weak for an intensive program. Arrangements were made with two of the stars at the *Lycée Francais*. I would spend two hours a week with each one of them, at their houses this time. They were masters at teaching. The mathematician Monsieur Pelissier's results were near-miraculous. I was able to enter the *Lycée Saint-Louis* in Paris, reputedly one of the most demanding, in the fall of 1937.

A week or so before the departure for Europe, Father and Mother took me for a picnic on our sailboat. It was one of the few occasions on which we had all gone sailing together. The day was radiant. Father was at the helm. We sailed out of the harbor and anchored well beyond the harbor's jetties, near the beach of Agami. We swam, we played water-polo of sorts and we had lunch on the boat: a cold *eggah* dish which was a well-browned, flat, rather dense omelet stuffed with bits of green peppers, onions and herbs. It was swilled with beer. We then rowed to shore in the boat's dinghy and went for a walk on the beach which could not be reached by road in those days and was deserted. We talked. Father mused. He compared the ripples to the dunes undulating along the coast as far as the eye could see.

"Both were formed by recurring winds. The dunes are but large versions of the ripples. Both are rhythmic and orderly; both are made up of an accumulation of shiny specks—grains of sand. For our part, we are made up of infinitely small particles, and we are affected by forces we do not understand—luck perhaps, and a superior order? And to an ever-astonishing extent, by our own will. But you'd better stay on the right side of God!" Papa came closer to me and spread his arms around me when he saw that tears were beginning to slide down my cheeks. "My dear boy, we will manage. I know you will succeed wherever you are if you really try hard."

Henri Dorra

Early years in Alexandria.

Early years in Alexandria.

Early years in Alexandria.

Henri with his parents, Clement and Aimée in Luxor, Egypt, January 1, 1935.

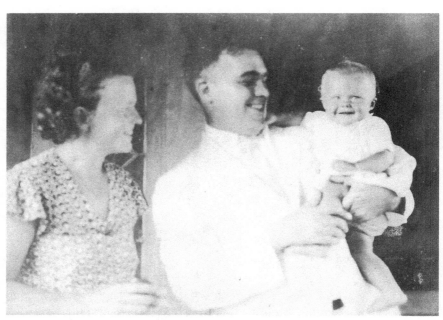

Susan and Joseph Tonetti Sr. with Mary, Macon, Georgia, 1934.

# II
# Fort Worth, Texas
EARLY BEGINNINGS ON THE SECOND CONTINENT, 1941

A CREAKING DOOR announced the Sunday evening radio program, "Inner Sanctum." Chills ran down my eight-year-old arms as the door opened slowly. The emphatic chords from the rumbling organ music always set off a Pavlovian response of fear in me the moment I heard those sinister sounds, and goose bumps appeared immediately all over my skin. But I wouldn't have missed a minute of the scariest radio program of the 1940s. I made sure I sat in the ample lap of Cassie, our housekeeper, cook, and nanny. Nothing felt more comfortable than having Cassie wrap her smooth brown arms around me, and together we listened to the creepy radio show. Every Sunday afternoon we both sat quietly listening.

When Cassie laughed her mouth opened so wide I could see the gold in her back teeth that matched her prize possession—her gold hoop earrings. Her large bosoms shook on those occasions when she was tickled by something funny. But listening to "Inner Sanctum" was not one of those occasions. The ghoulish chuckle of Boris Karloff on NBC rang in my ear long after Cassie turned off the large Magnavox radio. Still, even as Karloff's laughter dissipated, I wondered what Carter's little liver pills really did to earn the promise: "the best friend for your sunny disposition" and I tried to figure out what that meant to have a "sunny disposition."

One evening we heard the voice of the host, Raymond, the narrator of "The Tell-Tale Heart" tell his listeners: "It is early evening. Down the road comes a man who has just risen from the dead." The throbbing of the dead man's beating heart stayed with me, always making my own heart pound against my chest, just as "Inner Sanctum's" host Raymond said it would. I put Cassie's hand on my chest, "Listen, Cassie. Can you hear my heart thumping?"

"Now don't you worry, child. I'm here with you and that dead man's heart will stop beating when I turn off this radio. It's just pretend." But what happened next wasn't just pretend and it was even more frightening than "The Tell-Tale Heart." Suddenly we heard the kitchen door swing open, and then it slammed shut with a loud bang.

"Mama, Mama, where are you? I'm bleeding. I'm all bloody." The footsteps rang through the long hallway from the kitchen. Cassie's twenty-five-year-old daughter Dorothy burst into the living room. I saw blood running from gashes on Dorothy's arm dripping into puddles on the floor, and Dorothy's daughter, my playmate Sugar Pie, holding onto her mother's dress, was close behind. Cassie gently put me down on the sofa, then rushed to Dorothy who kept sobbing in anguish while her mother unwrapped the apron from around her waist and used it to tie a tourniquet on the bleeding arm. She turned to her granddaughter, and said, "Sugar Pie, get me some them towels in that downstairs bathroom." Dorothy cried out: "He done attack me again."

"Precious girl, he always do that when he be hittin' the gin."

"This time he said he was sure gonna kill me and I knew he meant it by the look in his eye. He said it was the last time he was gonna see me with that no good dancin' nigga who come to town from Galveston. I thought a callin' the police but…they ain't interested in helpin' black folks. I knew that." Cassie got out the first aid kit, cleaned the wounds and wrapped the arm with clean bandages, all the time she shook her head in disapproval. Dorothy wiped her eyes. I dared not move, and stood aside, twisting the curl on my forehead the way I always did when I felt scared. Never had I seen so much blood. I did my best not to lose my dinner. I looked over at Sugar Pie, and saw that she had begun to wipe away the tears trickling down her cheeks. Seeing this made tears begin to well in my own eyes.

Dorothy's voice reached a new level of rage while Cassie continued to bandage her arm. "I ain't studin' no dancing nigga from Galveston but if I was, then it ain't no business of Charlie. He ain't in my life no more, and I done told him that. And he got no business comin' round again after what happened last time. Come here, Sugar Pie."

Sugar Pie fell into her mother's arms, still staring with eyes as big as saucers at the bandages and the remaining bright red blood on her mother's arm. We exchanged glances not knowing what to do.

Sugar Pie and I played together often and we liked each other very much. Her favorite game was to play dress up in my mother's evening clothes. We pretended together that we were movie stars, and took turns ordering each other around as servants. Cassie finished the bandaging and was still

Mary with her first Nanny.

in full control. She told Dorothy to stop crying and get herself and Sugar Pie back to the little house. That's what everyone called the modest servant's quarters where Cassie and her family lived. I knew Sugar Pie was scared for her mother and I said, "No, Cassie. They should stay in here with us. Charlie might come back to get them." At first my own eyes felt as wide as Sugar Pie's, but I also felt very grown up. It was the first time I didn't agree with Cassie, and I needed to express it.

"He won't come back. He's fixin' to get into more trouble and those policemen by now must be on their way after him." Cassie's soothing voice produced the desired effect on everyone in the room. "Now ya'll go on. I gotta get Mary to bed cause it's a school day tomorrow and she's had enough excitement tonight." Dorothy and Sugar Pie seemed reluctant to leave but obeyed. Cassie walked heavily behind me while we climbed the stairs up to my bedroom,.

"Will you stay with me, Cassie, until Mama and Daddy come home?"

"Of course, my precious girl." Cassie held my hand and said, "I ain't goin' nowhere. I'm here with you all night if I need to be. Don't you get yourself all upset now." She stayed sitting next to the bed in the little pink room, singing softly until I fell asleep.

That dear woman, I knew, loved me as much as her own daughter, and sometimes in later years when we saw each other she said she thanked the good Lord that at least my life went untouched by the drama and dangers of her own daughter's life. Perhaps Sugar Pie would somehow escape the fears and troubles which seemed to crop up on a daily basis.

The next afternoon, I was sitting with my mother reading again my favorite book, *Tag-Along, Tooloo* when the doorbell rang. She answered it and was surprised when two police officers asked if they could speak to her. Mama invited them into the living room. After they settled themselves comfortably on the sofa one of them began, "We understand from a neighbor's report that there was some trouble here at your house last night. We have reports of screams out back in the servants' quarters. Is that true and could you tell us about it?" When the questioning officer saw the alarm in Mama's pretty face he continued in a gentler tone, "Sometimes things get pretty wild with the black folks around here…after they've tied on one or two." He ended this last remark with a slight chuckle.

"I was not here and have heard nothing about it, but I will ask our housekeeper who lives out back with her daughter and her granddaughter. She always tells me the truth. "Mary, go tell Cassie to come in here please."

Cassie's shoes slapped against the floor down the hallway as she came into the living room. When Cassie saw the uniformed police I saw that she was shaking. My mother put her hand on Cassie's arm to reassure her. Mama would tell me that "negroes in the South did not hold the police in high regard" and were never at ease in their presence.

"You needn't be afraid, Cassie. These men are here to help. Please tell them what happened last night, if you know."

She stammered out the story of the attack on Dorothy by her former boyfriend whom she declared as "a no-good ruffian—we're all scared of him." Her eyes seem to grow larger as she spoke. The police then tried to reassure her by saying that he had been found wielding a knife not two blocks away and the police took him into custody where he would remain. At least for now.

Cassie looked at my mother and said "I'm sorry, Miss Susie, for all this trouble."

"It isn't your fault, Cassie, and you mustn't worry. You and Dorothy and your granddaughter will be safer now that these officers have become involved." The police asked Cassie a few more questions and then turned to Mama saying that she needn't worry. They said the police were now on top of the situation. They had all the information they needed. Cassie breathed an audible sigh of relief, and left the room. Mama knew that Cassie really wasn't convinced that they would be safer.

The protection of the police was something she never counted on.


I ALWAYS LOVED the occasional shopping expedition into downtown Fort Worth. With just Mama and me, and no younger brothers tagging along, it was a rare treat. We were going to buy a new pair of shoes to replace those that already pinched my toes. Mama promised we could begin the downtown expedition with a stop at the library, my favorite place. How I enjoyed checking out books with my own library card. Even though I was only eight, I felt so grown up and loved the weekly pleasure I had come to enjoy for two whole years. The librarian always looked glad to see me bound down the stairs in anticipation of the expected new books. She took pleasure in telling me when she had new arrivals she knew I would enjoy.

Next to the family living room on Sunday afternoons with "Inner Sanctum," the public library was the extra special place in my young life. My mother always said I could read anything I wanted, and she let the librarian guide me with five new books to take home every week. It was like being on a great journey because those books took me to China, India, Italy, France and Spain, and more importantly, back in time to places I could never imagine, with kings and queens and boys and girls just like me.

They were so real to me it was like meeting a whole new group of friends who took me on wonderful adventures. Heidi, Peter Pan, Hans Brinker, the Wizard of Oz all came into my life with their joys and their sadnesses. It seemed hours had passed without my knowing it, and then suddenly Mama appeared saying it was time to go shopping for new shoes. She thanked the librarian, and so did I. The librarian whom I was so fond of always gave me a big hug and said "Enjoy your new books, Mary." And I always did.

The children's shoe department was always busy on Saturdays. When Mama and I got off the elevator on the third floor of Monnig's department store, no one was standing in front of the two water fountains opposite the elevator. I walked towards them, then stopped. I'd known how to read for the past two years but had never noticed the signs above each fountain. One said "White" and the other "Colored." I looked up at my mother puzzled, "What does that mean? Colored? Is the water colored, Mama?"

My mother replied. "No, dear. It means that fountain is for colored people. Now let's move along. There will be lots of children getting new shoes today, and we have other errands to do."

I knew I was frowning. "But why do they have to be separated for drinking water?" I remember my mother turned to look down at me and said, "I know. It doesn't make much sense, does it?" Later, she told me when I was much older that that was only one of the times I had reminded her of her own mother who always asked such difficult questions of everyone. My grandmother Hyde had been one of the first women graduates of the University of Michigan, and most people never felt comfortable in the company of her acerbic wit. "Why" had become my new favorite word.

"We will ask your father tonight at the dinner table. He can explain better than I can."

We returned home in time to see Daddy park the Packard in the driveway. He got out and held a package in his hand.

"I brought you a present."

I unwrapped the new roller skates and pushed the wheels against my palms. I threw my arms around my father's long legs and then sat down on the front sidewalk to put on my new skates.

"Good. Here's your very own skate key to tighten up the skates, to make sure they won't come off. And we still have time to have a skating lesson before dinner." The skating lesson proceeded with only an occasional minor tumble. I loved skating from the very beginning, made rapid progress, and skated into my father's arms, laughing and crying aloud, "This is more fun than anything." But the vision comes back to me of my father's serious and distant expression. He seemed to be thinking of something else far away.

I'd just learned a new expression and decided to try it out, "A penny for your thoughts." My father put his arm around me and said, "I am thinking of our country. Yesterday the Japanese bombed a harbor that belongs to us. It's called Pearl Harbor."

"Is it in Texas?" I stopped skating and sat down.

"No, dear. It's on the island of Hawaii, in the Pacific Ocean which is not actually part of the United States, but belongs to our country, and I am afraid those attacks mean we're at war."

While I removed my skates, Daddy put his hand on my shoulder. Though I remembered that I wanted to ask him about the "colored" drinking fountain, I somehow knew it wasn't the right time to speak about it because his mind was on the war. We walked together into the house and found Mama seated next to the Magnavox radio. We could hear President Roosevelt's booming voice: "Yesterday, December 7, 1941, a date which will live in infamy—the United States of America was suddenly and deliberately attacked by naval and air forces of the empire of Japan...."

I will never forget the worried looks on both my parents' faces. Both of them had furrowed brows, and although they didn't speak, they looked at each other with such intensity and anxiety, I knew the war was going to be very important in our lives. My eyes moved from one to the other, trying to figure out what this news would mean to me and to the family. The voice with the distinctly non-Texan accent continued on, and I was listening as hard as I could, trying to understand what Roosevelt was talking about. "It will be recorded that the distance of Hawaii from Japan makes it obvious that the attack was deliberately planned many days or even weeks ago...."

My father jumped up from his seat and poured himself a whiskey from one of the many bottles in the ornate liquor cabinet which stood in the corner of the dining room. Taking the whiskey in hand, and without saying a word he returned to settle into his seat next to the radio. The stern voice on the radio continued. "Hostilities exist. There is no blinking at the fact that our people, our territory and our interests are in grave danger." I was beginning to understand by the tone of the voice, and the looks on my parents' faces that it was a very dangerous matter. War, I knew meant soldiers going off to fight with guns, and people getting killed. Was that going to happen to us here in Texas? What a terrible thing! This was more frightening than "Inner Sanctum" or even Dorothy's bleeding arm.


ONE SUMMER DAY as a special treat, Cassie helped me up the steps of the bus. I loved riding the bus with her because it was always such fun, and

Mary in Santa Barbara with her mother, 1934.

she seemed to know everyone. While she was paying the driver, I looked around and spotted Cassie's friends sitting in a long row in the back of the bus. Oblivious to everyone else I shouted, "There's Willa Mae!" It didn't take long to run down the aisle and into Willa Mae's open arms. The row of Black maids laughed loudly and Willa Mae, Cassie's best friend, said "Who this pretty little girl runnin' into my arms? With them golden curls covering her head like one of Saint Gabriel's baby angels."

What could be more delightful than snuggling comfortably into Willa Mae's arms as Cassie greeted her other friends? It always seemed like a party when they were together—no matter where they were. "We're gonna get some religion, Mary and me. We're fixin' to go to church this evening. How 'bout you?"

"Yes, that's where we're headin' too. Brother Charles gonna preach a fine sermon this evening. He's gonna talk about the war and things."

I climbed into Cassie's lap as soon as she was settled into the empty seat next to Willa Mae, who herself took up almost two seats with her colorful orange dress spread out and clashing with Cassie's fuchsia polka dots. The whole row of women looked almost theatrical in their colorful church clothes, and their laughing and chattering filled the bus. Meanwhile I was looking around, from one to the other, and pleased with all the attention I was getting. At the time I noticed how quiet the people were in the front of the bus. They were not having as much fun as we were in the back.

A noisy group of boys, one who was a freckled redhead, sat in the seat in front of me. He was trying to open the bus window even wider and finally succeeded. He turned to his friend next to him. "Listen to this. See that little nigga girl over in the vacant lot." Before his friend could answer he yelled out the window at the slim pretty young girl, "Hey there, nigga girl. Two bits in the tall grass?" While they waited to see what she would do, laughing uproariously at their tremendous joke, the stunning teenage girl put her hands on her hips, turned slowly, and with an air of defiance she faced the bus with a glacial stare. "Dat what yo motha charge?"

Cassie, along with the whole row of maids in the back of the bus, hooted with laughter and shouted, "That's it, girl. You tell him." A wave of contagious mirth lapped over the seats, row after row, swelling into a cacophony of deep rolling laughter, belly-shaking guffaws bursting forth from gold-toothed grins, quiet giggles, and murmuring heads nodding in approval. As the hilarity reached the front of the bus, even the whites exchanged flickers of smiles at the young girl's repartee. Everyone seemed to be looking at the boys and shaking their heads. As if a blanket had been thrown over them, the boys became quiet and slunk down into their seats, whispering to each other.

Mary, 1937.

I didn't understand at all their joke or why everyone was laughing, but I remember I didn't much like the boys and thought they were show-offs. There was a lot I didn't understand at the time, but what I did like was being in the back of the bus with these happy people basking in their aura of warmth. I enjoyed listening to them even if I didn't know why they had to talk so much about their work week, and what they cooked, and their endless conversations about the people they worked for and what their menfolk did when they were drunk. Willa Mae was the star. Every time she opened her mouth the others burst into gales of laughter. I didn't know why it was so funny, but I laughed too. It was usually about her husband, Lester, dipping and spitting snuff.

Cassie, bent over with laughter, "Lawdy, girl. You bout the funniest woman I ever knowed. Good thing my little Mary here don't know what you talkin' bout."

The Pentecostal Holy Roller Church was the last stop, at the end of the line, and the only ones left on the bus were those in the back of the bus. Everyone descended the rear steps and proceeded to walk the short distance to the white clapboard church. I held Cassie's hand and walked alongside her. The nearer we got to the church, the louder the singing. Cassie began humming and turned toward me. "You gonna hear some fine singing tonight, precious girl."

I looked up at Cassie. "Is it as good as 'Boogie Woogie Bugle Boy' or 'Drinkin' Rum and Coca Cola?' I love those songs."

Cassie smiled showing all her even white teeth, "I know you do, Shuga. You know lots of songs from that radio you always listenin' to. But this kind of singing you ain't never heard. It gonna get right into your little soul." Cassie's face had a luminous glow, and her hair was plastered with shining sweat as she wiped her brow.

We heard strains of what I later knew to be "I'll Fly Away" drifting out from the church through the chilled winter air. Willa Mae, Cassie, and the others joined in the singing. "Some glad morning when this life is over I'll fly away, to a home on God's celestial shore I'll fly away."

Cassie and Willa Mae entered the church with me in between them, holding their hands tightly. They nodded to friends right and left walking down the aisle until we found places to sit in the crowded church. The wooden floors creaked as the parishioners walked down the aisle, and the hall filled up. Everyone nodded and smiled at us, and I smiled back although somewhat hesitant to see so many new faces—all looking happy as they sang, "I'll fly away, O glory…. When I die hallelujah by and by I'll fly away." The music was getting louder, and some folks were already swaying side to side.

I had never been to church before. My parents were not religious and never bothered to go beyond having us baptized. When Cassie asked my mother if she could take me to her church, my mother seemed hesitant but knew that Cassie would never take me any place that would be dangerous so she said "Yes, Cassie, of course."

After we were seated in the wooden pews, I looked up at Cassie and smiled, "This is fun and I'm so glad you brought me to your church. I didn't know church was like this." Cassie's gold earrings swayed from side to side as she hummed and threw her arms into the air above her head.

The colorful clothes the women wore were intriguing to me: orange, red and purple with big hats almost covering their faces. I saw that the men were sitting on the other side of the aisle, and they too were dressed not in work clothes but in dark suits. Soon I heard the repeated refrain "I'll fly away" and I could sing it along with them. Just as I was learning the words, the music stopped. Cassie looked down at me. "He gonna speak now. He's the preacher." As soon as he began to speak, everyone stopped singing and listened attentively. I was frightened when the preacher suddenly banged his fist on the pulpit and shouted, "Why don't you come to Christ Jesus? Why don't you come? Are you afraid?"

I squeezed Cassie's hand and looked at her to see if she was as afraid as I was. He seemed so angry. I whispered, "Why is he so angry?"

"Shush, my precious. He just talkin' to the sinners here tonight. Don't be afraid. He gonna help us all."

Someone in the congregation yelled back "We sinnas. God help us. Hallelujah we seen the Lord!" Others joined in with Hallelujahs and "We seen the Lord." I was puzzled by their knowing when to start singing again all at the same time. It started softly then became louder and louder, hurting my ears. My head was so light, and the noise was so loud I felt dizzy. Some of the women in front of me began to fall on their knees, one after the other. They reminded me of the dominoes my father used to line up on the dining room table and then toppled over.

Then the singing grew louder still. "When the shadows of this life have grown I'll fly away like birds from prison bars have flown, I'll fly away." The women in their fancy dresses began to writhe on the floor. I remember looking at them wondering if they were sick, or what had happened to them because their eyes rolled to the backs of their heads, and they shrieked "Hallelujah. Hallelujah!" Those who had not yet fallen to the ground continued singing, "To a land where joys shall never end I'll fly away." My head was spinning as the singing grew louder, and more people fell to the ground singing "Hallelujah." The black-suited preacher had stopped to wipe the sweat from his brow and take a sip of water.

The last thing I remember is seeing Cassie who had stopped singing when she saw that my face had turned white as snow. I expect she knew I was about to faint. When I was comfortably in bed that night she told me the whole story of how she grabbed me quickly into her arms and we hurried out of the church and into the fresh air. My body had become limp in her arms and my eyes were sealed shut.

Cassie said she had to think fast. She pulled a handkerchief out of her pocketbook and ran to the water fountain outside the church. She dampened the cloth with the cold water and began patting it onto my forehead. She repeated this several times, she said, holding me by the waist so that my curly head hung down while my face was being swabbed with the cool cloth.

"You don't know how scared I was when your eyes stayed shut. I thought you sure 'nough was dead. Then a miracle happened! Your eyes fluttered open, and a little smile opened up on your lips."

"'Oh Cassie, I'm so glad to see you.' Those were your very first words. Then you said 'What happened? I heard them singing Hallelujah and it got louder and louder and then everything went black.'"

Cassie continued, "Then I asked you, 'Can you stand up now, little one?' You answered me loud and clear," she chuckled: "'Yes. But I don't want to go back in there. Can we go home now?'"

"You sure 'nuff' don't have to, I told you. We're going home now. You've had enough religion for one night." Willa Mae and the others had followed close behind us as we climbed up on the bus and walked to the back without saying a word and proceeded homeward.

Although I never was taken back to the Pentecostal Church, at my mother's request I assume, I did choose to join and become confirmed in the High Episcopal Church at the age of thirteen, where I sang in the choir every Sunday. And at every communion service I feared what inevitably happened. At precisely the same spot in the service week after week, when the pitch reached an emotional climax with the resounding "Hozanna! Hozanna!" I fainted dead away and had to be carried out of the choir loft.


IT WOULD TAKE more than ten years before there was a Rosa Parks who dared to challenge the Jim Crow laws in Montgomery, Alabama by refusing to give up her seat to a white man on the bus in 1955. By that time Blacks didn't have to sit in the back of the bus even in Texas, and the memories of sitting back there were stronger than ever.

Chateau de Chardonneux which the Dorras purchased in the Loire valley in 1940.

# III

# "A Different Kind of Jew"

LEAVING ALEXANDRIA for good was not a terrible wrench for Maman. She had always wanted to live in France, and once all the foreigners were made unwelcome in Egypt our family had no problem deciding where to go. Since we had spent so many summers in France traveling with Grandmère, and also because we had always spoken French at home in Alexandria, I was delighted to be able to call France my home. I had been at the *Lycée Saint-Louis* in Paris for over two years and finally felt I was one of the boys there. When my vacation began that spring day in May 1940, it was a glorious sunny day, but we Dorras had no idea that our whole way of life was about to change again in an even more dramatic way.

I was sixteen years old and returning from a morning walk when I glanced up at the large dining room window of the Chateau Chardonneux that my mother had purchased in the Loire valley a couple of years earlier. The window looked out onto vast lawns and neatly kept parterres, and the huge magnolias that were now in full bloom. Everyone in the household was aware that Hitler had invaded Denmark and Norway only the month before, and everyone was worried about the future of France. I thought it ironic that so much energy was put into the new rose garden being laid out by the master gardener that morning as if there were nothing to be worried about. The smell of freshly dug soil promised such beauty the following spring.

I looked up at the nineteenth century Italianate chateau, with its elaborate red brick in strong contrast with the white stones and extensive slate blue roofs. I was pleased that it was to be our home but felt that the place drew attention to itself in a way that made me feel uncomfortable. To me, the colorful incongruity was vaguely unpleasant in the understated

31

L' Orangerie at Chateau de Chardonneux.

countryside of rural Sarthe. Nevertheless, Maman had delighted me when she bought the chateau during my second year at the *Lycée Saint-Louis* in Paris. It seemed too good to be true that Egypt was behind us, and that we now could call ourselves French. But what pleased me most was seeing my mother so engaged in the restoration of the chateau and its gardens. I smiled as I thought of what a different person she'd become since we left Alexandria, in contrast to the sybaritic life that she'd led in Egypt. Now she was rising early each morning, full of energy and eager to supervise the workmen or drive with me to the nearby nurseries to choose the trees and shrubs for the workmen to plant that day.

It was only that morning that Maman had told me the news that Neville Chamberlain had resigned after pressure from the Labour members for a more active prosecution of the war. Britain was at war, but this did not yet touch our lives at Chardonneux. Only the plans for the koi pond and the rose garden captured my mother's undivided attention--this and the addition of masses of hydrangeas beneath the large dining room windows. I knew that the workmen liked it when she was there, laughing at her good humor and her delight in their work. It was uncanny how everyone who worked for her always looked happy in her presence, as if it were a privilege to work for her. Her good humor was contagious. I had, in fact, never seen her in such high spirits.

In later years, I would think often of how quickly our lives so radically changed, and of our moving from the tree-lined Boulevard Hussein in the center of Alexandria to the beautiful chateau in the Loire. For now, the future seemed so promising. Was it only two years ago that my acceptance at *Saint-Louis*, the Parisian *lycée* had made my parents so proud? My Alexandrian tutors were ecstatic at the news, and the new teachers and fellow students were just as I had wished: engaging, entertaining and brilliant. For the first time in my life I would have close friends with similar values. I was proud to know that it was the only public French *lycée* exclusively dedicated to getting its students into the "Grandes Ecoles," and it was a foregone conclusion that Saint-Louis graduates would be the leaders of France in every field. It was also impressive to me that among its illustrious graduates was my favorite childhood author, Antoine de Saint-Exupery, as well as Louis Pasteur, Jean Racine, Emile Zola, the painter Yves Tanguy and, at the top of the list of distinguished alumni was Charles Maurice de Talleyrand, the great French diplomat and aide to Napoleon. My tutors in Alexandria had encouraged this admiration at a young age. To attend that great *lycée* had been my dream and it meant a future of imminent success. My parents agreed with the teachers at *Saint Louis* that I should prepare for a future in engineering at one of the *Grandes Ecoles*.

But interrupting those pleasant thoughts, a conversation came to mind that took place during the last week in May before I left school for the holidays. My friends and I followed the war news on the BBC from day to day. We were fiercely proud of the French army even in its glorious defeat. It was only at the very end of the conversation that they mentioned the enormous respect they had for Pétain and his ever-increasing agreements with Hitler. My good friend Alain looked at me long and seriously, his blond hair shining in the sunlight, his lean body perched casually on a stool and a look of what? Was it compassion? Was it tenderness, or what exactly was it?

"You mustn't worry, Henri. You're a different kind of Jew," he said with a slight smile. "You will be protected. You are one of us. Even Pétain knows a good Jew and one who will make France proud." I forced a smile. What an odd sort of compliment to be called "a different kind of Jew." Was it just because I was a *Lycée Saint-Louis* boy? Why was I a "different kind of Jew?"

What would they say now, those boys who had welcomed me so warmly at *Saint Louis*? And the ghosts of those successful men that wandered the halls in the mecca of learning on the *Boule Miche*, would they rise up in protest? Of course they would. Many of them were Jews also.

Then as I looked into the dining room I could almost hear the voice of Grandmother Castro who, only a short time ago, presided at the head of the long rosewood dining table at that last luncheon in Alexandria. She had awakened me from being lost in my thoughts, and pressed my arm gently. "Henri, will you not have some more soufflé? It is one of the cook's best." It was always she who encouraged me to indulge in the fattening pastries and other luxuries that she so enjoyed.

"*Merci. Non, Grandmère.* I've had enough," I remember answering, for the first time denying myself that pleasure. Today at that same table with the same silver candlesticks and the silver I had always known, I looked around at the other thirteen relatives and close friends from Paris who had come to stay at Chardonneux until the climate in Paris became more secure. All had left Egypt at the same time and were part of a small colony of displaced Alexandrian Jews who were now living well in Paris and making a new life. They were assimilated into the civilized milieu of Paris with the ease that their well-educated, cultured backgrounds provided. They were determined to stick together now as they did when they realized the political climate in Egypt would be unsafe, and that they had to leave.

My father, Clement, was the only one missing today. Not having him there was nothing unusual. It was the women of this family that carried on. I admired my father, who had already left for New York to work for the Voice of America translating Arabic and French and to prepare for the New

Left to right, Henri and two Parisian school friends.

York Medical School exams, but I longed to have him beside me. I missed Papa. There was no doubt in my mind that my father had the necessary discipline to pass the rigorous Boards in order to continue his practice in New York. He didn't seem to resent having to take the boards, even though he'd been head of the clinic in Alexandria.

I realize I must have looked from one to another of the familiar faces of those gathered around the table. I saw that some were whispering to each other. Others were speaking all at once as was the family habit. I heard snatches of arguments—all about the future of France, the rumored Vichy government and the power of the French Marshal Pétain. Uncle Jean-Jacques's voice rose above the others. It had an uncharacteristic somber tone that caused a hush in the room.

"The air strikes are devastating. Hitler has conquered the Netherlands and the German *Luftwaffe* has already made its presence known in northern France. He will not stop there."

I glanced at my mother and could see that her agitation was palpable. She rose from the table and paced up and down, occasionally stopping to fold her arms across her chest.

"It is *affreux*! Simply terrible! As we speak, the Germans are advancing from the north." The phone rang, causing everyone to jump and all conversation to seep silently into the walls of the large wood paneled dining room. Maman rose to answer the jarring ring, and was heard to say "*Ce n'est pas possible. Mais oui. Meme ce soir.*" Those still seated at the table heard the receiver click and the sharp snap of her heels against the hardwood floor when she returned to the hushed dining room.

"It was Raoul Aghion, in the Foreign Office. He says a British ship will leave with refugees from Saint-Jean-de-Luz within the week and that we must be on it. The Germans have already reached the Loire just north of us."

"That means we must leave tonight," Jean-Jacques interrupted. He knocked the ashes from his pipe, stretched his long legs, and moved towards Maman.

"Yes. And we must begin immediately to pack only what we cannot do without or what we can sell, if necessary." Maman had stopped pacing the floor and turned to face each of us, dictating what had to be done: We will have to leave France for England or even America. "No Jew will be safe in France." Her voice cracked with emotion.

After only a slight pause, she regained her composure and turned to me: "Henri, we will need you to drive one of the five cars. Yours will carry the fuel for the entire convoy." Her voice was now steady and firm.

I took great pleasure in hearing these words. I was, for the first time, being treated as one of the men—no longer a child. Father was not here and I had to assume a bigger role. This rush of excitement soon gave way to a wave of nausea beginning at the bottom of my stomach. I realized it was fear. I thought at the time, "How childish of me. I mustn't give into fear. Not when Maman is counting on me." It was knowing that my mother trusted me that pushed away the fear, the nausea and the self-doubt that had begun to overtake me. I looked at her with pride. I can still see her standing behind the caned back of a large Louis XV armchair as if seeing her for the first time. Not even my hero Talleyrand could have been more impressive at this moment. I realized how in spite of her diminutive stature she exuded a Napoleonic strength.

"Pétain has sold out to the Germans. It is the end of the French Republic, and Pétain will be the new chief of state—and Hitler's puppet. They have already begun rounding up Jews in the north."

She turned to face us all: "I'll drive the largest of the cars, which will be filled with as much baggage, and as many trunks, as we can fit. We'll all stay together, stopping only long enough to refuel."

Uncle Jean-Jacques interrupted, "We will have to drive all night without headlights so as not to be seen by the German fighter planes."

"Yes, according to Raoul, they have already begun air strikes as far south as the Loire." She added quickly, "We can reach Cognac by tomorrow night if we drive all night."

"Our friends will receive us. I am sure of that." My uncle had already moved towards the hall and the telephone. As one of France's most outstanding wine merchants, he had contacts all over France. Everyone loved his company. "I will call the Martins now, and the others who will host us the next three nights if we need shelter before we reach Saint-Jean-de-Luz."

At this news, some began leaving the table, anxious to begin packing. Grandmother Castro and I remained seated at the table, along with Jean-Jacques and Aunt Edmae. Maman turned to the servants who had been assembled. She addressed Angelina: "You will be in charge. You must empty the chateau of the valuables. Take the furniture from the salon and the dining room. Divide it, and all the china and silver, amongst yourselves. Keep it in your cottages or hide it if you can, especially our treasured Tabriz and Shiraz carpets." She hesitated and swallowed before continuing, "If we don't come back, they are yours."

"But Madame. You will come back."

Maman put her hand on Angelina's arm. The two women exchanged looks of tenderness mixed with anxiety before Maman turned to the other servants standing in a line nearby. She addressed each of them by name and

The salon at Chardonneux.

handed each an envelope which contained a substantial amount of cash. Wiping away the tears from their eyes they thanked her, and left the room to begin their work.

I held Grandmother Castro's arm to support her as she rose from the table. She turned to Maman, "I'm afraid I cannot go with you. I'd only be a burden." She was breathing heavily. "It's as easy for me to remain here and to be hidden by the servants, if necessary. They will take care of me."

I couldn't stand it. "But no. Grandmère, you cannot be left behind. You must come with us." I'll never forget the tears I saw in her eyes that day which unexpectedly produced a welling of tears in my own. Of all the people I loved, she was the one whom I would miss the most.

She patted my arm. "You must escape. It's too dangerous for all of you to remain. I'm an old woman and can easily be overlooked by the Germans."

I looked into her eyes and thought, what would life be without her? Ever since I could remember I'd relied on her gentle presence when my parents were unavailable, as they so often were. The nausea had returned. This time the cause was not fear but because of something else. I realized at that moment how devastating the effect of war would be on our family.

Someone had turned on the phonograph. Strains of the Kreutzer Sonata filled the room. Maman had asked Angelina to bring in champagne. I, who had not taken my eyes off my mother, saw that a courageous smile had formed on her lips.

"I thought we should hear something beautiful before we leave. It may be a long time before we hear Beethoven again. Listen to this music. For me it's always been an affirmation of life."

I heard the first movement and thought, how amazing. Beethoven had translated his lust for life into music. He brought to his music all the excitement and the darkness of life—even its danger just as we face it here today. But the melody also reflects the quiet and the beautiful in life too. Never has this music been more touching nor more sensuous. It must have had a similar effect on the others around the table because I felt there was a peace in the room that I'd never felt before. In later years whenever I heard the Kreutzer Sonata I recognized that it had indeed marked my soul that day at Chardonneux.

"Let us toast Beethoven and celebrate his joy of life."

The first movement ended and while we listened to the second and third, our moods lifted. We felt we could succeed and what had been sadness and despair had turned into a resolution of hope and even joy. I thought, let's drink to the music that inspires us to keep on going. As we must.

THE CARAVAN BEGAN its quiet exodus with only the light of the moon to guide us. We'd placed mattresses on top of the cars and turned off the headlights so that the German *Luftwaffe* that had already begun their night raids in the area would not spot us. The ominous quiet was broken only by the sound of crickets. We drove on and on, always checking in the rearview mirror to make sure the others followed. The caravan had to stop to refuel and to eat from the lavish baskets of food provided by Angelina and the kitchen staff.

During one of the stops, Uncle Jean-Jacques addressed everyone. "We will soon be at Cognac. The Martins have promised a welcome feast and will bring out their *grands crus* to keep our spirits lifted. 'It's the least we can do for you,' Edgar Martin told me on the phone." Jean-Jacques lowered his voice and continued, "But, *mes chers*, Edmae and I have decided to remain in Cognac. We will not be continuing with you to Saint-Jean-de-Luz."

This news astonished everyone. Then Mother was the first to speak, "But are you sure?" You are Jews and you won't be safe in France."

Georges Bernard broke in, "They will find you. You must come with us."

"We *are* sure. We will remain with the Martins, under their protection. They will hide us," he added with a slight waver of hesitation.

Then Aunt Edmae looked tenderly at Maman, and spoke, "I cannot leave France. England would be just too different. I'd feel lost."

Maman gave a sigh of resignation and grasped Edmae's hand. "As you wish, my dear. I won't beg you. It's your destiny. No one must be forced into the unknown. I feel I've made the right choice for Henri and myself but you and Jean Jacques must make your own decision." It was decided.

We left in the middle of the night. Once we reached Cognac, Maman, convinced that it was more dangerous to remain in France than to continue, brought up the subject again with Uncle Jean-Jacques. "You realize that the Germans are very near, don't you?"

"Yes, Aimée. But we're determined to stay here in Cognac."

The Martins asked if others in the group wished to stay behind as well. The chateau had lots of rooms, they insisted. The Bernards accepted the invitation and said they too would remain in France.

The caravan was dwindling. Now there were six remaining in our group of friends and cousins: the Aghions and my cousins Jacqueline and her brother and their mother and father, the Greens. These all said they wanted to continue on to Saint Jean de Luz with Maman and me. They were down to four cars now, including the one I drove which was half filled with cans of fuel.

A day of rest followed, and we again drove at night. We were expected at our friends' country house the next night at Saint-Emilion, where we all knew the greatest wine in Bordeaux was to be poured for us upon our arrival. The host, an old friend and client of Jean-Jacque was the Marquis de Rivarolle, who greeted us with great warmth when we arrived at eight, exhausted and famished. There was something unsettling about drinking the wines that had been treasured for so many years: Chateau Yquem, Chateau Latour Pauillac and Chateau Margaux among others. But I pushed the thought from my mind as I sipped, the flavor heady, the texture smooth on my palate. I only had the pleasure of the moment. That's all I wanted to consider. I didn't want to think of what was ahead of us.

An incongruous gaiety filled the Rivarolle country house. The Marquis's son, Robert, brought out an accordion and began to play Viennese waltzes. Mother pulled me on to the ballroom floor where we danced. Her sudden joy was catching, and I saw that everyone in the room was smiling at her. Others joined us, and I knew the gaiety masked the heaviness in all our hearts. We would not let each other know our true misgivings about the future. Who knew what it would bring? I didn't want to think about it.

When the music stopped Mother spoke in a confident voice, "It is 11:00 and we must all retire now. Sleep is our most precious gift if we can have it. Henri will knock on your doors tomorrow morning at 4:00. We must leave by 4:45."


I DROVE ALONE along the road that sliced through the acres of maritime pine trees and remembered that this part of Aquitaine was called the "Sahara of France." It bore no resemblance to the Sahara we had left behind on that other continent we used to call home when that other exodus took place. Another escape. How long ago that seemed. Would life always be like this, escaping from one continent to another only to find that we had to run away once again? My thoughts became sadder, and my heart felt heavy.

The next day was the same, a full day of driving in endless boredom. I couldn't wait for the end of this dry, flat, and sandy earth covered with the stark pines. I remembered from a geography class at Saint-Louis that it was Napoleon who had instigated the planting of this endless forest in order to stabilize the shifting dunes. We drove past sand and acres of pine trees. The forest seemed to go on forever. We passed no other cars, no other people, just our four cars forming a lonely caravan.

To make the time pass, I whistled the themes of every Mozart aria I could remember. This worked, because on the third day of driving and whistling I was jolted back to the present when I caught my first glimpse of the sea. I realized I was smiling. It was glorious to see the Bay of Gascogne, and I felt like celebrating until I looked at the gas gauge which showed empty and a new fear came over me. Even though Saint-Jean-de-Luz was only a couple of kilometers away I wondered if we would be able to reach the harbor before running out of fuel. The gauge showed we were down to a few liters. At the sight of the sandy beach that stretched for miles along the coast I longed to have a last swim in the beautiful blue-green sea. But I knew this would be folly. We were only a stone's throw from Saint-Jean-de-Luz and must move on to be in line for the British ship. The undercurrent of our present worries seemed to be echoed in the drama of the colossal waves that broke along the coast of Gascogne Bay as far as the eye could see.

We were delighted and finally somewhat reassured to see that the British ship was waiting in the harbor. So far so good.

"Oh my God! Look at the line of people hoping to get on the ship." I realized I was speaking out loud. I had been doing that, talking to myself, for the entire trip since leaving Chardonneux which now felt like a century ago. How would we ever manage to get aboard? So many people waiting to get on the ship! There were only six of us left, my Green cousins, the Aghions, Maman and myself but what were our chances of going aboard? Had we made the trip in vain?

We parked the cars and headed toward the ship's embarkation dock. While I was looking at the boats in the harbor, I suddenly spotted a tall young man with wavy brown hair who looked familiar in his dark blue jacket. Could it be? Yes—it was Anthony Adler, my old chum from Alexandria. We could hardly believe our eyes and ran to each other, arms waving.

"Anthony, what are you doing here?" I couldn't help laughing. We gave each other a warm hug.

"Probably the same thing you're doing, trying to find a way out, to save our lives. We were hoping to board a ship leaving for England from Bayonne but we arrived too late. It was completely full. They wouldn't take any more passengers. My mother became hysterical."

"I'm afraid that may happen to us here. My mother and cousins are there in line. Just look at that line of people."

Anthony raised his shoulders. "Where did they all come from? They don't look French, do they?"

"They must be Eastern Europeans, I would guess. Many are well dressed and some are even carrying fur coats."

"Some look as if they'd travelled halfway across the world to get here."

I nodded in agreement, "Well, that's how I feel, and it'll be a great blow if we're not allowed on the ship. But what will you and your family do now?"

"Our backup plan is to go to Portugal because we were told there'd be another ship leaving in two days."

"How will you get there? Do you have a car?"

"No car—we came by train. We're trying to figure out how to get to Portugal and then my father says we must go back to Egypt. He says that in spite of everything that would be the safest place for us."

"Anthony, we were planning to leave our Packard here. Would you like it? There is very little petrol but you're welcome to it."

Anthony beamed. "Of course we would. It would be our best way of getting to Portugal."

"Be my guest." I'd just learned this English expression and felt so happy for the chance to use it. "But I must go now. My mother will have a thousand things for me to do and hopefully she'll think of something to get us on that ship. It isn't a luxury liner but it's all we have at this point." He pointed to the large unpretentious vessel in the harbor. "Safe journey, *mon ami*."

"And to you."

The little group of Dorra friends and relatives were talking heatedly when I approached them. Maman turned to me and said, "We're off to England or Canada or wherever this ship is going. We're on our own now. The others, the Greens and the Aghions, after seeing the long line from here, decided that it would be impossible to get on the British ship. They've been talking to the Adlers, and I see that you found your friend, Anthony too. The Adlers convinced them that it made more sense to give up the idea of getting on the ship. They will join the Adlers going to Portugal and from there back to Egypt."

"But, Maman, don't you think we too should go back with them and abandon the idea of England or America or wherever this ship is going?"

"No. I'm convinced we must stay here and get on that ship. No matter what." We moved forward with the line and were now in the main building amidst a throng of people scurrying here and there. The noise inside was deafening. There appeared to be no barriers, only a vast area with a few British officers trying to keep order. Maman saw that there was a pile of luggage behind the solitary desk where the chief officer was stamping passports and allowing some to proceed to the gangplank.

"Go around to the other side of that British officer to see what they are marking on the trunks they passed for embarkation. We have no time to lose."

I walked around, through the crowds, unnoticed by the officers who were busy processing the people, dismissing those who didn't have proper papers and trying to subdue those who became angry. I took advantage of the pandemonium and slipped through the crowd. When I returned, Maman was still waiting in line, and I announced with pride, almost laughing, "They're marking the trunks with a yellow chalk, once they have been checked."

"Good. Now you must go into the village and find a hardware store. Buy some yellow chalk and get back here as soon as you can. *Vite! Vite!*"

I was able to buy the chalk after going to two hardware stores and returned to Maman with it in triumph. She beamed with delight, "Wonderful! Now let's get started. We both set about marking our trunks and suitcases with big yellow X's. No one paid any attention to me, an agile boy dragging the trunks around to the other side of the officer's desk. Meanwhile, Maman had moved up in line and gave me a wink of approval when she saw that I had accomplished what she'd asked me to do. Within half an hour we arrived at the desk of the officer in charge of checking passports and issuing embarkation passes. My heart was racing. I looked over at my mother and was baffled that she could maintain such an aura of calm, as if nothing at all was at stake.

In minutes, we were standing in front of a handsome British officer who asked for our passports. Maman smiled at him and wished him a good day and handed over our passports. I held my breath. How could she be so charming at this point?

"But, Madame. These are Egyptian passports. This is a British ship and we are taking only British subjects. You must understand. We're sorry."

My heart sank but she drew herself up with a dignity I had rarely seen. She looked straight into the eyes of the officer and said in perfect English, "My dear young man. Don't you know that Egypt is part and parcel of the British Empire?"

"Yes. Madame." He looked flustered at first but then we heard the blissful sound of the stamping machine hitting our passports with a loud click. He handed us our embarkation passes and told us to proceed to the gangplank. I followed my triumphant mother who marched with assurance, turning back only once to see if all our luggage was safely with the checked baggage. It was. And so we proceeded, hearts pounding and heads held high, to follow the other passengers who were boarding the ship.

THIS CHRISTMAS THREE WISE-MEN RIDE ON TO FULFILL
THAT HEAVENLY PROMISE OF PEACE AND GOOD-WILL
WITH A PERMANENT PACT· THEY TOTE IN THEIR LAPS
FOUR FREEDOMS·A CHARTER AND DE-NAZIED MAPS·
THE TONETTIS PREDICT THAT THE YEAR FORTY-FIVE
YOUR HOPES FOR THE FUTURE ARE SURE TO REVIVE·.

A Tonetti yearly Christmas card designed by Mary's grandfather, Robert Wilson Hyde

# IV
# Mid Forties in America
## ADOLESCENCE AND POST WAR SYNDROMES

"WHO ARE THOSE THREE MEN riding on the camels? That seems a funny Christmas card to me."

Celebrating Christmas in the Tonetti household usually began in early December with the addressing and stuffing of hundreds of Christmas cards. My mother and I were at the card table that had been set up in the light-filled sun porch for this annual project. The envelopes and 1945 Christmas card didn't look like the cards my friends' parents sent but I always enjoyed helping my mother with this project because it meant Christmas would soon be here. We had picked up the boxes of off-white cards and envelopes the day before and were beginning to stamp and stuff the envelopes. My mother explained to me that the three men riding camels across the front of the card were, according to the Christian Christmas tradition, the three wise men riding to Bethlehem to see the baby Jesus. You see the star above them. That was their guiding light. But when you read the message inside the card", she continued, "you see that the artist had three other wise men in mind as well. Those three are the world heroes who earlier this year ended the war that has been going on for years. They are our president Roosevelt, and the leaders in England and Russia, Mr. Churchill and Mr. Stalin. You understand that because of the message inside the card:

The message on the inside of the card is one of good wishes for a Merry Christmas and for a New Year of peace and prosperity in the coming year.

"You know that the artist who always draws our Christmas cards is your grandfather, Daddy Hyde. You remember him, don't you? He is my father who lives in Santa Barbara, California, and he is a very sweet man."

Mary with her father and brothers at the annual Fort Worth rodeo and fat stock show.

"Yes I remember him and I liked him when we met in California." I looked down at the card and shook my head. "I like the picture of the three wise men but why did Daddy Hyde put President Roosevelt and the others on our Christmas card?"

"Because it was just this year in February that those three met at what is known as the Conference of Yalta to discuss the peace terms after our enemies surrendered, and it was a very happy day. Daddy Hyde wanted to commemorate that event because he is a very peace-loving man. He hated war."

The Conference of Yalta was the first of several historic events that year. Only a few months after Roosevelt died in office in April the U.S. dropped the first atomic bomb on Hiroshima. Under President Truman who took over after Roosevelt's death a second bomb that would bring Hirohito to his knees was delivered on the city of Nagasaki just three days later, and finally on August 14, World War II finally ended with Hirohito announcing Japan's defeat.

But none of this world news affected the twelve-year old girls who went with me to see Rita Hayworth in "Gilda" or the "Road" shows with Bing Crosby and Bob Hope. Sometimes Veronica Lake became the object of our attention at the weekly Saturday morning picture shows. Our main preoccupation was to acquire the greatest number of autographed photos of our favorite movie stars: Van Johnson and Betty Grable. (I had 62 pictures of Betty Grable.) While my parents were tuned into the nightly radio news broadcasts, my friends and I listened to Frank Sinatra, the Ink Spots, Johnny Mercer and Vaughn Monroe. We knew the words to all the top songs of the day which were announced on "Your Hit Parade" every Saturday night and which had become a replacement favorite for "Inner Sanctum" as the teen age years approached. We memorized the words of all the "hits" including "Let it Snow, Let it Snow," "The Gypsy," and "For Sentimental Reasons," and when we were together in car pool transits, choruses broke out easily. We were also fascinated by the new skimpy bathing suit, the Bikini, named ironically after the atoll in the Marshall Islands where scientists had tested the atom bomb.

It was just before I entered the seventh grade that I received a phone call from an older friend whose parents were also friends of my parents. It was flattering to know that she called me because I so admired her. Angelique was her name. She was one of the most popular girls at Morningside, and usually the leader of the girls who ran everything. She was a senior, and I'd known her since we first moved to Fort Worth and looked forward to the lovely hand-me-down clothes that came my way from her. They never appeared worn or out of style. The party dresses were a great delight to me, and when I wore them I felt almost as pretty as Angelique. Her mellifluous voice was always a treat to hear, and when she told me she was calling to invite me to join a secret society I couldn't believe my ears.

"You should join. It will be lots of fun," Angelique said on the phone.

It is a very select club called Sigma Chi Sigma or SCS. And it's secret. I'm the president this year," Angelique said with a touch of annoyance at having to explain her importance to her younger friend. She herself was all of fifteen. "All the leaders and the most popular girls at Morningside Jr. High School are members: the cheer leaders, the class presidents, the editors of the newspaper and the yearbook. Only a few seventh graders are taken in every year and I'll put you up."

"Well. It sounds great," I said, but with some hesitation. "What do I have to do?" The word "secret" made it intriguing but a little scary.

"You'll be invited to parties during rush week so the other members can have a look at you, and then you will have to be a pledge for three months... and there is also an initiation. Pledging can be a hassle, but I'll be your big sister to help you through it. Oh, and Mary, who's that cute girl you're always with at the picture show on Saturday morning?"

"She's Gloria Shuman, my best friend. She's smart and really good at the piano. Much better than I am."

"Great, give me her number and I'll call her too. You'll love it. There will be meetings after school, of course."

"Well, I already have my piano and dance lessons after school but I guess it could work. I would love to do it. I have a strange feeling that I don't think my parents will like all this, a secret society and everything. I know my mother was in a sorority at Stanford but it wasn't secret. It had a Latin name... Kappa Kappa Gamma sounds like to same thing to me. Maybe she will let me do it." Angelique had become impatient, and abruptly closed the conversation with, "You'll just have to work it out, Mary. I have to go now."

Gloria and I began our pledging during the summer of '45. It continued into the fall but I didn't speak much about it at home because I knew my father didn't like the idea at all of secret societies and believed Angelique was one of the silliest girls he knew. Sometimes at the dinner table when we were encouraged to talk about "what happened in school today?" I was teased by my brothers in front of our parents: "Mary belongs to a secret society. Tell us about your pledging and your secret society." I usually shrugged off their teasing and changed the subject.

The SCS meetings took place on Thursdays after school in the shade-drawn, candlelit living rooms of the members' houses. At one meeting about midway through the pledge term several inactive members appeared. They were older girls who were already in high school and in another sorority but who loved coming back to receive the reverence they got from the Jr. High school members. Enjoying their Cokes that were miraculously produced in spite of the shortage and rationing, they gossiped and took a sadistic pleasure in grilling the pledges about whatever the misdemeanors were that we'd committed during the past week. A high level of drama filled the room when we pledges were brought in before the twenty or so active members who sat cross-legged on the floor and held candles when it was their turn to speak. The pledges stood in a line in front of them. I learned later that terrifying the younger girls produced a thrill that was encouraged by the "pack" of older girls.

"Why didn't a certain pledge speak to a member at the picture show last Saturday? You know who you are. Please step forward and confess."

I gulped. Could it have been me? I thought I'd seen and spoken to all the members but maybe I'd missed one. Not having seen that member was not a sufficient excuse, I knew. Five of us pledges felt guilty enough to step forward. The members laughed.

"I am referring to only one of you and she has not yet stepped forward. All of you can step back into line and will the guilty pledge please step forward. No doubt you have other things to confess."

After the usual grilling of the pledges, we were grateful to be dismissed. As we filed out of the living room I heard my name called. "Mary, will you please remain."

When the door was closed, the president, my friend Angelique, spoke in a low voice in the darkened room, "Gloria Shuman is your friend, isn't she?"

"Yes. She is," I stammered.

"And is she Jewish?" asked a severe sixteen-year-old inactive whom I had never seen before.

"Yes. She is."

"Well we have to tell her that she can't become a member of this sorority because of that. Did you know that the Jews killed our Lord?" A silence followed for what seemed an hour to me. Then Angelique spoke, "You may go back to the room with the other pledges."

Gloria was then brought in and told the reason she could not continue to pledge. When my father came to pick us up after the meeting he saw that Gloria had been crying. On the way home, she didn't say anything, and just looked quietly out the window. I looked at Gloria's long fingers entwined in her lap, the only sign of her inward agitation. No one spoke on the short ride to Gloria's house until she said when she opened the door of the back seat, "Thank you, Mr. Tonetti, for the ride." She turned her tear-stained face to me. "Bye, Mary."

"Good bye, Gloria. I'll call you. " I felt sick to my stomach as I watched her going up the sidewalk to her mother standing in the doorway. I didn't know what to do and felt so sorry for my dear friend who had been hurt so unjustly. I knew it was unjust. What did Jesus's dying on the cross have to do with my friend's having to leave the sorority? Yet how could I change what happened? How could they be so cruel? Daddy and I waved goodbye to Gloria and her mother as they entered the house.

Daddy put the car in gear and I heard him say: "Damnit! What have they done to that little girl? You know I disapprove of that sorority and those silly girls."

"I don't understand why but they told her they couldn't have her in the sorority. They said it was because she is Jewish."

My father looked as if he was about to explode. "That's the most absurd thing I've ever heard of. I was afraid of something foolish like that. I can only say that I'll never have any respect for you if you don't get out of that sorority immediately."

"But I can't! It's the most important group of girls at Morningside. All the school leaders are in it, and not everyone gets asked." I began to cry, somehow knowing that my father was right. The SCS members had done something that was cruel. But I couldn't give it up.

My mother greeted us at the door and knew by our expressions, something was wrong., "What's happened? Something must be terribly wrong."

My father answered, "Yes. Terribly wrong. We have to talk." He told me to go to my room, and began to make the nightly Tom Collins for the two of them. I listened at the top of the stairs and heard my father say, "We cannot allow her to continue in that atmosphere. You know that." His voice dropped and I couldn't understand what came next so I moved further down the stairs.

My mother's voice was growing louder. "But why should she be punished for the bad judgment of the other girls? I think it would be too hard on Mary to leave." I peeked through the railing of the stairs and saw that she had risen from her chair, and was sipping her cocktail. Then I was relieved to hear her say, "She loves it so. She knows that being a member of SCS is almost a pre-requisite for everything. They actually control who gets elected president of the student body, the cheer leaders, and even editor of the school paper."

My mother was right but I heard my father answer, "You may do as you like but I'll always disapprove of the sorority and wish she would have nothing to do with it."

When I came downstairs for dinner Mama said, "Call Gloria Shuman right now and tell her you want her to go to the picture show and have lunch

with you tomorrow. Tell her that we will pick her up at 9:30."

The next morning I looked carefully at my friend.

"Gloria, are you all right?" I asked, my voice quivering.

Gloria looked me straight in the eye with an expression so peaceful it stunned me. I'd never seen such an expression on the face of a girl our own age.

"Yes," she said, and then there appeared a smile that curled softly on her lips. "I'm fine. Don't worry about me." I wondered what Gloria's mother said to her to make her so confident. Whatever it was it was powerful, and I wished I knew what it was. But I knew that my friend, over the past twenty-four hours, had become an adult.

BY THE LATE NINETEEN-FORTIES, polio in Texas reached epidemic proportions. Evidence linked the rise in polio victims to crowded public swimming pools and to temperatures that reached over 100 degrees for days on end. We were not allowed in any public places like the movies, or pools. My parents became so alarmed that they had to get us four children out of the heat and away from the crowds as soon as school was out. It seemed logical to my father that we spend our summers in Martha's Vineyard in the rustic camp built by my uncle, Bobby Hyde, who'd married my father's sister, my aunt Lydia. Cement was in such demand for the postwar construction boom that Portland cement was backordered for as much as six months. My father, the affable General Portland Cement salesman, had very little to do, other than taking orders, and telling his customers they had a long wait for delivery. His secretary could do this while he took his family to the Vineyard.

Daddy spoke often of his carefree summer days as a child in Martha's Vineyard and took pleasure in telling us about his teenage years sailing and going to beach parties and dances on the island. He loved it so much that he and my mother went to the Vineyard for their honeymoon in nineteen-thirty. I knew even at the age of thirteen that the Vineyard was where my father had been his happiest.

Driving from Texas to Massachusetts in a Ford with a rowboat secured on top of the car became an annual June event. It thrilled me to smell the salt air for the first time each summer when we stood on the upper deck of the ferry crossing the Vineyard Sound. I soon came to think of the voyage as going to another world, so different were the people, the way they spoke and what they said. My new friends had opinions on every subject. It's not that they didn't have opinions in Texas—they did have them and they were strong. I only remember that I disagreed with most of them and they always seemed to be putting someone down for no good reason, I thought. And the

Sixteen-year old Mary at Martha's Vineyard.

new Vineyard friends seemed to appreciate me in a way I wasn't appreciated in Texas. They talked about things I'd never given much thought to, and wanted to know what I thought about world events I had heard my parents discuss at the dinner table but which I had not really paid much attention to before. They listened to me when I dared to give my views. I also became aware that it was better to think before I spoke, but this was often difficult. My New York cousins made fun of me at first because of my Texas accent, but soon, because I had a knack for languages, the accent almost disappeared, and never fully came back.

My parents established a pattern: that the entire family, before going up to Martha's Vineyard, would spend a week at Snedens Landing in New York on the Hudson. My grandmother had left my father in her will several pre-Revolutionary houses. He rented out these houses to the same people for years. One, "the Pirates' Lair," was always saved for our visits.

The summer I was fifteen I fell in love at Snedens. Dave Langston was my first real boyfriend. Not only was he tall and blond, but he was a great dancer, and played the guitar. My three younger brothers and younger male cousins who were always at our house were fascinated by this new relationship. They chanted his name in singsong whenever the telephone rang and giggled when they saw him coming down the path to the house. Dave and I became "a couple" and danced most of the time we were together.

When we first met at a dance at my cousin Sarah's house he crossed the room to ask me to dance. It was a slow dance: "Moonlight Becomes You." When he took me in his arms for that first dance I was impressed by the way he immediately took charge. He held me firmly and knew how to "lead" and moved me around the dance floor with assurance.

"You follow so easily," he said. "It's as if we've danced together many times before. It's nice," he whispered in my ear, and smiled down at me.

I remember smiling back and saying, "And where did you learn to dance so well?" I rested my hand on his shoulder and thought, "This is so much fun and the evening has just begun."

"What are you smiling at?"

"I like dancing with you."

In fact I realized later that it was because he was such a good dancer that I was attracted to him. We never missed a step whether it was the rumba, the samba, jitterbug or fox trot. I saw that my cousins were watching us. Their expressions, I noticed, seemed to show that they were pleased with me. Their new Texas cousin was a success. Later my cousin, Sarah, who was the same age said, with a touch of envy in her voice, "Well, that didn't take long. You already have an admirer."

I thought the tenants were all fascinating people, Jerome Robbins and the pianists Arthur Gold and Robert Fizdale among them. They apparently found me amusing too because one summer day Mr. Fizdale invited me to come and stay with them after my parents went back to Texas, if I wanted to stay on in New York. They lived in the "Ding Dong," the name Granny gave to the beautiful white house with a bell attached at the entrance under the arching grape arbor that ran along the length of the house. I was honored and never forgot this invitation, but my parents wouldn't hear of such a thing. I loved standing outside their house listening as the sound of Bach's two-piano duets came floating out the window, and sometimes I could hear when the two men laughed quietly together after finishing a piece. Wonderful smells also came from the house, telling me of the couple's love of cooking. One day Mr. Fizdale remarked that their friend, George Balanchine, was coming for lunch. When they discovered I was a dancer, they told me about their friends John Cage and Jerome Robbins. Both men came out to the country from New York to luncheon parties that Gold and Fizdale gave. Mr. Fizdale said he would show me how to make chicken tetrazzini that John Cage so loved. To me, theirs was the most thrilling life I could imagine. They'd travelled everywhere and knew so many people. One afternoon I stopped on the way up the hill to the bus stop just to listen to the two amazing pianists playing a Chopin duet. I breathed in the smell of a rich French stew coming through the grape arbor from their house. When I smelled that delicious aroma, heard that music and somehow knew how happy the two men were together, I decided that theirs was the life I must have one day. Everything they did showed their love of life, and I could see how much they cared for each other, these two friends. A realization came to me suddenly when one afternoon I was invited to listen to their practicing. They had just finished playing a beautiful duet and they seemed particularly pleased with themselves. They suddenly threw their arms around each other and kissed on the mouth. I had never seen two men kissing before and it embarrassed me. They must have forgotten I was there in the living room.

That summer was a magical one and I seemed to have become an adult in one big spurt: falling in love, losing my Texas accent, meeting the famous pianists, and invited to lunch without my parents, on my own like a grown up, with Gold and Fizdale—all in one summer. In addition to other things, Mr. Gold and Mr. Fizdale showed me how to cook in a wok.

Letters went back and forth all winter between my New York beau, Dave Langston in New York and me back in Texas. The first meeting of the summer was always filled with trepidation, neither of us knew whether the other would feel the same as we'd left the year before. But we needn't have worried: the same feelings were always there and our faces showed it. We fell into each other's arms and the world became a different place. Over the next four years we were increasingly starry eyed, excited to see each other, and to dance together again. Dave took me to parties where we drank soft drinks, then beer when I turned sixteen. Of course we danced to the popular songs of the day. Soon Dave suggested that we have "our song." It was "What'll I Do?" which he'd chosen that first summer when he knew we'd have to part for another year. Whenever I heard it on the radio, and that wasn't often, it brought a few tears.

The sojourns at Snedens were shortened by the determination of my father to get to the Vineyard as soon as possible. That pattern beginning in 1948 of stopping at Snedens for a week was all we were allowed. It later crossed my mind that Daddy might have wanted to separate the young couple as everyone knew it had grown into a serious romance.

It was at the Vineyard on one of my solitary sessions on the dunes that I realized my tastes and interests had changed. Even I realized that I was changing and growing up during the high school years. Instead of rush parties, acquiring movie star photographs, and going to the picture shows my summer days were now filled with "rusticated" living. The "Tonetti camp" as it was called by the islanders and summer people alike, was on a rural road two miles outside Vineyard Haven. It was surrounded on three sides by water. From the front porch, on a clear day, we could see Woods Hole on the mainland beyond the Vineyard Sound. The sandy beaches stretched in front of our three-bedroom house or "camp" down to Herring Creek which was banked by two man-made jetties. The current was so strong it was a challenge to swim across without getting swept out to sea if the tide was running out. Behind the camp, Lake Tashmoo, always miraculously filled with clams, came almost up to the back door.

Swimming several times a day in the salt water was a substitute for the daily bath. We had no telephone, no radio, and no plumbing. Each of us had to carry a bucket of seawater to leave by the toilet for the next person's flushing. Daily treks into Vineyard Haven were a necessity when we filled gallon jugs with water for cooking, and sponge baths after the morning dip in the Sound. I didn't mind the sticky salt crystals that dried and flecked on my sun-browned body. I did, however, look forward to going to my cousin's house for a weekly shampoo in fresh water and a luxurious hot bath.

The elegant white sand dunes dotted with native grasses and beach plum shrubs provided ample protection from the wind, offering privacy for nude sunbathing and reading that had both become addictions. Nude sunbathing was a common practice on the Vineyard although I was the only one in the

Mary showing her freshly made blueberry pies.

family to make it a routine. My brothers knew I lay nude in the sand dunes and were embarrassed by it at first but then eventually accepted it as just part of my being different from the sisters of their friends. Tolstoy, Dostoevsky and George Eliot replaced Betty Grable, Van Johnson and Veronica Lake in my new hierarchy of interests. I listened to my mother who suggested these authors to me. I knew my mother had worked for Scribner's Publishing Company as the secretary to Max Perkins in New York before she married. Mama told me wonderful stories about the writers she'd known at that time: Thomas Wolfe and John Dos Passos were two of them. I loved hearing about my mother's life in the publishing world of New York before she married Daddy. I remember thinking how different her life had been before she married my father. When I asked about this she said simply "I knew when I first met your father that I wanted to marry him. He was the 'cat's meow', I never looked back."

The idyllic Vineyard life produced healthy bodies and long dinner table discussions about novels, politics and the world. Nourished young minds began to show signs of independent thinking. When I wasn't reading novels I fished for flounder with my father and brothers on the shallow "middle ground" half way toward the mainland in the Sound. Or I went on sailing dates with new friends, or to elaborate clam bakes and beach parties in the evenings. It was at those beach parties that I realized Dave was not the only boy in the world. There were others who interested me just as much.

Because of the plethora of wild blueberries and freshly caught fish I was developing my skills as a cook. Required blueberry picking for the whole family brought enough berries for the pies, muffins, cobblers and jam that made up my repertoire. The daily catch of flounder and bi-weekly clamming expeditions were so productive that our family was able to live almost entirely off the land for the two and a half months we spent each year at the Vineyard. We never found a better way to prepare the freshly caught flounder that my brothers scaled, gutted and filleted as soon as we got back to shore. Then immediately they ran with them to the tiny kitchen where my mother and I dotted them with butter and minced red onion before popping them under the broiler. We always seemed to have enough fish to share with neighbors and relatives and even the Martha's Vineyard hospital.

BACK IN TEXAS during those years at Morningside Jr. High and the first year of high school my passion for dance filled my mind and my days. By the time I was sixteen I was dancing in the Fort Worth Civic Opera Corps de Ballet. When, Leon Varkas the head choreographer of the Metropolitan

Opera, came to Fort Worth to audition dancers, I was ecstatic when I was one of those selected. I was happier than I had ever been in my life and loved the routine of rehearsing every day after school for "The Bartered Bride", "Faust," and "Carmen," Those rehearsals and the letters I received from Dave three times a week made my life complete. Through the rehearsals, I came to know and admire the older girls in the corps de ballet, most of whom I'd seen in the hallways of Morningside Jr. High. They wore leotards under their calf-length skirts, and I noticed that even when walking, they looked like dancers. They were considered "artsy" by the sorority girls who turned up their noses at the non-conformists. Neither group paid the other much attention, and each felt superior. The dancers all knew at an early age that they wanted to dance professionally. I was not as committed but I worked hard and loved the exhilaration of putting on my leotards and dancing every day. I worked so hard I forgot all about the pettiness of SCS and the new high school sorority I had also pledged. Gamma Delta was just more of the same in spite of the fact that the girls were older. I kept hearing my father's voice saying how silly all of that pledging was, and I couldn't help remembering the tear-stained face of my old friend Gloria, who moved away the year after she was asked to leave SCS. I realized that I no longer felt it necessary to be part of that life. Dancing was all I wanted to do that first year at the High School.

When the Opera productions finished for the season, the choreographer called me aside. "You could become a professional dancer if you wanted to, but you will have to work much, much harder than you are doing right now."

"I realize that." It came out suddenly and unrehearsed, "And I don't think I have the talent to become a really good dancer. I don't think I have the discipline that I'd need. There are so many other things I'd like to try."

"Are you sure of this?" he asked.

"I want to go to college and study subjects I know nothing about, learn languages and, also travel, you know, see the world."

Leon Varkas looked at me with a serious expression, "You are lucky to have figured that out at such a young age. I hope you accomplish what you want in life." He put his hand on my shoulder and looked me in the eye. "You are a focused young lady and I think you will get what you want."


DURING THOSE TEENAGE YEARS, most of my friends and I were always in love. Sometimes it wasn't for very long but it felt serious. The boys I met on the Vineyard were all in Eastern prep schools, planning to go to one of the Ivies just a year or two away, and although I was still loyal to Dave I found the boys vacationing on the Vineyard very attractive. We were innocent, but at the dawn of the 1950s the muscles and sinews of the tanned teenage bodies were developing beautifully and both sexes appreciated each other's attractions.

I thought more than once that I was not missing Dave as I had in the past. I didn't rush to the mailbox to devour his letters. When I wondered what had happened to me that summer before I went to college to cause this change in feelings a startling thought hit me: what I loved about Dave was that he was such a good dancer. We never talked about books or ideas or what we were going to do with our lives. It was always the pleasure of the moment—the parties, the new dance steps and the movies. I saw clearly that the Vineyard boys interested me in a completely new way. And I was fascinated by what they had to say. For example they all seemed to know about what was happening in the world. I had no clue about the divergent views of Trotsky and Stalin, and I wondered about the expression "Better to be dead than Red." I brought these subjects up at the dinner table and asked my father to explain them to me. He was usually delighted to see that I took an interest in such things.

I knew for certain that what I looked forward to more than anything was the idea of going to Vassar in the fall. It would be a new life.

That last summer before college brought changes. Instead of reading most of the day I had a summer job as a receptionist at the Havenside Inn overlooking the Vineyard Haven harbor where the patrons came back year after year from Philadelphia, Boston and New York. I sorted the mail for the guests, did the flower arrangements for the dining room and answered the phone. It was a quiet sinecure I enjoyed, and I could continue to bring my novels to read when I wasn't busy at the inn. The guests were mostly over 75. I'd never seen or talked to people of that generation and I was fascinated by their gentle manner towards each other. At the Inn, I noticed, no one interrupted. The pervasive atmosphere was one of subdued kindness, which I saw as a welcome change from the noisy talkative family life at our crowded camp where we four siblings vied for attention and to hold the floor.

Whenever we went to the other side of the island, to Edgartown, I loved walking around the harbor, observing the people in the shops or in their yachts. I saw immediately that the crowd of young people was different from my friends who lived in more isolated cottages and camps near Vineyard Haven and Chilmark. They appeared to come from a different world, one that was wealthier and, I thought, more worldly. I'd study them, fascinated by the way they spoke to each other and the way they laughed in a hollow, self-conscious way. I discovered quite unexpectedly that they seemed to be competing with each other. On the one hand I felt intimidated by them and overcome with shyness. But at the same time I sensed, as I watched from a distance, that they were not as nice to each other as my friends on the other side of the Island were. They were just like the people in Fitzgerald's novels. At a dance at the Edgartown Yacht Club, I learned that these were the children of the Edgartown summer residents who sailed into the harbor from Bar Harbor, Kennebunkport, Long Island or other affluent watering holes on the East coast. I noticed how elegantly they dressed and how my own clothes never seemed quite right. And I preferred the other side of the island where my girlfriends wore simpler cotton dresses to the dances in the evening and unpretentious jeans or shorts during the day. Running into two of my friends on the street in Vineyard Haven the next day I was relieved to see they were genuinely glad to see me and seemed to appreciate me just the way I was.

That last summer before college brought "Dolly," the worst hurricane the Islanders had seen in years. Heavy rains hit us the morning of the hurricane. This was not unusual at times in late August, and I didn't think much about it. I sat in a cozy part of the camp reading *Gulliver's Travels* to my youngest brother, John. I leapt up when I heard the excited voice of our neighbor. "You'd better leave. We heard on the radio that a tremendous hurricane is due to hit the Island this morning. The weather advisory was mandatory: everyone should go into town as soon as possible. Look at the sky. It looks really bad."

My father agreed. "Thanks for coming to alert us. We'll follow you into town right away." Then he told me and my three brothers, to get in the car immediately. Within minutes, he had dashed to the car, and got it started after a few pushes on the choke. With the motor running, my mother, my brothers and I took our usual seats in the car, slammed the doors shut and we were off, leaving behind everything. There was such urgency that I forgot my handbag in the excitement—and that is what my brothers and I felt it was—an exciting adventure that we'd never experienced. "It's just like Gulliver's storm, isn't it, John?" I said this to my youngest brother with a touch of drama in my voice.

My three brothers and I turned to look through the back window at the waves crashing against the camp battering it with a force we'd never seen before. When the car kept stalling in the flooded road we all held our breath. Driving into town Daddy had to drive through pools of water, causing frequent stalls. The waters came together from the Sound and Lake Tashmoo with such force that I could feel the car labor to keep from getting us all swept off the road. During what seemed like an endless ride into town no one spoke. When we finally reached the paved road on the edge of Vineyard Haven there was a collective sigh of relief. We could see the harbor and watched boats crashing into each other. Some were completely overturned. Others looked like oversized prize fighters hitting each other again and again. Later that afternoon when the all clear was announced we piled back into the car to return to our house. The last curve in the road towards our little house opened up a vista that horrified us all.

My brother Joe was the first to speak, "Look. The water is still high."

Daddy spoke: "Yes. We won't be able to park in our usual space near the camp. We 'll try to get as close as we can."

I was thunder struck: "Look at the camp. Can you believe it?" It's turned on its side!"

We couldn't believe what we saw. The house had been ripped from its pilings, and looked like an intact matchbox pushed onto its side. When Daddy finally got close enough to park the car, we all jumped out and ran to the front of the house to look at the devastation. Then as if in a Dali painting or a Duchamps sculpture, we saw the bathroom toilet sitting upright on the beach in front of the house, uprooted from its privacy in the cubicle off the master bedroom. I ran down to the beach to see what else had been swept from the house and was floating in the flotsam of the now calm water. While the other members of the family gathered up shoes, bathing suits, towels, books, a few dishes and other random belongings that had been strewn over the beach grass and onto the beach, I sat in the sand, thinking "What will we do now? We can't stay here." My thoughts travelled miles away and I ran my fingers through the sand. I touched something, pulled it out, and saw a piece of paper with my own handwriting. At that moment my mind came abruptly back to the present. I read: "You have been there before but there will be an unusual amount of water." A chill came over me when I understood that it was one of the pages of notes I'd taken in Texas when I visited the numerologist, Miss Norris. On the beach I pictured Miss Norris who had gone into what appeared to be a trance-like state when she spoke of what she saw in my future. Such predictions as "There will be an unusual amount of water." I didn't understand at the time, but I, like the other clients who visited her regularly, did as Miss Norris insisted, and wrote down everything she told me. It was eerie how confident she was of her predictions. Sitting there in the sand two months later, after the morning's frightening event, I knew how uncanny it was that I should sit at just the right place on the beach to uncover the paper that I'd thrust into my handbag before leaving Texas. I ran up to the house where my parents were standing to show them the mysterious note.

"Look at this. You made fun of me when I insisted on going to the numerologist. And look what she said and what I wrote from that last meeting. I found it in the sand just now." My father and mother exchanged glances, and they both shook their heads in amazement. No one could believe the workings of fate. And I never found my handbag or any of the things in it. Although the house was righted the following year, the summers were never quite the same. We Tonettis never again returned for the entire summer as a complete family of six.

Mary at Martha's Vineyard, 1940s.

Aimée Dorra

# V
# England, June 1940-45

*"We shall not flag or fail, we shall go on to the end, we shall fight in France,*
*we shall fight on the seas and oceans...we shall fight on the landing grounds,*
*we shall fight in the fields and in the streets, we shall fight in the hills;*
*we shall never surrender. And even if...this island...were subjugated and starving,*
*then our Empire beyond the seas armed and guarded by the British fleet,*
*would carry on the struggle, until, in God's good time, the new world,*
*with all its power and might, steps forth to the liberation and rescue of the Old..."*
—WINSTON CHURCHILL, MAY 11, 1940

DAYS AND DAYS PASSED. We could not know how many, for nights were sleepless and melted into the daylight hours mixed alternately with tedium and fear. We zigged and zagged though the Atlantic waters, avoiding both the German submarines cruising the Atlantic and the Luftwaffe above us. Dogfighting between the spitfires and the *Messerschmitt* were a daily occurrence. All of us huddled together, even complete strangers, not knowing whether we would drown in the ocean or suffer the direct attacks from the barrage of bullets launched from the *Faocke-Wulf* biplanes above us. The noise was horrendous.

We had no idea where we were being taken. Food was almost non-existent; tempers were rising amongst the passengers, and everything was beginning to smell, something abhorrent to Maman. I noticed that she saved the last drops of *Vol de Nuit* to dab on her wrists and handkerchief. She buried her nose into the linen handkerchief to stifle the smells that, even in the open air, so offended her. It's hard to know whether Maman missed Papa or not. She never talked about him and I didn't bring up his name very often. She really seemed happier when he wasn't around, I thought.

Maman seemed to particularly enjoy the company of her neighbor who turned out to be one of the last of the Romanian royal family. The rings on three fingers of each hand first attracted my attention. They were all different, gold settings of Alexandrite, opal and lapis, and the fingers were slender, long and beautiful. Her name was Maria and she discussed Proust with Maman, to keep their minds off the present. A rust colored woolen shawl covered her thin, blond hair streaked with gray, and she spoke to Maman between violent shudders that racked her entire body. "Where are we? When will this misery end? I have no more drugs and you can't imagine what it is like to be without my heroin."

I looked at her shaking hands, not at her eyes, and at one point when I did look up at her she looked me straight in the eye and said, "It is like Christ on the cross, what I am suffering." Maman and I could find no words to comfort her. Never have I seen anyone shaking so uncontrollably.

The nights were cold, forcing us to huddle close together to keep our bodies warm. The thundering sound of airplanes overhead caused an anxiety that made our hearts beat faster and caused us to forget the pangs of hunger that were a constant reminder of the meager rations we received. I tried to think of the warmth of the fire in the library at Chardonneux. It helped.

"Maman, I have kept track of the days by the sunrises each morning and we have been at sea for seven days."

"We must then be approaching Canada, if we have been at sea that long. If we were arriving in England, we would have done so before now, don't you think?"

Others, overhearing our conversation, nodded in agreement. Before anyone could answer we heard a bright Englishwoman's voice on the loudspeaker welcoming us to we knew not where. One of the better English speakers declared with excitement, "That is my cousin Lady Astor. I would recognize her voice anywhere. We must be in Dover." Announcements followed telling us that we were about to arrive in England and to be prepared to disembark within half an hour.

The excitement was palpable. Although exhausted, everyone felt a new infusion of hope as we gathered our belongings around us and prepared to disembark on English soil. Our hope was countered, however, by the shortwave radio that blared news of Mussolini joining the Axis powers on June 11. We listened with dismay to the news that France was bombed mercilessly two days after we left Saint-Jean-de-Luz. Churchill's voice on the shortwave radio insisted on keeping up the fight, no matter what. Even the devastating news of the attacks on France had not deterred him. We all agreed that if there were any hope at all for the survival of the civilized world it would be in Churchill.

AS WE DISEMBARKED at Dover, each passenger was given 20 pounds. Each of us received a strong handshake from the British officers, and the Captain of the ship along with his officers offered their good wishes. Maman looked out from the top deck admiring the white cliffs, dabbed a bit of *Vol de Nuit* on her wrists, pushed her chic cloche hat further down on her head and thanked the crew while I managed to find a sturdy cart and began to load our luggage onto it. Somehow, we managed in the next few hours to get ourselves by train to London and to a modest hotel where we collapsed with a fatigue we had never known before. We decided that above all sleep was what we needed. We left instructions with the desk clerk not to be disturbed under any circumstances. It was after a day and a half that we finally descended the stairs and out into the street. In contrast to the darkness of the future the day was a brilliant sunny one.

"The first thing we must do is buy a new hat. I have no suitable hat for London," Maman said with a new energy befitting our new life. "Then we will go to Simpson's in the Strand for some wonderful English roast beef. Then tonight we will go to the Savoy for dancing. We must celebrate having got this far."

I couldn't resist smiling.

She continued, "You like that idea? I have invited Colonel Flanders to join us for lunch. You remember who he is, don't you?"

Of course, I remembered who he was. He was the RAF pilot whom Maman gave a large sum of money to if he could arrange to get it out of Egypt and into a British bank in her name. It had been very dangerous for him because if caught, he would go to prison for helping the émigrés. It was also a risk for Maman. I don't know how she knew she could trust him. That seemed so long ago, and I remember thinking Father would have a heart attack when he heard what she had done. I marveled at Maman's risk-taking but of course she was right. The money was in the bank in her name.

In a cloud of anticipation for the roast beef at Simpson's, we were unaware at first of a disheveled old woman who was crossing the street towards us shouting.

"I know who you are and I know what you are. You are refugees. Like me, I have been a refugee here for thirty years."

The old woman came closer, and we tried to escape her menacing finger pointed at us. "And don't think the British will accept you. I am still a refugee. I am a Pole, and I will always be a Pole."

Our footsteps clattered on the rough sidewalks as we hurried to get away from the loud shouting old woman who was following us, still talking either to us or to whomever was within earshot. Suddenly with a frightening laugh she added in a strong, self-satisfied tone, "You are Jews. I can tell."

I put my arm around my mother, and we continued as if we didn't notice her. I turned to Maman and whispered, almost laughing, "It is like a witch scene from Shakespeare." Others in the street had stopped to listen, but seeing the agitated state of the woman, they too wanted to get away as quickly as possible. When the old woman saw that everyone was moving away from her and all were rather frightened, she stopped her haranguing and said to no one in particular. "It's because of the likes of you that we are in this dreadful war."

I could feel Maman's arm shaking against mine. She was distressed, I knew, although she would never admit it to me. I remember thinking, "Is this what we must face for the rest of our lives?"

Colonel Flanders was waiting for us at Simpson's and had been seated in a sunny corner near the window. We would both have recognized him even if he hadn't been wearing his uniform. He looked handsome as he stood to greet us, smiling broadly. "You made it," he said with genuine warmth. "I am so happy to see you. I was afraid you wouldn't be able to come."

"Yes. And we have much to tell you, Colonel."

He grasped Maman's arms with both of his and seemed about to embrace her when she pulled back and continued, "Much has happened since we last parted in Alexandria at the Sporting Club. I never believed that you could really manage to get the money safely into my bank here in London." She looked intensely into his eyes. "We are so grateful that you were able to help us."

I saw that the Colonel's hair was beginning to show a little grey at the temples and had to admit I thought it exceedingly attractive. I knew he was around 40 years old, only three years older than Maman. I knew this because Maman had told me for some reason that they had discussed their ages in Alexandria when they were last together—an eternity ago.

"You look wonderful. One would never know you had just been through such a harrowing experience."

Maman blushed with pleasure and looked at me to see if I had noticed how much the compliment pleased her. I wondered if the compliment were not just another example of his good manners. I remembered her telling me that his good manners had been what she had first noticed and attracted him to her at the Club three years ago. The Colonel looked at her with admiration and turned to me, "You know your mother is one of the smartest women I have ever met." Then, turning to Maman, "Please be my guests today for lunch. I know that you made the reservation, but I would like to be host and want to celebrate your arrival in London."

The waiter had arrived at our table. The Colonel, turning to Maman, "Shall it be champagne to start or a gimlet? As you may know the latter is a remarkable creation here."

I had been admiring the wood paneled walls, the warmth of the fireplace, and the feeling of English comfort and stability the restaurant offered, all of which added to my good spirits. I felt happy indeed for the first time in a long while. I smiled at the Colonel, "I have never had a gimlet and would like to try it. It sounds so British."

We regaled our host with the tales of our escape, passing the afternoon feasting on rare roast beef, Yorkshire pudding and cabbage along with many glasses of a good Burgundy wine. Before we had reached the famous treacle sponge with Madagascan vanilla custard, the conversation turned serious.

Colonel Flanders looked at me with an intense expression. "I trust you will continue your studies at the University of London or at Cambridge. I remember hearing that you were studying in Paris and that you distinguished yourself as a student."

"They exaggerate." I frowned at Maman.

"Now, don't protest. Both your parents are so proud of you. I would love to know what your plans are for now."

I looked at Maman, my mouth open, preparing to speak. Before I could answer, Maman retorted with evident pride, "He will of course continue his Engineering studies while working as an engineering apprentice at the Thomson Houston Company in Rugby."

*"Mais, non,* Maman. Let me talk." I was always angered by her speaking for me and particularly in this situation with the Colonel, the only man I had conversed with for months.

"I suppose you will be studying at the Rugby College of Technology and Arts there. It has a very good reputation. But is it still functioning during these difficult times?"

"I don't think the air raids in Rugby are as frequent as they are in London, if there are any at all. I hear it is pretty quiet there."

Colonel Flanders was visibly impressed, and continued to ask about my future plans. "But what about Cambridge? I thought that was the plan—that you would eventually go to Cambridge."

"I wanted to go to Cambridge but when I was interviewed the dean said it would be an extraordinary exception to his principles to admit me. He said there would be no future for me in England."

"What did he mean by that? There is always room for a smart engineer."
"I think he meant because I am a Jew. I was stunned when he said 'Jews can

Henri and Aimée Dorra, 1940s.

be intuitive, but they're not really…It's not solid. They don't have that kind of precise, steel-like mind that makes a good scientist or engineer.' I saw for the first time that he was an anti-Semite, and it surprised me that he spoke his views so honestly."

"Didn't that make you angry that he made such a distinction? It would have infuriated me." I saw that the Colonel was bristling with anger, and I couldn't help being pleased that he was showing such anger on my behalf. His voice grew louder. I looked around nervously and noticed that the waiter had been standing nearby and listening attentively to the conversation. When I caught his eye, the young man started and moved away discreetly.

Then lowering his voice, the Colonel continued his questioning.

I too lowered my voice. "It didn't make me angry, and I felt glad that I had begun to learn what makes the world tick. It was an important lesson, I realized. It had suddenly occurred to me, maybe I'm in the wrong field. Maybe I should go into business or something." I had hardly paused between sentences. The words came tumbling out.

"If you want to be an engineer you should forget what that old fart of a dean said to you. Follow your dream. Do you understand me?"

Before answering, I drank a sip of the golden Chateau Yquem that had been placed before me and closed my eyes to savor the sweet wine to its fullest. "I will of course come back to London and to the University when the war is over and hopefully get my Bachelor of Science there. Instead of at Rugby."

The dessert had arrived and was being served. The Colonel regained his control and lowered his voice still further. "You are right. You must keep on working and I know you will do well."

Maman who had become unusually quiet during the previous conversation changed the subject abruptly.

"Nothing could be more English than this dessert," she said with a smile. "Let us begin."

"And you, Aimée? Will you remain alone in London despite the danger or will you, too, go down to Rugby?"

"How could I think of being buried in Rugby. No. Henri needs to be alone to finish his studies. There is nothing for me in small towns. I will stay here in London which I love, and I will get used to the air raids. Henri will come to see me on vacation." She looked at the Colonel with tenderness for the first time all evening.

"And what about Clement, your husband? Have you news of him?"

She responded without smiling in a staccato voice, "He is still in New York and we were finally able to wire him this morning that we are safe. We will join him in New York if this war is ever over."

"Then I will have the pleasure of your company often until then, I hope?" I looked from one to the other and saw that the Colonel could not take his eyes off Maman. We both saw how the candlelight had created a halo around the soft curls that framed her face and the dazzling smile that appeared on her lips when she answered "Yes. Of course." She was appreciating the moment and had never looked lovelier.

Aimée Dorra, 1940s.

Mary Lawrence Tonetti, 1954.

# VI
# College Days in the Fifties
## OLD VALUES WEATHER NEW EXPERIENCES

ON THE TAXI RIDE to the Middlebury French summer school I saw streams with willows bordering their banks, stands of silver birches shimmering along narrow roads winding through the hills. Wildflowers colored the fields. The whole effect was breathtaking. It must be like driving through France, I thought. I wondered if perhaps the countryside might be similar, and smiled at the idea, and at myself for thinking that everything that was beautiful must be French. As the taxi approached the Middlebury College campus my heart beat faster. I knew that summer in Vermont was going to be thrilling because I was free to live my life on my own. *En plus* it would all be in French and I would be free to experience it. French expressions were already beginning to pepper my mind and I was excited at the idea of signing a pledge to only speak French for the entire six weeks. It was the next best thing to going to France which was my goal in life. Yet I had an unsettling premonition that something new and different was going to happen that would require me to be a thinking adult rather than an irresponsible fun-seeking teenager.

I found my Vassar friend Abigail Norton and the two of us registered for classes, signed the requisite pledge to speak only French, and headed for the ivy covered building where we would spend the next six weeks. On the way to the dorm we struggled to think in French and get the right words for what we wanted to say. Hopefully that would become easier. We were met at the dorm by Abigail's younger friend, Mimi Anderson, who knew Abigail from their Long Island summers and, unlike us, would have another year of high school before entering college. She seemed pleasant enough although I found her constant, confident chatter irritating. She hadn't even signed the pledge yet but began immediately once we were introduced, "*Enchantée de vous connaitre,*" she said tossing her long hair over her shoulder. Then she went into a non-stop description of her ride up to Middlebury on the train and the handsome boy who sat opposite her who had been reluctant to speak to her. I could certainly understand why he didn't respond to her as she continued to tell me in great detail how cute he was and what he was reading, etc. Poor boy, he was probably wishing he could move to another seat to get away from this chatterbox. She was completely unaware of our inattention to her endless rambling. Instead of listening to what she was saying I was listening for her to make mistakes in French grammar. There weren't any, however, and her French although spoken in an irritating Park Avenue accent, was perfectly correct. She just kept on talking, not waiting for us to interject any sort of comment. Once inside the dorm we all climbed the stairs and began to look for our assigned rooms along the corridor on the second floor.

At the top of the stairs I was met by an unexpected surprise. Kate Miller, a girl I had known briefly at the beginning of freshman year stood there as if waiting for us. She had been an odd person who was known to frequent the cemetery across from the campus and down half a bottle of gin nightly while sitting among the tombstones. She wasn't someone a person was likely to soon forget. Her short dark hair stuck out in all directions and was singularly unbecoming.

"When I learned you were coming to Middlebury, I thought it would be fun if we were on the same corridor since we both were in the same class at Vassar."

I was at a loss for words. The last thing I wanted was to be on the same corridor with this weird Kate and that naïve Mimi for the entire summer. Inwardly I groaned, but remembering my manners, I introduced Abigail and Mimi to Kate. The latter had begun to stare intently at Abigail in a way that made all of us rather nervous, that is, except for Kate who continued to address Abigail directly.

"Yes. I think I remember seeing you at Vassar last year," she said to Abigail. "I remember you play the piano rather well."

"Yes. I play but not very well," Abigail responded with an embarrassed smile. "I hope there is a piano around here somewhere because I do enjoy it, and my playing would benefit from some practicing."

Holding her head high and with an air of superiority Kate continued, "I shall look forward to hearing you play; I believe there is a piano on the first floor." I was surprised when the haughty expression disappeared, and her face changed with a smile that was almost beguiling. She looked more agreeable than I had ever seen her.

Perhaps she isn't as strange as I remember, I thought to myself as I picked up my suitcase and began to search for my room along the corridor.

"*A bientôt,*" Abigail offered to Kate as she followed us along the corridor.

One of the many beautiful Vermont watering holes that is enjoyed by summer visitors. Photo courtesy of Mike Mahaffie

"*Bien sur. J'attend avec plaisir notre diner toutes ensemble. A bientôt,*" Kate returned cheerfully.

We were all anxious to unpack and get settled before meeting for dinner, so we quickly dispersed to our respective rooms.

MY CLASSES in phonetics, advanced grammar and conversational French met every morning for several hours, followed by lab work in phonetics and homework assignments which took most of the afternoon. Except for the wakeup call for Abigail, "*Bonjour. C'est l'heure de se reveiller,*" I hardly saw Kate or Abigail. We had agreed when we first arrived to have dinner together once or twice a week but that just didn't happen. Meanwhile I had made it a point to get to know some of the other students who were in my classes. As for Mimi, I actually saw more of her than I wanted to. She seemed to be present wherever I turned, as if desperate for my attention. I felt sorry for her because she seemed so lonely. A few times I asked her to come along with some of my new acquaintances for picnic sandwiches down by the river's edge. It was there almost two weeks after our arrival that Mimi confessed she was very lonely, and was being ignored by her friend Abigail.

"It was because of her that I signed up to come here for the summer session. Now she appears to prefer Kate's company and I hardly see her."

I didn't know what to say. "Oh, I think she is still your friend, but I think they have bonded over Abigail's playing. I see them together often in the music room and they seem always to be enraptured by the music. The way Abigail plays Chopin is very impressive, don't you agree?" I hoped I had successfully changed the subject.

Mimi did not seem to be distracted by my comment and continued, "You don't think it strange that Abigail appears to see only Kate?"

I reflected, and then mused aloud in somewhat disjointed sentences, crossing and uncrossing my legs as I tried to think of something comforting to say, "Abigail is so outgoing. I am sure she sees other people. It does seem strange, however, that I see so little of Abigail except when I wake her in the morning. Perhaps it is my fault. I should remind her to join us for dinner the way she used to."

"But I have asked her to have dinner with me and she always seems to have an have an excuse not to join me alone. She said I could have dinner with her and Kate but, you know, I really don't like Kate. She is so odd. Have you noticed how she looks at Abigail? And how she never really looks at anyone else. And that curious all-knowing smile of hers is so annoying." Mimi's voice had reached a new pitch as she stood, arms folded in front of me.

I had to admit that since she arrived at Middlebury my initial opinion of Kate had not changed. Her behavior was still strange. It was as if no one was quite interesting enough for her except Abigail. And Abigail was such a gregarious person it was now mystifying to me that she wanted to spend so much time with Kate. I noticed Mimi's puzzled frown and said aloud "They are so different. But then there's so much about people I don't understand.

"Nor do I, but obviously I haven't given it as much thought as you have. I am sorry."

"No need to be sorry. It's not your fault." Mimi was really hurt. I saw that she had turned to look out the window and that her lips were trembling.

"I know Abigail was your friend, and it is sad when one feels a friend has just disappeared for no reason."

She turned to face me and I saw there were tears in her eyes.

"You just introduced them but they were bound to meet anyway, I guess. The music and all."

I could see how upset she was, and that she didn't want me to see the tears that were now streaming down her face as she stumbled back to her own room.


IT WAS 7:30 AM, the usual hour that I knocked on the door of Abigail's room for her morning wakeup call. There was no answer. I knocked again, and when there was still no answer I pushed the door open. What I saw caused me to clutch at the doorjamb to balance myself. I felt faint. The shades had been drawn making the room so dark I could barely make out a figure stretched across the bed, with a head hanging off the mattress. It was Abigail, and her face was streaked with dried blood, her eyes almost swollen shut. I could see welts on her arms and. I shrieked, "What happened to you Abigail! You have been attacked. We should call a doctor."

"No. That won't be necessary. I ran into a door."

"Sure! I believe that," I said with a heavy tone of sarcasm. It was no time for a joke.

"I'll be all right. Don't worry."

"I am going to call your mother."

"No please. I don't want her to know anything about this." She turned on her side writhing in pain, and it made me uncomfortable just to look at her.

"But someone has to know about this. You may be even more seriously hurt than you think."

"Promise me you won't call her. I'll lay low for a few days until the swelling goes down."

"But, my god, have you seen your face? It is a mess. Can't you tell me what really happened?"

"I can't." She lifted herself up with great effort and grasped my hand. With a tearful voice she pleaded, "I know you mean well but I am right in this case. You mustn't call my family. My mother would die if she heard anything about this."

"But you must tell me who did this to you. Did you know the person? Was it another student?

Abigail fell back on the bed, "I don't think it will happen again...Kate only did what I asked her to do...and...things got out of hand."

I gasped, "What do you mean, Kate did what you asked her to? Why in the world would you ask Kate to do this to you?"

"I can't tell you anymore. And I have to sleep now. But you have promised not to tell my parents, right?"

"Okay. But it is against my better judgment." I could think of nothing else to say so I squeezed her arm and said, "I'll look in on you later."

That morning I could hardly concentrate on my classes. My French conversation class went badly because all I could think about was Abigail's beautiful blue eyes almost swollen shut. Right after class I cornered Mimi and steered her into the ladies' room where we could talk without being heard.

"What is it, Mary? You look worried, almost scared."

I began the story breathlessly. "You can't imagine how frightening it was. I discovered Abigail lying, almost lifeless, across her bed. She looked as though she had been in some terrible fight, and had dried blood all over her face which was so swollen I could hardly recognize her. "

"But who would possibly have done such a horrible thing? Oh no. The only person she has been seeing these days is Kate. Oh my God! She is such a strange person I wouldn't be surprised at anything she might do."

I struggled to find the right words and remembered only the worried look that came across Abigail's face as she tried to speak. "She didn't seem to want to blame it all on Kate and said she had asked for it. Can you believe that?"

"And what does that mean, 'She said she asked for it?'" Mimi's expression had changed quickly to an angry one. Her mouth hardened as her words escaped through her clenched teeth, "I can't imagine Abigail asking to be hurt like that."

"Who knows? I certainly don't understand the strange power Kate has over Abigail." I suddenly thought, "Why am I involving Mimi and disturbing her? She is not even out of high school. What could she possibly know about this kind of behavior? But then I thought I have no one else to talk to about

COLLEGE DAYS IN THE FIFTIES

this and she has known Abigail much longer than I have.

"Mimi, I don't understand her power over Abigail. But, I do think Abigail's mother should be told, and unfortunately she made me promise not to tell her parents."

"But you didn't promise not to tell the Middlebury authorities and I think we should go to the Dean's office together and explain the whole horrid thing." Mimi was now pacing the floor and thinking aloud.

I was beginning to see Mimi in a different way and was surprised by her clear thinking. Silence fell over both of us. "I guess you are right. Kate is so strange. I should tell the authorities here at the school. There's no telling what she is capable of. It might happen again." My plan was becoming clearer to me and I was determined to carry it out. I walked towards the door, opened it, and turned to face Mimi. "I must go now to the Dean's office."

"And you know, you didn't promise not to tell me, and I certainly should inform Abigail's parents and I will. Do you want me to go with you to the Dean's office? I will cut my next class if you need me."

"Oh, Mimi, thank you for offering to go with me. I do think it would be better if there were two of us. I have never been through anything like this." I was thinking how grateful I was to have Mimi and how I had misjudged her at first. She really was quite sensible.

At the Dean's office we were told to wait. When we finally were admitted to speak to the Dean I began to tell the story of how our friend had been beaten to the point that she could not go to class. As I was recounting what happened, as calmly as I could, Mimi interrupted.

"It had to be another classmate, and we know who was responsible for the attack. She is a very strange, even sadistic and probably shouldn't be here at the College."

I glared at Mimi, annoyed with her interruption, and cut her off. "There must have been a disagreement between the two girls and apparently it had got out of hand."

The Dean was listening carefully. Now and then she pushed her glasses down on her nose to look at both of us more directly. Finally, she spoke.

"The College can do nothing about this. It is a personal matter between students, and the College has a non-interference policy when it comes to student relations."

"But this might be really dangerous!" I insisted.

"I am sorry but the College feels that its summer school students are all adults and cannot become involved in their affairs." She looked at her watch. Mimi gasped in disbelief. "So you will not speak to Kate Miller or try to find out what happened?"

"That is correct." The Dean rose from her chair and motioned us towards the door. "And now if you will excuse me…"

Dazed by the Dean's remarks, we left her office without another word. When we were out of earshot I turned to Mimi, "I know what we should do. There is a girl in my phonetics class, Edna Macy who is very smart. We have been having coffee together and I have come to respect her very much. I think we should ask her what to do."

"It wouldn't hurt to ask someone else, I think. We can't stand by and do nothing."

"Edna has just graduated from Bryn Mawr and is Phi Beta Kappa to boot. You will see how smart she is."

"Well, that is impressive. It wouldn't hurt to ask her what she thinks."

We found Edna in her room who was fortunately there studying. I recounted the entire story of what happened that morning and waited expectantly, anxious for the older girl's advice. Edna stood up, a good four inches taller than either Mimi or me, and with a wry smile, looked patronizingly down at us. "This is something you could not possibly understand. Sometimes there are games people play that are not understood by outsiders. Love can be, and often is, painful. If I were you I would just forget the whole thing."

Mimi and I exchanged shocked glances, both stunned by this remark. Once again, we had been told, in short, to mind our own business. We looked at each other and at a loss for words both of us turned to leave the room. I turned back hesitating, "Maybe you are right, Edna. I never thought of it that way." But I was thinking to myself, I must really be naïve, and Mimi too, if Edna, the brilliant Phi Bete, and the Dean both think we should mind our own business. Of course, they've had more experience with life than we have. And yet, dammit! They hadn't seen Abigail's face and body all covered with welts and dried blood. No. It was not a question of naiveté and it was our business. We would just have to proceed elsewhere. I opened the door to leave, and Mimi followed me out of the room. Neither of us said a word.

When we were alone I turned to Mimi, "I am feeling more and more uncomfortable about having told Abigail that I would not call her mother." Mimi's face lit up. "You said you wouldn't call, but *I* didn't. Do you see what I am getting at?"

"Yes, I do. If you were to make the call it wouldn't be a betrayal."

I agreed. Mimi called Mrs. Norton that evening and Mimi put the phone between us so we could both hear Mrs. Norton's response. She was extremely upset but composed enough to thank Mimi for the call. I listened as Mimi tried to prepare Mrs. Norton for Abigail's appearance. It was difficult not to tell the truth about the condition of Abigail's face and body yet she didn't want to alarm Abigail's mother more than she had to.

Mrs. Norton replied rather off handedly, "You have shown good judgment and I appreciate your letting me know." Mimi realized that, in her attempt not to alarm Mrs. Norton, she had not expressed the severity of the situation strongly enough. Mrs. Norton wasn't getting it.

"I think you'd better come up as soon as you can." Mimi spoke slowly and clearly.

"Okay, Mimi. I hear in your voice that it is rather serious. I will have to cancel some meetings but I'll be up to get Abigail as soon as I can get away." She closed by saying that she was not to say a word about it to Abigail or to Kate.

Mimi and I looked at each other in relief when the receiver had been replaced on its hook. "You did a good job, Mimi. I am impressed. We must get some sleep now. I'll see you in the morning."

"Yes. I am ready for sleep. That took a lot out of me. I feel I have aged ten years."

I smiled at her. "Me too. This whole thing has been a frightful experience, hasn't it?"

That night as the day's events ran through my mind I thought to myself "How could Abigail have let herself get into that situation? I know that Kate and Abigail have come to care for one another in a way that I don't really understand. But I could never let myself be so subjugated to the will of someone else that I am no longer in control of my own thoughts and my actions. Could Abigail have been brainwashed by Kate to allow such things to happen? And what did Edna mean by 'games people play?' How could anyone let this happen, let alone her smart Vassar friend, Abigail? I began to envision the two girls together when they were alone and felt greatly disturbed by these thoughts. I felt a great sense of relief that Abigail's mother was now informed and would be arriving soon. That was the right decision; I was certain of it. Why Abigail was beaten was incomprehensible to me. What had led up to this? How long had this been going on? It must have been a very strong and passionate relationship. And Abigail was adamant in not wanting her mother to know what about what happened, or even about Kate's and her relationship, whatever that was. Could such a relationship be a good one? I thought not. In a strange way I felt grateful that I had been able to learn from this experience and felt a little more knowledgeable about the world. I also felt a strange reassuring confidence that I had the kind of self-preservation instinct that would prevent my ever being in such an abusive relationship. With this comforting thought I drifted into a more peaceful mode, emptying my mind of the whole horrible situation, and finally fell into a deep sleep.


I WAS NOT IN THE DORM when Abigail's mother arrived to take her daughter back to New York. When I returned to the dorm after my late afternoon phonetics lab, passing Abigail's room, I noticed the door was open. Leaning against the door looking at the empty room, I stood thinking how in just a day and a half so much had happened. The shades had been opened; the bed stripped, and I felt the emptiness of the room stifling. I didn't know how long I had been standing there but I was startled by a hand on my shoulder. Kate had appeared as if out of nowhere and said, in an almost hushed yet dramatic voice, "Yes. She is gone."

I turned abruptly and shrugged Kate's hand from my shoulder. We looked hard at each other for a few seconds, and I left the room without saying anything more.

During the last two weeks of the French summer session I hardly saw Kate, and when I did, I noticed she was always alone. She stood staring into space, her shoulders sagging, and she seemed shrouded in melancholy.


MARTHA'S VINEYARD at the end of summer was always the best part of the year. After Middlebury and its unhealthy atmosphere it was especially restorative to spend the end of summer vacation with my family at our summer camp on Martha's Vineyard. But this summer it felt like coming home from the hospital after a severe illness. Just breathing the clean salt air was a pleasure I never forgot. Even the sharp-toothed leaves of the beach plums seem to respond to the salubrious atmosphere as the gentle breezes made them dance in the air over the sandy dunes. Our cousins and friends envied the simple life we led in the little camp right on the Vineyard sound. They didn't know that on the other side of this carefree life we were awakened by the sun streaming into the bedroom early every morning, as we four children scrambled into our bathing suits to have our obligatory morning swim before breakfast. The fresh blueberries with our shredded wheat or blueberry muffins were a memorable Vineyard breakfast before we brushed out the sand every morning from the roughhewn floors and brought up buckets of sea water for toilet flushing.

The idyllic life on the Vineyard came to a close, but I still had much to look forward to. Since my family was leaving for the drive back to Texas, and I had a whole week before I had to be at Vassar for sophomore year, my parents decided I should stay at Snedens with my older cousin Angie, already in her twenties, and we would be chaparoned by our Aunt Annette. Needless to say, I loved this idea because I could spend all my days with Peter who at the end of the week would be escorting me up to Vassar. I had met Peter earlier in the summer before going to Middlebury. He was a junior at Harvard and very handsome with his curly brown hair. But the main appeal was his intellectual curiosity. We enjoyed each other's company on so many levels, and when we weren't swimming or playing tennis, we spent hours just talking to each other about the books we'd read and the movies we'd seen. His political views and his literary tastes were like mine and we loved being together. We were both reading Camus that summer and I had never met any boy who could discuss books as impressively as he did. He seemed to value my opinions too even though he was much better read than I was. We took from Camus's philosophy that summer: "You will never live if you are looking for the meaning of life." We just wanted to live and be happy and that's what we were in addition to being in love. It was a joyous end of summer.

Since my parents had returned to Texas, Peter, my new beau, drove me up to Vassar for the opening of the sophomore year. When we arrived at my new dormitory that September Sunday morning, there were already leaves of brilliant fall colors dotting the ground underneath the enormous trees all over the campus. The air was crisp and stimulating. It made me want to begin new classes and new ideas immediately. Everything looked just the way I remembered it except, as if in a bad dream, when I looked up to see a familiar figure standing at the entrance of my dorm. It was Kate with her arms folded across her chest looking for all the world like Medusa guarding the Virgin Palace. Her androgynous, angular body tensed when she saw me, and she bounded down the stairs to greet me as if she were the head of an official welcome committee.

"We're all here in Strong together," she said cheerfully. "I am waiting to see the surprise on Abigail's face when she learns that I am back at Vassar. I have been readmitted and requested to be here with the two of you in Strong."

My voice quivered a little as I managed to ask, "But how did you learn we were both going to be in this dorm? You haven't been in touch with Abigail have you?"

"No of course not. Her mother swooped her away from Middlebury in the early morning hours, and I have not seen her since. I did try to contact her in Long Island but was never allowed to see or even talk to her." Kate moved closer to me and spat out her sentences in bullets.

Meanwhile Peter had just stood nearby, aghast at the vehemence of this new person who had appeared so out of the blue and who was so angry. He looked at me and must have determined that I could probably handle the situation for he moved away and began to unload my suitcases. He took my hand and simply said, "Call me if you need me." I wanted to get away from Kate and to follow him but was at a loss of how to stop the conversation with Kate. I was already trying to figure out how I could get word to Abigail that Kate was here and living in the same dorm. I certainly didn't want to have more of the same drama that we had experienced at Middlebury. Something had to be done. The College had to be notified.

I never liked seeing people kiss in public and I certainly never had done so but somehow, I didn't mind when Peter held me and kissed me passionately right there on the steps of my dormitory before he drove away. There were other girls standing nearby looking at us and giggling, but I didn't care. This must be another new sign that I was changing. I was concerned about finding Abigail to warn her of Kate's presence on campus, and Peter had to drive up to Cambridge that afternoon which meant it was time to say goodbye. We kept thinking of things to say but finally let go of each other, promising to write often. I waved to him as I climbed the stairs before going to Abigail's room to find her or her roommates in order to alert them of Kate's presence. I didn't know her roommates well, but knew who they were, mostly Eastern boarding school girls who were always well dressed, rather snobby and exclusive.

"When is Abigail arriving?" I asked with more energy than I had intended and knew my voice was alarming to the first roommate I encountered.

The roommate looked startled "She should be here this afternoon. Why are you so excited? Is there something wrong?" Her crooked smile was wry, and her tone had a disdainful edge to it. She literally looked down her nose at me.

"Just let her know I am looking for her. I must talk to her."


IT WASN'T UNTIL late that night that I went to find Abigail in her room. She looked utterly exhausted, but her face lit up when she saw me.

"I'm so glad you came. I have been distraught beyond words. Did you see her? I did and was horrified. Can you believe she was here?"

"I tried to find you and warn you but your roommates didn't know when you would arrive and Kate was there keeping vigil outside the dorm. She was determined to see you."

"Well, it didn't take my parents long to go to the dean. I was stunned to see her at the top of the stairs when we pulled up in front of the dorm. I told my mother who she was. My parents are effective if nothing else. They immediately turned the car around and headed straight for the administration building and the dean's office."

I told Abigail that I knew her parents must have acted immediately and accomplished their mission. "I saw Kate later this afternoon outside the dining room where she was apparently waiting for me. She was fuming and I was frightened by her anger. She fairly hissed, "Abigail hasn't seen the end of me. I will haunt her for the rest of her life. She will never be forgiven for getting me kicked out of Vassar and for all the other things she did and didn't do at Middlebury."

Abigail's eyes widened with fear or shock when I finished. "Yes. My parents were incensed and determined. They always take charge, and in this case, Kate was asked to leave immediately."

"Even though she's not here on campus you'd better be warned," I broke in, "The last thing she said to me was that she would be waiting for you every Sunday night at the Poughkeepsie track in Grand Central Station."

"Oh my God! How frightening! I'm so glad you told me. I won't be coming back on the train from New York if that is the case. I'll hire a driver." She took my hand and sighed, "I am sorry you have had to be dragged into all this."

"Don't worry. I'm okay but we should get some sleep. It's all over now." I hoped it really would be over, but the image of Kate standing at the Poughkeepsie turnstile at Grand Central like a praying mantis waiting for her victim kept reappearing in my mind. I was afraid that I too would run into her again.

"Yes, it's been an emotional day. Now let's hope we can forget about this, and last summer too," she added, hesitating. "Don't say anything about this to my roommates." She added rather haltingly, "They know nothing about what happened at Middlebury and the less said, the better."

I agreed although I myself never had understood what really happened and didn't want to ask Abigail. I walked slowly up the stairs to my room where my beautiful Italian roommate, Alessandra, was sitting on her bed putting cream on her legs as if there were nothing more important in the world to be accomplished. "Ciao," she said with an engaging smile. I was suddenly aware of how lovely she looked: her deep brown eyes and lovely olive skin were set off by a soft green silk nightgown trimmed in lace. At the same time I thought to myself, life experiences are such a hassle and take so much out of one. I always thought one was supposed to learn from these experiences, but I didn't know what I had learned from the impact of Kate and Abigail and whatever their relationship had been last summer. And here again, I was drawn into the role of a sort of go between, with Kate telling me things I felt I had to report to Abigail for her own safety. Why did I get myself involved in these things? It made me realize how little I knew. But what else could I have done? This confusion left me very sad as images of that harrowing Middlebury experience came back to me. I hoped that whole chapter in my life was over now that Kate was on longer on campus. Then all of a sudden, I realized that unpleasantness would never be completely over. That is what life was about, short periods of calm and happiness broken by serious conflicts, even dangers that came totally unexpectedly and with such a force I certainly could not control them. "What will happen next?" I asked myself. It was time for some new good things to happen and hopefully it would be a period of joy and discovery with my new courses. I was particularly looking forward to Philosophy 105 and to beginning Italian.

Before going to bed, I carefully took out from the long cardboard tube a poster I had bought at the French bookstore in New York the previous week. It was a beautiful, lively street scene in Montmartre that I immediately tacked on the wall opposite my bed so that it was the last thing I saw before dropping off to sleep. I imagined myself walking down that street almost every night.

# PARIS
UNE RUE DE MONTMARTRE

Harvard Co-op bookshop. Photo coutesy of Harvard Book Store.

# VII

# Cambridge and The New World

"THE STUDENT who lived here before you was just like you—a foreigner—and he didn't keep the place very neat," my new landlady, Mrs. O'Hara said, looking at the stains on the carpet and sofa. "I hope you will be cleaner—even though I think you foreigners are all the same." Her dyed red hair was curled into ringlets giving a clownish look to her that almost made me laugh.

Her eyebrows were arched, and her look of skepticism became more pronounced as a new idea seemed to occur: "And since the war, there are more and more Jews coming into our country. Surely that cannot be a good thing for America."

I remember thinking how ignorant she was and hoped there would be very few encounters with her. It was best to just let it all pass, which I did.

"You are like all the others, the foreigners who have invaded Cambridge since the war. Be sure and clean out the bathtub each time you use it, and don't let the hair from your greasy brush clog the toilet." These were Mrs. O'Hara's final words, giving me the key to the apartment and marching out the door. No one had ever spoken to me like that. When she said "foreigners," I knew she meant more than that. Anti-Semitic and resentful feelings were usually expressed in an indirect way and not as directly as Mrs. O'Hara had voiced them, but I came to understand the hidden meaning of the recurring euphemisms so prevalent not only at Harvard and in Boston, but probably in the rest of America too.

What was I doing here? Americans were so different, even though we spoke the same language I had left behind in Britain. It may have been a mistake to leave Europe, although everyone advised me once I got my engineering degree from the University of London that I should try to get a Masters at Harvard or MIT. These thoughts preoccupied me on the day after arriving in Cambridge, where I had found a large apartment on Garden Street—not far from Harvard Square. Walking into the lifeless beige room, I knew the person who had lived here before had been as lonely as I had been. I moved my few things including my records and phonograph into the place on one of those muggy September afternoons that are so common in the Boston area in early fall when the summer hasn't quite disappeared. Immediately, I plugged in the phonograph and selected one of my favorite records to cover up the loneliness in the characterless room. As the first sounds of the late Beethoven sonata filled the air, I took a deep breath and felt immediately better. I sat down in the one comfortable chair in the room to enjoy the familiar sounds and plan where I would put the rest of the furniture I would have to acquire. I couldn't live with the landlady's sagging, overstuffed couch and the other motel-like bits of furniture. I decided I would have to go furniture shopping the very next day.

The heat was stultifying, the kind that leaves one exhausted after reading only a few paragraphs of the Sunday Times. Here in Cambridge, the pervasive dampness reminded me of Alexandria's, but without the softening of the Mediterranean breezes. Remembering those breezes brought back happy memories of walks with Papa along the Cornice, some of my most treasured times with him. We laughed a lot and always stopped for ice cream when we reached the Qaitbay Citadel. He enjoyed it as much as I did. Even as a grown man just thinking of the *noisette* ice cream at the Bahary ice cream parlor caused me to salivate. But before I could taste even one spoonful, Papa always made me answer the same questions. "When was the Citadel rebuilt and why?" He loved teaching me. I knew he would ask me these questions, and I was always ready with the date 1480 and "to protect Alexandria from the Turks." Laughing, he would pull my ear and ruffle my hair to show I had given the right answers. Then, "What is the name of the Seventh Wonder of the Ancient World that stood where the Citadel is now?" I scratched my head. I knew it was the Pharos lighthouse but it always puzzled me that the lighthouse remained one of the Seven Wonders even though the original no longer existed. Yet, now, Alexandria makes sense to me, here in Cambridge.

Once it was a city of great importance, but because of wars, it was no longer a cultural and religious mecca for Muslims, Christians and Jews alike. To the world at large, it became just another dirty city. War does make the difference, just as it had in my life. My other life came to an end, and when I first arrived in this gloomy city after a big war, the hope I had for a better life vanished. I felt ill prepared for the tough engineering classes at Harvard, and it hadn't yet occurred to me that I didn't really like engineering very much anyway. I would much rather have been reading Voltaire or delving into the art of ancient Greece for the art history class I actually wanted to sit in on.

As the sunshine suddenly streamed into the room that day, my mood also lightened. I smiled and thought, "At least I am alive and better off than I was in England. After all, I've survived the exodus out of Egypt and then the escape from France. World War II is over. The Jew hater Hitler and his Nazis are supposedly now history, but I realize remnants of that Jew hatred still exists here in Cambridge." Once again, Mrs. O'Hara and her ignorant remarks came to mind, and I realized that her hatred was unconscious, and that anti-Semitism dated back to the Middle Ages. "Think positive thoughts," I kept reminding myself. "I am free, on my own, in civilized Boston, and about to begin classes at Harvard University, the pinnacle of intellectual life in America. Why should I feel sorry for myself? What is wrong with me? I drive a Packard and have money in the bank, and should feel ready to start my new life in a new country." But perhaps I was just too tired and hot to savor my good fortune.

Looking on the bright side, which I forced myself to do occasionally, I remembered that the date had been set for my citizenship hearing for the following month. Then, I would be a real American—almost.

Who was I kidding? I will never be a real American, but always a man without a country. I thought of the two speeding tickets I got driving from New York to Boston—must be careful not to get any more. That cop really gave me a lecture. "Foreigners who speed are not welcome here," he said while writing out the ticket. "Where do you come from anyway?" He had a stubble of a beard and his leer was frightening. If I had said to him what I was thinking, he would probably have handcuffed me. My hand was shaking as much as my voice, but I had managed to mutter "yes sir." Why did all these unpleasant thoughts crowd into my mind when I was about to begin my new life?

The doorbell rang, jolting me out of my reverie, and I jumped to answer it. I couldn't imagine who would be calling because I hadn't given my address to anyone I could remember. When I opened the door, there was a red-haired youth dressed in a Western Union uniform. "Sir, a telegram for you," he announced in a cheery voice. I fumbled for a tip and offered what appeared to be more than enough, judging by the boy's expression. "Thanks, and good day to you, sir."

The telegram was from Jean-Roger Herrenschmidt. I met him through the real estate agent when I first arrived. Jean-Roger was a Frenchman, and we'd both laughed when the agent said, "You two should get along fine. You're both foreigners." We felt an immediate rapport and agreed it would be a good idea to get together once in a while if only to exchange ideas and hear French again. Jean-Roger appeared to be as absent minded as I was, and we soon learned we had other things in common. We talked about books, the influence of Camus on our lives, courses we would be taking, how we loved to eat and how difficult it was to understand the Boston telephone operators.

His telegram extended a polite invitation to dine the following night at the local French cafe. "Two other French friends who have just arrived will be there. You will like them because they too are bright." My spirits revived immediately at the thought of seeing my new lanky Huguenot friend and getting into some serious conversation. My gloom disappeared. Was this what it took? A friend reached out to me, and I felt life might be worth living at least for the time being. The curtains at the window fluttered in the now cool breeze, and I experienced my first sound sleep in months.

THAT DINNER with Jean-Roger and Sylvan Wickham was the first of many weekly dinners. Beginning with an aperitif became a ritual we couldn't deprive ourselves of, and this was usually followed by a delicious onion soup which we had to admit was even better than the same *soup a l'ognion* in Parisian bistros. This one had a much thicker and crustier topping of cheese that melted in one's mouth and kept the soup deliciously hot much longer. Even though the restaurant became busy as the evenings wore on, we were always welcomed by the ex-pat French owner who sometimes joined us for a glass of wine. He was jovial, and his large belly actually shook when he laughed, which he frequently did. I know he found the three of us enormously entertaining and enjoyed our gallic, often scatological humor. We felt special in this charming French atmosphere. Perhaps the other diners understood the French because I noticed from time to time that they too were smiling or chuckling to themselves. We were, I learned later, immediately recognized as foreigners by our tailored English suits, our shoes, and the French ties from Charvet that we wore.

We always treated ourselves to two glasses of French wine, and the conversations moved quickly from the seriously philosophical to the roaring-with-laughter stories we shared about our own experiences and *faux pas* in this very different world. By the time we had devoured the main course of a perfectly prepared steak with *pommes frites*, I felt I was at home and with friends whom I could trust. I looked forward to those gatherings, the bright spot of my week, and I often saved both my funny stories about America and my thought-provoking questions for them. Several months later, I invited a new acquaintance to join us. The American Newell Mitchell proved a stimulating addition to our group because he was amazingly well informed on a variety of subjects and had a great sense of humor. His field was city planning, but he could converse on the French Enlightenment or modern poetry or Haussmann's contributions to the city of Paris with equal charm.

His French was impeccable. I learned from a fellow student that Newell was the most promising student in the Harvard School of Design. I felt so lucky to have found this new group of friends who filled the abyss of loneliness. For that was what I suffered from: loneliness in an exciting, but strange new country.

I had no family here, no girlfriend, not even my mother Aimée. The affable joshing of these new friends got me back from the depths and helped me get over the isolation I felt, at least for the evening. They loved my "dream" stories. I told them that recently I had dreamt I was an art historian and that a collegue asked me if I would like to join him at Buckingham Palace for an evening with the King and Queen who had taken a fancy to Art Historians. I was delighted with the invitation, but had to decline—"I would love to go but I have no shoes." Then the solution occurred to me: my friend should go ahead of me in his car and ask if it would be all right if I came with no shoes on. I would meanwhile walk the mile to the Palace (with no shoes) and wait for the answer outside the gate. When I got there, the guests were all leaving, and my friend said, "Oh too bad you didn't come with me. It was all very relaxed, so much so that the King and Queen took off their shoes."

And then there was Francesca. Francesca Green came into my life with an energy I had never seen before, except in Maman. We met in the Co-op bookshop where she was perusing a copy of Voltaire's *Candide* in French. She was absolutely stunning, and I was immediately attracted to her. Her dress was short and clung to her body revealing her tanned, perfectly formed legs. When she reached to the top of the shelf for another book, I saw her breasts were equally well formed under the soft silk dress.

I thought it odd that a beautiful American girl would be reading such a thing and mustered the courage to speak to her. "*Aimez-vous Voltaire?*"

She smiled at me, tilting her head, "*Bien sur.* And you?" The sudden switch to English was enticing. Never had I heard such a flirtatious response. She took the conversation onto a level of intimacy that surprised me. Before I knew it we were discussing the homosexuality in Shakespeare's sonnets. While the outward exchange cavorted from Voltaire's other works to Leibnitz and French literature in general, I delighted in her testing me with beguiling responses, her witty play with words and her charming provocations that came in such an easy manner. She peppered me with breathless questions. "Do you agree with Leibnitz that it is the 'best of all possible worlds?'" I wanted the conversation never to end, and she seemed interested in me too. I was encouraged, then thrilled, when she agreed to have coffee with me.

The coffee shop was filled with all levels of Harvard life: professors, graduate students, and undergraduates. The girls were all attractive with their

The northwestern corner of the Old Yard.

clean, shiny bobbed hair, but I was only able to look at Francesca. We drank our coffees—both of us having Italian rather than the usual weak American coffee that I never learned to like. We continued speaking about French literature, both agreeing that we enjoyed Racine much more than Corneille. I became increasingly impressed with how well she knew the French classics. The next two hours passed in seconds and the coffee shop began to fill up for lunch. Physically, Francesca was what all European men thought of as the stereotypical American girl: pretty in a healthy, free, voluptuous and energetic way. I was overcome, and I wanted to see her as often as I could. "You do speak English in such a charming way, and it's absolutely perfect," she said with a beautiful smile. "However, there are occasional lapses that all Frenchmen make. Would you like me to help you correct those?" We exchanged telephone numbers and then, as quickly as she had come into my life, she was gone.

THE NEXT TIME we saw each other was a week later when she invited me for dinner at the Greens' house in Longfellow Square. The place was filled with books, furnished with Victorian antiques and uncomfortable chairs.

Francesca's parents, Henry and Rosalind Green, were as affable as their daughter and just as well read. And their French was even better than hers. They'd lived in France and were perfect examples of what I was beginning to think was a uniquely American gift: they made me feel I had known them all my life. I never left their house without Mrs. Green's inviting me to come back for dinner again soon.

"You must call me Rosalind, and please call my husband Henry," Francesca's mother said in the most casual manner I had ever heard from an adult voice—so different from the French changing from the polite *vous* to *tu*, which took years to change in French. "We must meet your parents when they come to Boston," Rosalind said. "They sound very bright, and we'd love to have them here for dinner too. And Francesca tells me that you love the French classics as much as she does. You have read Proust, of course?"

I hesitated with embarrassment because I had not yet read Proust but told her that Proust was my mother's favorite author. "No, but I hope to as soon as I get settled."

"You mustn't wait. I will lend you the first four volumes of *A La Recherche du Temps Perdu* tonight. You may keep them until you are ready for the next three volumes, and I know I can trust you with them," she smiled. Our conversation moved easily from French to English and back depending on the subject. When I told them that my mother's philosophy was Voltarian,

I slipped back into French and described how she always said no distinctions should be drawn. Certainly, she felt that all people should be treated equal.

Henry, who had been quiet for a time while his wife continued to make me feel at home, cleared his throat and looked directly at me, "But then you said, didn't you, that distinctions were drawn between Christians and Jews when you were growing up in Egypt. Your family saw no differences there?"

I picked up my fork and ate slowly while I reflected. I had to think about this. I noticed that Francesca was watching me and waiting to hear how I would respond to her father. It was a contradiction, I realized. "Oh, but there were no distinctions between the educated people. Christians and Jews were treated alike if they were cultured or 'civilized,' as my mother would say."

That conversation was to be rehashed over and over again. I had found my element. These were the kind of civilized people my mother wanted me to be with, I thought. I had discovered the "best of all possible worlds" in America. How amazing America is, so informal, so friendly to strangers and so civilized! Unlike Europe, where your background makes you what you are forever, and where it is impossible to move from one class to another, American society seems so fluid. Classes are established in other ways, and it appeared one can move from one social stratum to another quite easily. In France, even if you are an intellectual it was almost impossible to move away from one's background. And if you are Jewish, you stay in your own group. And, certainly, you wouldn't be invited to dinner, having met in a bookshop. How miraculous that I should have met this wonderful family.

Francesca seemed to know everyone at Harvard and played an active role in the intellectual circles in Boston. She gave me good advice: "If you want to meet interesting people, you must give a cocktail party and invite everyone you've met since you've arrived."

"But I've never been to a cocktail party, let alone given one. I don't have the vaguest idea how to begin." She put her hand on my arm. "It's very easy. You make a big punch bowl of very dry martinis, and it will be a rollicking party. Go ahead, try it." It was then decided that night that I would give a cocktail party.

This idea gave me the push I needed. When in Rome, and when in America, give a cocktail party. Francesca wrote down the recipe for martinis. "They must be dry," she insisted. I called the fifteen people I'd met since arriving in Cambridge and was surprised when they all said they would be delighted to come and could they bring a friend.

"Of course. The more the merrier." I was pleased to have the opportunity to use the expression I'd only recently learned. I spent the morning of the party rearranging the furniture in the small living and dining rooms. Next,

I went out shopping: expensive peonies were irresistible for a huge bouquet I planned for the dining room table, just as Maman would have arranged. I found a cheese shop that carried good imported French cheeses, pates and real French baguettes, perfect for the hors d'oeuvres. After rushing from one store to the next, I finally completed my list and returned home laden with several pates, a tray of cheeses, the baguettes, and martini ingredients.

Making the martinis was the most challenging and nervous-making task of the whole day, since I had never before tasted one. But I was armed with Francesca's recipe and felt sure I could do it. An hour before the guests arrived, I washed out the punch bowl, borrowed from my landlady, and began to make the martinis. I pondered the statement that Francesca had tossed over her shoulder as she left "Don't forget that the martinis should be very dry."

How could a drink be dry? I couldn't come up with a logical answer. It disturbed me, and was just one more example of all I had to learn about the English language and America. I began with the gin—pouring glasses of Gordon's finest over the ice. After the fifth glass I added 5 tablespoons of dry vermouth. Then I poured myself a small glass to taste. I liked it. I drank it down quickly and thought with pleasure how great my party would be. I then continued to double and triple the recipe, each time drinking a half glass of the concoction, which I began to think the best drink ever.

My guests arrived all at once, streaming into the apartment, expressing their appreciation for the peonies and the few drawings I'd acquired in New York. Then came more compliments as they sampled the martinis and the French cheeses. I was beside myself with happiness to see everyone having such a good time. I moved from one group of guests to another checking to make sure everyone was included the way I had seen my father do. I poured more martinis into their glasses if I saw they were empty and filled my own more often than I should have. They were all helping themselves to the cheeses and that pleased me. I saw that Francesca was watching me, smiling broadly. She nodded her head in approval. All I remember was that I felt suddenly dizzy and I stumbled, falling into the arms of Jean Roger standing next to me. I was drunk and didn't know it.

THE NEXT DAY I wondered if I had ruined my chances with Francesca by passing out. I was mortified. Everyone called to say what a wonderful party it was and they all expressed tactfully how sorry they were that I'd been in-disposed and unable to enjoy the company. My head pounded, but I tried to put up a good front with each call, and thanked each with enthusiasm, never

Henri at Harvard in the 1950s.

letting on that my head was splitting with the worst headache of my life.

"I really blew it, didn't I?"

Francesca laughed gaily. "No, you simply showed everyone how European you are. In fact I thought it was quite charming—your first experience with martinis. I remember now that Europeans drink very little hard liquor—mostly wine."

"Well, it won't happen again. I'll never have another martini. They are deadly, but I must admit, delicious." I was feeling relieved that she was so understanding. But then that too, I would soon learn, was part of her charm.

"Francesca, will you have dinner with me tonight? I need to recover my self-esteem."

"Of course. I'm good at restoring self-esteem. We'll never mention martinis again. And besides, we both love Beaujolais."

"I'll pick you up at seven."

WE USUALLY SPOKE several times a week, but there was no regular pattern. I was surprised one morning a month after my cocktail party when Francesca called, and her voice sounded irritated. "Why didn't you tell me about the prize? I had no idea."

"I was going to tell you but I forgot. How did you hear about it anyway?"

My parents saw it in *The Boston Globe* this morning. The Bowdoin Prize is a really big deal and they were ecstatic to see your name as the winner."

I fell silent and flushed with pride. Francesca was still speaking, "Are you still there? You may not be aware that the Bowdoin prize is the most esteemed literary prize that Harvard offers students."

"Well, Professor Hanfmann did tell me it was a great honor."

"I knew you were taking Professor Hanfmann's class in Greek art but you never mentioned that you'd submitted your essay for the Bowdoin competition."

"I know. It would never have occurred to me to submit my essay. I didn't even know about the Bowdoin prize. It was Professor Hanfmann who submitted it. I called it 'The Power of Line and the Evolution of Greek Drawing in the 5th Century,' a subject that fascinates me but I never thought anyone else would be interested."

"Greek vases are so esoteric, and I've always loved the red figure paintings. My parents are so impressed and want to throw a celebration party for you. They'll invite all their most learned friends from Harvard."

Francesca couldn't see the pleasure on my face. "Your parents are the best. So kind, but they shouldn't. It's just a prize."

"Don't be absurd. That's just the kind of thing they love. My mother was so excited she started reeling off the names of the previous recipients...Ralph Waldo Emerson, Edward Everett Hale, Henry Adams. You are the perfect excuse to gather their snobby oh-so-intellectual friends together for a festive night."

"That's so nice of them. I don't know what to say."

"Next Tuesday then at 6:00? It will be great fun. We'll have a ball."

"My parents are coming from New York to Boston next weekend," I managed to squeeze in before she hung up.

"Oh. Have they already heard about your prize?"

"No. It's hardly that. My father has an appointment with one of the leading pulmonary doctors at Mass General. He's been diagnosed with lung cancer. They want a second opinion."

"Oh, Henri. I am so sorry." Her voice trailed off.

"It's probably because he smokes so much. There are new studies that show the connection between smoking and lung cancer but he won't stop smoking."

"I know. My parents always urge me to stop but it's more difficult than you think." There was a moment of silence, then I lowered my voice. "I wish you would stop, Francesca. It's a terrible habit. And both my parents smoke like chimneys. It's been that way for years. My father is a doctor and he should know how bad for him smoking is. I am worried about him."

"But maybe it won't be as serious as they think. Maybe the second opinion will confirm that."

I shifted in my chair, drank a sip of water for my mouth seemed suddenly very dry. The next words came out after a long pause and I cleared my throat. "Well, anyway this may be a good time for them meet you. I'd like them to get to know you while they're here."

"Of course, I'd love to meet them," Her cheery voice helped me to recover somewhat and I realized again how positive her attitude was about most things.

I laughed, "My father will make a big fuss over you. I'm sure of that. He loves attractive women. But I'm off to class and must dash. Will you have dinner with us Saturday?"

"I'd love to."

"We'll pick you up at seven."

"Meanwhile enjoy your fame. You deserve it." She hung up.

I looked out the window to watch the raindrops splashing against the window pane. Cambridge was covered in a blanket of grey that oddly reflected the opposite of my present sunny mood, an anomaly for me. The combination of Francesca's encouraging phone call, and having won the acceptance of her wonderful civilized parents did wonders for my state of mind. Life was good. Who would have thought that my theories on the Fifth century Greek vase painter Thanatos would reverberate as far as Cambridge in 1949. And who would have thought that the artistic visions of that Greek painter on love and death would have such an impact on the literary critics of Harvard University, that a prize would be offered to a newly arrived, unknown Egyptian Jew.

Professor Hanfmann's note on my first paper written for his class startled me to say the least. Just above the A on the paper, he'd written "Come see me immediately." The next morning when I arrived at his office I was still nervous and wondered why he wanted to see me "immediately." I knocked on the scruffy door.

"Come in." It was definitely the office of the elderly German professor. I recognized the throaty voice.

"Oh, it's you. I've been vaiting for you. Do sit down." He ran his fingers through his thin silvery hair and fairly spat out, "Dorra, vee in the Art History department don't understand you. Who are you? Vere do you come from? Your paper was quite remarkable."

"Thank you, sir."

"No, it is true. Now vhat do you need? Do you need money? Vy aren't you in the Art History program vere you should be?"

"Well. I don't know," I stammered, "I've almost finished my courses in engineering and will do so next term."

"You don't know? Well, I do know." Hanfmann's face wrinkled into a smile. His eyes sparkled. "There is no question about it." He slapped his thigh with a loud crack. "You must transfer. Finish up those engineering classes. Get your masters there and then forget Engineering."

I looked straight into the eyes of the nervous white-haired man facing me. Was this really happening? Could the great professor be encouraging me to do what I'd been thinking of doing but lacked the courage to do?

"Then you must come over to our department for your Masters in Art History and then your PhD." Then he chuckled, "You have a great future ahead of you. I will help you with the transfer papers if you wish."

I knew I'd been offered a great gift. That conversation changed the course of my life.


SEVERAL DAYS LATER I went to the small hotel where my parents were staying. Maman's voice had been ominous when she called earlier that morning. She ushered me into the sitting room of their hotel suite, motioning for me to sit down on the stiff Victorian couch. I looked around the room that somehow seemed more European than American. There was a standing floor lamp that threw light upwards to the tall ceiling which I had never seen in America. Antimacassars were everywhere, bowls of nuts and hard candies were on every tabletop. The heavy crocheted curtains covered rain-spotted windows and reminded me of the ones my grandmother had made in Egypt. I did as I was told and waited patiently to hear the report on Papa's health. Maman asked if I wanted tea while Papa sat in a large overstuffed chair in his familiar red silk smoking jacket. He had not risen to greet me, so I went over and kissed him on both cheeks. He smiled weakly and asked if I was enjoying Harvard, almost as if we had seen each other only the day before. Finally, Maman sat down with her cup of tea, smoothed her tailored skirt and folded her hands in her lap. She quickly began to explain that they had been to see both the oncologist and the pulmonary specialist that morning.

"We wanted you to know as soon as possible of our decisions. The doctors here have confirmed the diagnosis of the New York doctors. Papa will have to begin treatments for lung cancer immediately." It was all said without even a pause between sentences. Yet she was completely calm and unemotional. I noticed the raindrops appearing on the windows, and outside the morning had turned to a dull gray.

Maman had continued to talk, but I wasn't really listening to her. Finally, I heard Papa interrupting her. "I have decided to retire from my New York practice. It's time. I've been at it long enough. Your mother and I will move to Florida." It was as if he had rehearsed what he was going to say to me and had to get it all out at once. Then there was silence.

I turned from one grave face to the other. "I knew that you were having to make serious decisions, but I'm stunned that you are retiring, and moving to Florida of all places. Do you really think the Boston doctors are right? You do have cancer?"

Papa looked into my eyes for what seemed many minutes. He finally spoke. "You know when you receive information like this you have to reevaluate everything. Sometimes you have to start over in a new place. I think it's time for your mother and me to spend time together. We haven't done that for a long time." He looked at Maman with an expression of tenderness I'd never seen him show towards her, and he took her hand in his.

Maman broke the awkward silence with an unusual cheerfulness, "You know everyone says Florida is a bit like Alexandria. It has a welcoming climate, lots of oranges, sunshine and beautiful beaches. We will soon feel quite at home in this new and strange country." Once again, I was aware of how strong my mother was, and how she was like a field marshal who could control even the moods of those around her. Her willingness to move to Florida to start a new life was amazing to me and her apparent resilience in spite of this turn of events was contagious.

"YOU WANT TO write about what?" My professor of 19th century European art looked down at me, with an air of disbelief. He was the most autocratic professor in the department. He was never questioned and certainly not by a new graduate student in his first year.

"I have found evidence that Gauguin painted one of his Tahitian Eves in 1890—even before he went to Tahiti," I said with confidence and a touch of pride.

"That is impossible. There is no such evidence."

"Professor N., with all due respect I found that Gauguin visited the 1889 *Paris Exposition Universelle* and spent hours in the Java pavilion. He was profoundly influenced by the beauty of the voluptuous Javanese dancing girls and the impact the images of Buddha had on him was enormous."

The professor stroked his beard and looked with evident skepticism at me, the confident young man sitting opposite him. His foot began to tremble and he re-crossed his leg.

I noticed the professor's nervous foot and continued, undaunted by this response. "Gauguin's whole style changed after that. That experience added to his interest in exotic cultures stemming from his childhood memories of Peru and his 1887 trip to Martinique. His paintings of women, like that first Eve, take on an exotic far eastern look. His letters from that time are full of his enthusiasm; in fact, I suspect he could think of nothing else. And this was at least a year or two before he went to Tahiti."

"I know you are fluent in French and can read those damn letters that not one of us can make out. His slang is appalling and his handwriting is undecipherable. You have an advantage."

I went on as if I hadn't been interrupted. "He was captivated at that Paris Exposition by the reconstructed Indonesian village and the Borobudur sculptural reliefs that he saw for the first time. I can prove those became a model for many of his future figures including his most important work 'Where Do We Come From?' He blatantly imitates a Buddha from the frieze of a Javanese temple."

Professor N. looked at me with disbelief, and I am sure he must have been thinking, "This young foreign student is so cock sure. I've never seen anything like it. He is from another world and certainly not like the usual Anglo prep school boys we are used to seeing here at Harvard. Harvard is accepting an entirely new kind these days. Most disconcerting, I think."

"You know, Dr., I think Gauguin probably considered the bush alongside Buddha and next to Eve to be the Bo tree under which Buddha was rewarded with 'the great enlightenment.' It was considered the release from suffering, you know, and occurs again in other of his Eves."

I could see Dr. N.'s thoughts were racing, and he was hardly listening to me, the young man who was sitting comfortably next to him enjoying himself. He must have been thinking, "He's even beginning to lecture me! But could he be right? Humph, he can't be right!"

The professor shook his head, got up from his desk, walked to the door and opened it, indicating that the interview was over. "I am very doubtful that you can prove that, Mr. Dorra. But go ahead and try if you wish. I have to say, I think it is a waste of time." I followed, drained of all enthusiasm, and simply uttered a brief "Thank you for your time, Professor" before leaving the office.


ON THE TRAIN RIDE down to New York, I was too excited to read, and kept going over the brief conversation I had on the phone with Professor John Rewald. The great art historian—the world-renowned expert on Cezanne and Gauguin—was in New York and had invited me to come to talk about my Gauguin theory. As I entered the apartment on the upper west side, my mouth fell open in surprise. Dirty dishes were on every table, half-filled glasses and coffee cups sat next to stacks of books everywhere—on the floor, on the tables, in the chairs and on the stairway leading to the second floor. Ashtrays were filled with cigarette butts, and the wastebasket was stuffed, overflowing with crumpled papers. I noticed a layer of dust under the lamp that showed a cleaning person hadn't been there for some time. But the great Rewald ushered me in, pointed to a chair and after shaking hands blurted out, "So let's read your paper together."

We read, we talked, and we laughed throughout the afternoon and then into evening. There had been no suggestion of eating and there appeared to be no food around of any description, not even a cracker. After the first five hours, I finally asked if I could use the toilet. "Oh. Of course, right upstairs and to the left." The upstairs rooms might have been attractive, I noticed, if they had been cleaned. There were books stacked in every corner and on the floor next to the overfilled bookcases that lined the walls. The streetlamp outdoors cast a stream of light into the bedroom and onto the rumpled unmade bed.

When I returned to the living room, I saw that Rewald was holding my

*Ève exotique,* Paul Gauguin, 1890.

Gauguin papers in both hands, flipping through the pages with great energy. It was after a few minutes that he looked up from the papers and noticed me standing there. "This is great stuff. You are definitely on to something. Sit down and you must continue to read it aloud to me. You write beautifully!"

I read for the next three hours. When I finally finished, I looked at my watch. The last train back to Boston was at 10:00 and if I hurried I could make it. I couldn't believe that we had spent the entire day together just talking about art. It had been the most amazing day since I arrived in America. Rewald had more energy than anyone I had ever met. When I looked up from the last page of my thesis, Rewald was staring at me and smiling, "You say that your professor doesn't accept your theory? He must be an idiot. You have proven without a doubt that Gauguin at least drew some of those Eves before he went to Tahiti. I am convinced, and we will do something about it." He got up, walked around the room and returned to the table where we had been sitting. "I am supposed to send something to the *Gazette des Beaux Arts* this month and I don't have anything ready yet. I am going to submit your thesis on Gauguin instead of my work. They will publish it."

I couldn't believe my ears. If my "First Eves in Gauguin's Eden" were to be published by the esteemed *Gazette des Beaux Arts*, and with Rewald's letter of endorsement, then the doubting Professor N. would have to accept my theory. That was all I needed.

A month later, I presented my thesis which would become a published article in the May 1953 issue of the *Gazette des Beaux Arts*. The professor's eyes bulged when he saw that the lead article entitled "The First Eves in Gauguin's Eden" was by Henri Dorra. "Well, well. That is just fine, Dorra. I am so glad you changed some of the dates."

I couldn't hold back a smile. I did resist, however, the temptation to say that the dates had not been changed and were exactly the same as those I had mentioned earlier before meeting with John Rewald and which were scoffed at by Professor N. I must have been maturing because I held my tongue. I realized that even the great Professor N. had to save face.

*Autoportrait a l'idole*, Paul Gauguin, 1893.

Miss Mary Tonetti in Bermuda shorts and high socks as she bicycles across campus for the *Fort Worth Star Telegram*, 1956.

# VIII
# The New World at Vassar

AFTER THE INITIAL dramatic beginning of the sophomore term, I settled into a busy schedule of classes all of which interested me enormously.

My first trip into Manhattan was for a dance concert performed by the
New York City Ballet. Tanaquil Leclerc was stunning in "Afternoon of a
Faun" choreographed by Jerome Robbins and the weekend was a glorious
one—reminding me of how lucky I was to be at Vassar and so close to New
York, to the theatre, to the Metropolitan Museum and to all I packed into
the weekend. I was thinking just that when I arrived at the Poughkeepsie
track in Grand Central that Sunday night to return to Vassar. Then came the
shock: there she stood. Kate looked the same and just as threatening with her
spiked hair, arms folded in a stance of defiance, and eyes beaming her powerful will. Her sardonic smile belied her anger, which I knew was there, as
dangerous as ever. Again, there was that cheerful voice as if nothing ominous
had happened, "Hello, Mary. How are you? I have been waiting for you and
for Abigail. I knew you would turn up sooner or later." The tone of her voice
was clipped, and she looked at me with those piercing eyes, never shifting
them from my face. The collar of her camel's hair coat was turned up so that
her cheeks were framed into a narrow point at her chin, giving her a fierce
diabolical look.

Even though I was very nervous I somehow found the courage and the
strength to say what I had to say and what I had planned for many weeks if
and when I would be face to face with Kate. The words streamed out of me.
"Kate. Abigail wants you to erase her from your memory. You will never find
her here in Grand Central so you might as well forget that… and her, if you
can."

"You must know I can't forget what she has done to me, and I will
haunt her for the rest of her life wherever she is. I have means, you know, of
tracking her down."

The train had just pulled in, and people were already boarding. I could hardly think but had to end this conversation and get away from her.

"Kate, I can't imagine how you must feel, and I am sorry for you. Please try to understand that whatever went on between you and Abigail at Middlebury must be forgotten. It's over."

"It will never be over. You should tell her that. She will be punished."


MR. AMBROZINI was the tall Sienese Italian teacher who had joined the Italian department that year. His rather protruding blue eyes made him look like a Byzantine mosaic, and he walked about the campus with a black cape swinging from his shoulders, giving him the appearance of an actor in an Oscar Wilde play. He had taken a fancy to me and asked me to have coffee with him almost as soon as we met. We began to meet regularly in the student cafe once a week, speaking Italian. I loved the opportunity to speak Italian, and never thought I had put myself in a compromising position. But just the week before, Alessandra had reported to me that she overheard a conversation between two freshmen when they saw me in the hall, "See that girl there. She's Mr. Ambrozini's girlfriend." I laughed at the story. Of course, that was not true. He did lend an air of glamour and mystery to the campus, and I liked very much being a part of that. Before the Christmas vacation he asked me to have lunch with him. We ordered our sandwiches and sat down in the smoke-filled café. I was startled to see that he had a large parcel under his arm which he offered to me.

He was smiling as he offered the large package he had been carrying, "You must open it now. It's my Christmas present to you." The big book of beautiful Giotto prints was a treasure and totally unexpected. I responded shyly, "*Ho vergogna*, I am embarrassed. You mustn't give me presents."

"But I see in you a part of myself. I want to give you this present because I feel that very strongly." My reaction was immediate. I didn't want to hurt his feelings, but it finally had become clear that he was interested in me in a romantic way, and I had to figure out a way to let him know I wasn't interested. I felt it was inappropriate to accept the gift but knew he was a sensitive person, and it would be difficult to disengage myself. My naiveté had kept me from understanding the reality of the situation and that his interest in me was not platonic as I had assumed. I took the gift reluctantly and noticed that some students sitting nearby were listening with great interest to our conversation. My embarrassment only increased as I managed to smile briefly at him and excuse myself awkwardly. "I must go to class now. Thank you so much for the present. I will treasure it." I kept walking without looking

THE NEW WORLD AT VASSAR

back, and knew that I was still red with embarrassment, knowing that our conversation had been heard by the other students nearby.

When I returned to our room later that afternoon Alessandra was there already. She was not only beautiful but spoke such lovely Italian and French that I was elated to have her as a roommate. I had also loved my freshman year roommate who was bilingual in French, spoke Russian and knew Greek. Those were just a few of her accomplishments. Nina was one of the brightest and most sophisticated people I had ever met. We had however decided not to room together the following year but would remain close friends for the entire four years at Vassar and thereafter. On the door of the sophomore room that Alessandra and I shared, we had placed a card that said "Tonetti and Castelli" which we thought sounded rather like a Mafia headquarters. We were tempted to add "*Lasciate ogni speranza voi che entrate.*" We laughed about this Dantescan warning which we hoped offered immediate notification of our Latin roots and powers. We were both proud of our Italian heritage.

I had hoped that Alessandra and I would be speaking Italian together when we were alone, but we always had such important things to discuss and my Italian was so new that it never happened. We were both in love that year. At least I thought I was (again). Certainly Peter was attractive and intelligent and was more attentive than any previous beau had been. He called regularly just to chat about his and my classes, and to make plans for being together when I had a free weekend. He had already asked me to put several important weekends at Harvard on the calendar for the winter and spring. Alessandra's red headed beau was at Dartmouth and on the ski team. I couldn't for the life of me figure out why she thought he was attractive. It seemed to me that Alessandra spent all her time on the telephone with him and that seemed to make her sad most of the time. This perennial melancholy gave her a forlorn air that made her even more beautiful. Her lively face was usually glowing with smiles but after a telephone call from her Dartmouth boyfriend she was mostly drained and depressed. Even on those occasions her beauty was never diminished. Her Catholic family didn't approve of her leaving the campus to see young men and particularly this one, so they had cut off her allowance to keep her from going up to New Hampshire, even for Winter Carnival. Every evening she was either working in the library or in the kitchen scraping plates to earn enough money to get to Dartmouth.

One of Alessandra's classes was in French drama. Instead of an exam the members of the class had to perform in a play at the end of the term. That year's play was Musset's "*On ne Badine Pas Avec L'amour.*" "One Doesn't Play Around with Love" would be given in French in the main auditorium and Alessandra loved her role, the rehearsals, and Madame Ross who directed

Students take a study break, 1950s. Photo courtesy of Vassar College, Archives & Special Collections.

the play. It was one of the few things that seemed to engage her, so I was surprised when she appeared the week before the play and said in a grave voice, "I have to ask you a big favor. It turns out I have the German measles, and I hate going to the infirmary. I have decided I am going to my parents' apartment in New York to wait this thing out and recuperate. I can't face Madame Ross. Would you go tell her that I've got the measles and am in New York. And that I am so sorry I can't be in her play."

A brief flicker of disbelief came into my mind. She didn't look the slightest bit sick. "Okay. I'll tell her tomorrow after my French class." She then picked up a small suitcase and gave me a hug saying, "I must go. Bruce has come down from Dartmouth to drive me to New York. He is waiting for me downstairs."

I HADN'T SEEN IT COMING when it happened. The next day after French class when I was still trying to figure out what Proust meant in his beautiful French that I could understand only with difficulty, I asked Madam Ross if I might speak to her privately.

"Of course, what is it?"

I hesitated before speaking because I really wasn't sure I was telling the truth when I delivered Alessandra's message. "My roommate Alessandra asked me to tell you that she was so sorry that she can't be in the French play on Friday. She has the measles and has left for New York to stay in her parents' apartment until she is well." I added my own embellishment to make it seem less fictional: "She was really sorry because she loves your class and was looking forward to being in the play."

Madame Ross's bright blue eyes seemed to double in size. She pursed her lips, stared out the window for a few minutes, and then turned abruptly to face me again, "That's all right. YOU can take her place! You are the same size, know French reasonably well and the play must go on. There is no one else who would fit the part as well."

"But the play is day after tomorrow!" I stammered. "How could I learn all the lines."

"You don't have to. You are the ingénue and you can simply write the lines out on index cards that you can hold in your lap. You can look down at them now and then as ingénues do."

"But..."

"There is no other way. You must begin immediately to practice the lines. There is a rehearsal this afternoon, and we will explain the situation to the others in the cast. *Allons.* You must meet the challenge and you will be terrific. We will make an announcement to the audience before the curtain goes up and the audience will be particularly sympathetic to you for stepping in at the last minute."

I was dizzy and could hardly think of what to say. "But there are only two rehearsals before the play?"

"That is right. *N'importe.* I will coach you privately after lunch today before the rehearsal at 4:00. You can do it!"

"The dress rehearsal is tomorrow. May I see the costume I am to wear?"

Mrs. Ross nodded, "*Bien sur.* We will try it on this afternoon." She turned towards the door and with my stomach churning, I followed my teacher slowly from the classroom thinking, "What have I gotten myself into? It is not possible! But then Madame Ross is my teacher and she needs me."


THE MUSSET PLAY went well, and everyone was particularly nice and very complimentary about my performance afterwards. Those who spoke French said I was "*Superbe,*" "*Sensas.*" But I did decide then and there that I would never take a speaking role on the stage again because I got such stage fright. It would be as a dancer or nothing at all. So, for the next two years I danced whenever I could, choreographing the theses for some of the drama majors and performing in modern dance concerts whenever I could.

Life in the Vassar cocoon in 1953 meant that some of us were completely unconcerned with the outside world and so involved with our studies we never even gave politics a thought. I knew the McCarthy hearings were going on and although they interested me, I was not one of the politically active who gathered around the one TV on campus to see and hear the reports of McCarthy and the House of Un-American activities. Ever since that November day during freshman year when our President Sarah Gibson Blanding called the entire campus together to tell "Vassar's side of the so-called Fellers case," I had become passionate about defending Vassar against the attacks of being "Communist, atheistic and even anti-American." I had been shocked when President Blanding told us our parents might be hearing about a negative article in a publication called *The Freeman* entitled "God and Woman at Vassar" written by Nancy Fellers, a former student at Vassar who had been inspired by William F. Buckley's inflammatory "God and Man at Yale." No one had ever raised my conscience before as Miss Blanding did that day in her defense of academic freedom, pointing out so articulately that many Vassar students came from Republican homes and continued to be staunch Republicans at Vassar. In fact, when a straw vote was taken among the students, it was two to one for Eisenhower. As for religious thought at Vassar, contrary to Miss

Madame Ross. Photo courtesy of Vassar College, Archives & Special Collections.

Fellers' statements, the great majority believed in America and in God. I was still figuring that out for myself but contrary to Miss Fellers's beliefs, I had no doubt about the academic freedom at Vassar and knew firsthand that we hadn't been brainwashed. When my father called to say he had received some negative letters about Vassar as a "hotbed of Communists" I was able to give him some real facts. I think he was proud of me although he *was* a Republican. He even paid my Texas poll tax so that I could cast my first absentee ballot. I think he knew I would vote for Stephenson.

Becoming more aware politically was only one of the changes during those four years at Vassar. As the Vassar years melted away in a blink of time, I yearned for the freedom to travel and be a part of the outside world and a different life. I believed that change is a life force and wanted it to propel me into a new foreign world. It seemed inevitable that the subject of my Philosophy thesis would be "Sartre's Notion of Freedom." At the end of four Vassar years, I realized how much I had changed and was anxious to get on with still more changes. My roommate and I both agreed the last thing we wanted was to be married. My goal, unlike that of so many of my classmates, was to travel—that was the only aspiration I had when I graduated and walked away from Vassar in 1956.


"YOU ARE MAKING it very difficult for me, Mary." These were my mother's gentle words when I burst into tears, upon learning that there was no way I could go to Italy the following year. I was not a depressed person by nature, but I was devastated. I was also scared for the first time in my life at the thought of a completely new life separated from my family, working in New York and expected to be an adult, completely independent and self-supporting. It was my mother, in the living room at our house at Snedens, who had to bear the brunt of an emotional collapse just days after I left Vassar. Sobbing almost hysterically, I told her how I really didn't want anything in life, except to go to Europe, while she comforted me and held me in her arms.

Then my father came in joined in the conversation. He spoke to me honestly, "You know that your three younger brothers have to be educated, and that will be a big financial strain on the family and our limited finances. Of course, we *could* manage somehow to send you to Europe, but your mother and I feel strongly that that would not be the right thing for you at this point in your life." He was looking at me intently, and perhaps seeing that I was about to burst into tears again, added "You will get to Italy eventually I know, but now is not the time either for you or for our family."

I wiped my tears and said, "I know I am being selfish and am sorry,

Daddy. I wasn't thinking of my brothers." I didn't tell him that I was afraid I couldn't get a job in New York. Who would want to hire a Philosophy major who didn't know shorthand and whose typing speed was barely adequate to be a secretary?

He put his arm around me and said, "That's my girl. You don't know it now, but I know that you will be happy in New York. It is a great city, and you will have a wonderful life there. You will see."

He reached for the pack of Lucky Strikes on the table in front of us, lit a cigarette and continued in a calm and convincing voice, "We will be leaving for Texas in a week's time, and you will take the bus into the City tomorrow to have the job interviews that have been set up. But we won't leave until you do have a job."

I couldn't imagine the next part of my life if it didn't include my dream of being free and living in Europe.

Empire State Building, 1956. Photo courtesy of Library of Congress

# IX
# New York and the New Life
# Beyond Harvard

"HENRI DEAR, I must tell you before anyone else. Henry and I were with Francesca in the hospital this morning." My heart nearly stopped beating. There were no tears, just gasps as I listened to the quiet voice of Rosamond Green saying that Francesca's cancer had finally led to her sudden death. I looked at the Gauguin print of the Breton women that I had tacked above my desk. Gauguin caught them praying in his "Vision after the Sermon" and I felt suddenly the true Christian piety that he must have seen in those Breton women and a sudden urge to pray came over me—not for myself but for the Green family and for Francesca, now finally at peace.

I had lost not only my first American girlfriend but also a friend who made me a better person. Francesca had become a light in my life and that light had now gone out. Her advice on almost every subject was invaluable during the brief three years we knew each other. My mind was swirling back to the last time I saw her. She was so changed, even then. Yet still there was that beautiful gentleness in her eyes when she spoke. "I am going to die, Henri, and you must know before anyone."

"No. You mustn't say that. The doctors at Mass General know what they are doing."

"But listen to me. I have been to several doctors and they all say the same thing. It may be three months. It may be six, or it may even be a few more months, but it is certain. Now you mustn't tell my parents. Understand?"

Those words echoed in my brain. I remember she smiled at me and kissed my hand while tears flowed from both our eyes. We made love for the last time.

That was four months ago. Now four months later the tears were flowing again as I heard Rosamond's voice explain that Francesca was gone. Francesca and I had spoken only the day before as we did almost every day, and she seemed weak but not about to die. I had asked if she wanted me to come up to Boston although it would have been a real hardship because the Met kept me so busy, and I was trying to finish the Gauguin article *Ia Orana Maria* (Hail Mary) that would be published in the Met's Bulletin in May. She said, no, of course, that she didn't want me to see her the way she looked then. We told each other we loved each other and with tears streaming down my cheeks, I told her I loved her and missed her. "You will get well, I know." I managed to say without much conviction.

"And if I don't you must carry on with your work, and I hope you will find someone who loves you as much as I do."

That was the last time I heard her voice.


NEW YORK was the only place I wanted to live after leaving Harvard. It seemed to be the world at large, rather than a mere city in the United States. There were so many layers to New York, and I loved exploring all of them. Central Park alone still attracted all of humanity to enjoy its beauty that Olmsted so ingeniously created. And no need to go to China because Chinatown in New York had the same exotic flavors with the narrow streets exuding energy at every turn. Since I had no interest in going to Germany at this point in my life, and because I loved German food, it was a treat for me to mingle with the newly arrived immigrants from Germany in the suburb of Astoria, which I found was in Queens. Just walking down the streets there one could smell the kielbasa hot off the grill, and the aroma of grilled bratwurst and sauerkraut always made my mouth water.

For me, to have a fellowship at the Metropolitan Museum of Art was a dream come true. I soon found out that Manhattan was like a mini world with people who came from everywhere, and New Yorkers didn't seem to care where you came from. When I walked to the Met from my small cold-water flat in the East Seventies, I loved seeing the well-dressed young Americans all of whom seemed to be successful and confident. There were of course others, like me, who looked foreign and lacked that American self confidence. One could tell by their shoes that they were not American—just different. Yet we were all privileged to live and work in this melting pot of a city where one could be anonymous if one wanted, or one could talk to perfect strangers, or sometimes one could even make friends, as I had done here in Manhattan.

My colleagues at the Met invited me to small dinners and cocktail parties and from those, I was invited to others. At those parties I was impressed by how many spoke French well, had read Proust and had traveled extensively.

Central Park, 1952. Photo courtesy of Library of Congress

It was Maman's Voltairean world. There were no differences, only similarities of values and interests. And yet when I had a real conversation with any of them I discovered that they too were lonely or had bouts of depression. Americans are so honest and surprisingly often it really didn't take much to get to another level of intimacy where revelations were forthcoming even from strangers. After a few glasses of Scotch and soda I learned that others had parents who were estranged, sibling rivalries, and sometimes they even confessed they had had thoughts of suicide. Strangely enough, it made me feel comfortable and less alone, rather than depressed, to hear that others had my same doubts and insecurities.

When I had time I loved exploring all the different ethnic sections of New York. Sometimes, I let my mind wander instead of focusing on the Greek vases in the current exhibition I was preparing. I thought of my last trip to Little Italy and the wonderful mussels *picantino* at the charming *Grotta Azzurra*, which had been on Mulberry street since the early 1900s. The seafood there was fresher than anything in New York except for the Italian waiters who flirted incessantly with every female client in the restaurant.

Maman and Papa had postponed their move to Florida and decided to rent an airy apartment on West End Avenue. It seemed to me they had conquered New York because they were always in a social whirl, with dinner invitations, theatre parties, concerts and the opera almost every night. Maman looked radiant. I hadn't seen her so happy in years. Their apartment on the upper west side was just across the street from Central Park where she walked every day. She loved the crisp fall mornings with the magenta, vermilion, amber, and sunburst yellow leaves streaking the paths, the children on their way to school laughing and giggling with each other in total freedom.

And then there were her salons, even better than those in Alexandria. I marveled at my parents' diverse collection of friends: other Sephardic Egyptians, French diplomats, distinguished archaeologists, musicians and Columbia professors. Of course, included at theses soirees were also their stockbroker and lawyer whom they had come to respect and see as friends. I never heard fewer than three languages in the large drawing room overlooking Central Park, and I loved seeing Maman preside with such charm over these elegant soirees. Her French, Italian, Arabic, and English came forth with equal ease as she moved gracefully from one guest to the next. Her new Chanel dress was the perfect attire, and she wore it often. Papa made sure that he complimented and flirted with all the women present, always assuring even the least attractive that he could hardly wait to rendezvous with them at a later date. Papa's practice was apparently a great success.

The story about him in the *New Yorker* "Talk of the Town" when he first began his practice must have given him a boost for he had more patients than he could take care of, and they loved him. Maman hid a giggle when she read the article out loud to him. It described him as an affable, multi-lingual, debonair Egyptian gynecologist who had moved his practice to Park Avenue. It also described him as "pudgy" which of course was true, but which he didn't like at all. On the whole, the article made him sound very appealing, and I noticed it never mentioned he was Jewish. I remembered the "quota" at Harvard, and thought it wise of him not to mention his ethnicity.

I had been working hard at the Met when I received the letter announcing that a stipend for travelling was also included in the fellowship I had won, and that it was the first one the Met had offered. It would allow me to travel any place in the world to visit museums. I read the letter over and over because I couldn't believe it. Papa had roared with joy when I told him about it. "You mean you will get paid to go to museums? *Sans blague!* That is fantastic, my boy," and he gave me a big bear hug, whispering he was so proud of me. I remember Maman smiling at me over his shoulder, and she too nodded her head in agreement.

"But you must understand," I interrupted and recrossed my legs. "It won't happen until the end of my year at the Met. And they give only a portion of what it would cost to visit all the museums I need to see." I ran my fingers through my hair and saw that they were both eagerly listening, so I continued, "I have already decided where I need to go and my list is a long one. Holland is a must for my work on Van Gogh, and then I wanted to study some of the museums in France, Norway and, of course, England." It all came bubbling out and then the enthusiasm trailed off, ending with just a note of sadness as I added, "It will be very different from when we were in London last, Maman, with bombs exploding everywhere."

"That is over now. Thank heavens. You mustn't think of that time past… look to the future." She rose from her chair and asked if we wanted a drink, saying that she did.

After pouring small glasses of Scotch for each of us she raised her glass and toasted "to our dear Henri, who makes us so proud." Maman's sudden and cheerful voice had a contagious effect on me so that I was able to continue in a more optimistic tone, "I am anxious to see the paintings hanging in their usual places again, and to see all those Renoirs next to each other as they should be seen—not just one at a time as we saw them during the war. Now they are back safely hanging at the Tate, the British Museum and even at the Louvre."

"I don't think they are where they should be in Germany," Papa interjected. He stroked his chin and began to pace the room. "It will be some

The Metropolitan Museum of Art, NYC

time before the Germans release the stolen works from the Nazis." He and Maman exchanged glances and drank more of their whiskies.

"No it doesn't seem likely. That will take some time, both for the reconstruction and new installations in the museums, but also for me to want to go there. I am not going to Germany or to Austria yet," I said emphatically. "That will have to wait and..." I continued after a slight pause. "There is plenty of work for me to do in the other museums."

The time in New York just flew by; I enjoyed my work at the Met, and although Papa's health seemed better I knew he was in temporary remission. The doctors said so. Papa talked enthusiastically about moving to Florida, and it amused me to hear Maman agreeing and saying, "It will be like Alexandria, palm trees, lots of oranges and lemons, and sunshine." They had been inquiring about real estate in Florida even though I knew that at least superficially they were enjoying New York, and seemed relieved that I was moving along well in my new museum career. I desperately wanted to belong to this new vital country and now that I was a legal US citizen I saw more clearly what still wasn't working for me. In learning more about myself I was able to cope with new realizations: I was not at all like the extroverted American male and never would be. Reading the comic strips every evening helped me find out how the American mind worked and about their humor, which was always incomprehensible to me. I concluded that the American was a product of his new continent. He had to adapt himself to the often brutal rigors of his new surroundings just as I had, if I were to survive here. It was so different from Europe, and thank God I could return to Europe to see the more familiar and be part of the culture I was brought up to know. And yet, I did want to stay here, to be American and to be a success in the art museum world. Far greater scholars than I had tried to understand the American mind, and perhaps that was too difficult a goal for me. But one thing became clear to me about the American character and the aesthetics of American art. I was beginning to understand what de Tocqueville meant when he wrote, "Americans will habitually prefer the useful to the beautiful and they will require that the beautiful should be useful." I thought to myself, perhaps one day someone would let me curate a show on American art and the complexities of the American mind. The more I studied American art the more I respected it—both the paintings and the literature. There was real genius there. I loved de Tocqueville's notion of what Americans require of "the beautiful", and that utilitarian element could be at the core of an exhibition on American art and architecture. And I saw that along with the jollity and genuine good humor of the average American there is also a sense of idealism and spirit that touched me deeply.

THE LOSS I FELT for Francesca during those first months often brought tears to my eyes, but work helped alleviate the pain. While I looked forward to the European trip for the museum research, I realized that discipline and my daily work at the Met had a grounding effect on me and was just what I needed to keep from being depressed. My time at the Met was limited, and I knew that I would have to move on to another real job after the travel was over. My applications for the Florida museums were sent, and hopefully I would hear something to determine my future when I returned from Europe.

Long Island, 1952.

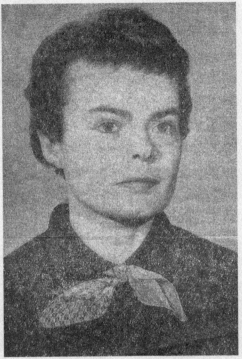

Miss Mary L. Tonetti.

## Miss Mary Tonetti Will Join Envoy's Staff in Costa Rica

Miss Mary Tonetti, daughter of Mr. and Mrs. Joseph Lawrence Tonetti, 2412 6th Avenue, Will leave Sunday first San Jose, Costa Rica, to be tutor and companion to the children of Mr. and Mrs. Robert F. Woodward. He is US ambassador to Costa Rica.

Miss Tonetti, who has been entertained while visiting in Fort Worth with her parents, is a graduate of Vassar College. She made her debut at the 1954 Steeplechase Ball, and has been employed in New York City since her graduation.

# X
## Freedom in New York
### THE WORLD WIDENS

THAT SUMMER OF 1956 passed like lightning. When I left Vassar after four years, armed with a degree in Philosophy and a good foundation in French and Italian, there was only one thing in the world I wanted to do: to live in Florence or Rome. I left word at the Vassar vocational bureau that I would be willing to leave New York immediately if they found a job for me in Italy. Meanwhile my mother and her friends arranged to have me meet Mrs. Andrews, owner of an employment agency in New York which dealt almost exclusively with graduates of the "Seven Sisters" colleges (Vassar, Smith, Barnard, Radcliffe, Wellesley, Mount Holyoke and Bryn Mawr, so named for the Pleiades, the seven daughters of Atlas who were "changed into stars"). The interview was set for three days after I left the security of the Vassar campus.

Feeling quite strongly that no one would want to hire me, much less that the Vassar degree had "changed me into a star," I was sick to my stomach on the bus ride into the City from Snedens. I had no idea what I was going to be asked during the interviews, but Mrs. Andrews was so reassuring and insisted any employer would be lucky to have me. Of course I didn't believe her, but was willing to go to the interviews she set up for me because of the newfound confidence she inspired in me.

Mrs. Andrews was so "polished," I thought. She was elegantly dressed in black, and her posture exuded confidence which was contagious. It made me sit up straight just listening to her. "You can just be yourself, smile, and tell them about the languages you speak. That will be appealing to both the Editor of *Gourmet Magazine*, and to the shirt company VP who is looking for a secretary who knows Spanish and French."

I spent the rest of the afternoon being interviewed at both companies, and I was thrilled to receive job offers at both meetings. The job at *Gourmet Magazine* was the most appealing because I would be working in the glamorous penthouse office of the Plaza Hotel and working on an Italian cookbook they were beginning to design. I had subscribed to *Gourmet* for the last two years at Vassar and loved the magazine, cooking from it as often as I could. It was a perfect job for me except for the salary, and I thought it was the next best thing to being in Italy. I wasn't sure I would be able to support myself in New York on $50 a week. The shirt company offered more but sounded so boring in comparison. I called Mrs. Andrews back to thank her for making these opportunities available to me and told her I would accept the *Gourmet* offer with pleasure. Apparently, *Gourmet* editors were impressed that I had had three years of Italian at Vassar and even my Italian name must have helped get the job. Little did they know my Italian was based on the studies of Ariosto, Tasso, Petrarch and Dante, which was a long way from the vocabulary I would have needed for writing an Italian cookbook.

"Not so fast," she interrupted. I have another possibility for you with a salary of $25 more a week than the *Gourmet* offer. Before you go back to Snedens, go to the Corning Glass office on Fifth Avenue at 718 Fifth Avenue. Their export department needs someone with languages and you are perfect for the job."

"But…"

"No buts. Just go for the interview, and then we'll discuss it."

I was used to taking orders, particularly from my seniors whom I knew had more experience than I had. Walking through the plush air-conditioned showroom of Steuben Glass I felt the eyes of the chic saleswomen on me as I looked around at the beautiful glassware. The Steuben ladies were all thin, smartly dressed in black, with pearls at the neck and their hair immaculately coiffed. I was already impressed, when upon asking where the Export Division was, one of them approached me and smiled pleasantly as she led me to the elevator at the back of the showroom, saying, "Their offices are on the third floor."

On the third floor, the receptionist said they were expecting me and led me into a large office where I was met by the Director of Personnel, the head secretary and the VP in charge of the Export Division. Everything went well after that, because I had profited from the counseling of Mrs. Andrews and the practice I had had in the other two interviews. It was with the crisply efficient head secretary that I was to spend most of the interview time. I liked her confident, cheerful manner, but didn't feel as at ease with her as with the two men, the VP in charge of the Export Division or the

Director of Personnel. I could feel almost immediately a competitive edge to her, disguised by an overly enthusiastic manner and the insincere smile that covered her face. Right away I knew it was her I had to impress, and I had to make her like me.

"You will learn from your boss, who is a very nice man, and he is head of our Export Division," she said with pride. I sensed she really liked him, and I was pleased that she had already assumed I would be given the job as his secretary. She, of course, was secretary to the President of the Company and had let me know that when we were first introduced. "Have you ever used a Dictaphone?"

I didn't say I really didn't know what a Dictaphone was, but I answered, "No I haven't but I can certainly learn and hope you will teach me."

"Of course. And maybe you will teach me some Italian," she smiled. "I would love to go to Italy." I was already feeling better, knowing there was something I could teach her, something she didn't already know.

After an hour and a half with that interview and the other two I was thrilled when I was told I had the job at $75 a week if I wanted it! It was scary to think I had to write business letters in Spanish and Italian, but I knew just where to go to get the right formats for the letters. My Spanish and Italian friends would be invaluable in the translating of the business letters. I would be ranslating and typing business letters each ordering so many cases of Pyrex to be sent "FBO" which I later learned meant Federal Business Offices. This job meant I would have money to pay for taxis, clothes, my weekly hairdresser, and some theatre. I wouldn't have to ask my parents for money, so I felt rich and privileged. I wished I could work for "Gourmet" but knew I wouldn't be in New York for long if an opportunity to go to Italy came up, and I didn't want to ruin my chances for working at the magazine later in life.

It was a great time to live in New York. To add to the luxurious lifestyle, I had the use of a "country house" at Snedens that my father kept open for the family and which my brother at Princeton and I could use. I loved being able to invite my New York City friends out for Sunday lunches under the grape arbor where I often produced roast chicken with polenta and lots of Chianti. And spending weekends with friends on Long Island or in Connecticut seemed glamorous. I hardly had a free weekend to stay in New York for museums, concerts, or the endless cocktail parties. All of that was very typical of the life we led in the 50s in New York.

My cousin Lydia had invited me to live with her and two other girls all sharing the rent of a luxurious three-story town house in the upper East 90s. The owner was a niece of Buckminster Fuller and a friend of our families at Snedens. She was a divorcee who had enough money to travel extensively but soon learned that the four of us were having such fun in her house that she kept the master bedroom for herself and stayed on to enjoy our cocktail parties and dinners. Her four new tenants were all young, energetic, and we all had jobs allowing us to pay the modest rent which was low enough that we even had money left over for luxuries. Cooking was something we all loved, and each of us was responsible for preparing dinner one day a week. We shared the expenses for the once a week grocery shopping and entertained each other's friends, had cocktail and dinner parties, generally enjoying New York in a privileged way. I ran into Vassar classmates almost every day in midtown Manhattan and our social circles widened through these accidental encounters. We were always meeting new people and revelling in the cosmopolitan life in New York through friends at the UN, and those we met at our various jobs.

The secretaries in the Export Department at Corning Glass made up a small but very diverse group: one secretary was Russian, one German, and then there was Madge, a sexy blonde from Brooklyn who stood out in various ways. She took by far the fastest dictation, wore the tightest and shortest skirts, and her accent was the most distinctive. When the marriage of Arthur Miller and Marilyn Monroe was announced in the tabloids it caused great excitement in our office.

"I can't imagine why Arthur Miller actually married her," I remarked ingenuously to those standing around the water fountain.

Madge's mouth fell open in astonishment, "Well, why in the world did she want to marry HIM!" The difference in our two worlds could not have been captured more clearly than in this exchange. I admired her for her lack of inhibition, her confidence and once again I was reminded of my own narrow perceptions. Revelations of a larger world were to come from further exchanges with Madge, whose humor and worldviews I came to understand and appreciate as we worked together.

Elena, the attractive young Russian girl exactly my age had emmigrated from Saint Petersburg to New York with her parents, gone to public schools in northern New York state, graduated with distinction from Uppsala College in New Jersey, and was highly thought of at Corning. She was hired for the Russian translations. Despite our very different backgrounds we became fast friends early on, and discovered we had more in common than we had originally thought, including the fact that we were dating men who were brothers, but who lived and worked in different worlds. Mine worked at Time Life as a copy boy and hers was a struggling actor. We shared our problems and delights daily.

Another friend I made at Corning was Ursula, a chic older German lady unhappily married who shared her marital problems over our frequent morning coffee klatches. I recognized it immediately as a repressive marriage but so comfortable financially that I knew why she stayed with him. She told me that my life as a free young American girl with no marital problems was enviable. I understood when I saw a sudden sheet of sadness appearing on her face, and I pitied her. Reaching for her hand to squeeze with affection, I saw her life through her eyes, and had another confirmation of how lucky I was not to be married.

I hadn't heard from the Vassar vocational bureau until about six months after leaving Vassar. Then out of the blue a special delivery letter arrived that surprised me. It also disappointed me to the extent that I didn't even answer it right away. The idea of going to Costa Rica instead of Italy never even entered the realm of possibility in my mind. A couple of days later at our usual coffee klatch with not much to report to Ursula, I brought the letter to show her and told her I had done nothing about it or even answered the letter. The letter strongly recommended that I go to Washington DC to meet with the American ambassador to Costa Rica and his family.

"What? You didn't even investigate the possibility of that job?"

"But it is in San Jose. I never even thought about living in Costa Rica. Why would I want to go there?"

"You don't have to take the job, you know. And you should certainly find out more about it." She lowered her voice and continued in a stern tone. "I am surprised at you. You should meet the family and then decide. Why you haven't even been to Washington, DC! That alone is a reason for going to have an interview."

I thought about it for a few minutes and was embarrassed that I had been so lacking in curiosity. "Of course, you are right. I should go and then decide." Years later I realized that one of the handicaps of the young is not being able to think outside the box. That realization was thanks to Ursula, my older German friend who introduced me to the idea that I should be willing to try things I had never considered. Before I knew it, I had set up the interview and was on the train to DC.

THE INTERVIEW WENT WELL, and I was most impressed by the Woodward family. Ambassador and Mrs. Woodward were not only charming; they were the most sophisticated people I had ever met and I knew immediately that I would enjoy living with them no matter where they lived. Mrs. Woodward, petite and with streaks of silver in her short brown hair, had an engaging smile and such a natural manner that made me like her immediately. I couldn't help noticing how gracious she was in the simple act of pouring tea for both of us while explaining what my job would be. I would be preparing Bobby, their twelve-year-old son, in all subjects with the help of the Calvert School Correspondence course. The goal was to give him a seventh-grade curriculum that would prepare him for a top American boarding school when the time came for him to return to the US.

Bobby and his 10-year old sister Mary ambled into the drawing room to meet me and were quietly polite after the introductions were made. They had, I learned later, met several potential tutors and were rather bored with the idea of meeting yet another. There was an edginess to Bobby who spoke in a staccato voice, and pushed his large horn-rimmed glasses down on his nose. He had just been to a science fiction movie and was particularly excited to tell us about it in great detail. His mother looked at me and smiled, "Bobby loves movies." To their great relief, the children were excused, and we returned to the interview after they left the room.

The options they offered me were more than generous. To begin with, the salary was more than I expected, and I knew I would have very few expenses so most of that could be saved for my never to be forgotten trip to Italy. It would be an open-ended commitment on both sides. If it turned out that I was unhappy and wanted to go home in less than a month, or if they didn't feel I was doing a good job, I would pay my own way back to the States, and if one of us decided after three months that it was not a good fit, they would pay my way back. It was important to me that Mrs. Woodward explained at the onset that I would be treated as a member of the family by the servants, and they would introduce me to their friends as such. I would be free to do whatever I wanted after Bobby's morning classes were over. I could go to the University if I wanted to. I could even continue to have Spanish guitar lessons with a local instructor they would find for me.

I was delighted with all the proposed arrangements, and we both agreed it would be worth a try. A diplomatic passport would be procured for me and would be sent to my address in New York. I could hardly believe my good fortune, and we agreed that day that I would join them in three weeks after I gave the required two weeks' notice at Corning, and a return trip to Texas to say goodbye to my parents for perhaps a year.

The Berlitz Spanish classes I had been taking for the past two months proved to be fortuitous both for the Spanish I needed at work and also now for my new life in Latin America. By increasing the number of classes per week Spanish gradually overtook the Italian, which faded into the back of my mind. I hoped it wouldn't be totally forgotten as so much of the Spanish from my Texas elementary and Junior High schools had been. Hopefully

Italian would remain dormant until I needed it for my eventual trip to Italy. My parents and all my friends were happy for me, and I was particularly pleased with the reaction of my boss at Corning who said he knew I wasn't going to stay at Corning forever and was delighted with this new opportunity for me. Going away parties, lunches and dinners kept me in a constant state of excitement before leaving for Texas. My friends Ursula and Elena were happy for me but at the same time a little saddened at my leaving. Ursula had a special luncheon for me at a Spanish restaurant for all the secretaries, where she gave a special toast to my "future life in the diplomatic world." She insisted that I write about my new life and said she would live vicariously through my letters. I felt a tinge of sadness knowing how most of them were envious of my going into a different life but I was touched by all their good wishes.

When my "Special" diplomatic passport arrived by registered mail I was relieved, and knew it was all not a dream but actually going to happen: my first adventure in what I hoped would be the beginning of an exciting international life. As I clutched the new red leather passport case holding my passport to a new life I knew it was going to be a fabulous experience even if it wasn't in Italy; I had never been more convinced of anything in my life.

# Harvard Engineer Leaves Field To Head Art Gallery

**By Doris Reno**
Herald Music and Art Critic

A young man who had planned all his life to be an engineer got a sudden yen for paintings, plunged into art midstream, and last week arrived in South Florida to hold down a director's job that had been created especially for

**HENRI DORRA**

Henry Dorra had never thought of art as a career until after he received his master's degree in engineering at Harvard about three years ago.

Today he finds himself director of the Society of Four Arts in Palm Beach, a newly created post that to him is as breathtakingly exciting as the first circus to a 6-year-old.

Dorra's appointment was announced last week by Mrs. Paul Moore, chairman of the society's art committee. He took over his duties the day following the announcement.

In Miami last weekend to participate in Lowe Gallery's southeastern directors

meeting, Dorra tried to explain how he happened to switch to a Gallery director's career after thoroughgoing preparation for life work in an entirely diverse yeah field.

"After I'd finished my master's", he reminisces of the now 3-year-old happening, I just took a course in fine arts for fun, for refreshment from the engineering grind, and there I was right where I belonged I was so happy I couldn't give it up.

The enthusiastic young discoverer, into whose ken a new planet has swung, immediately transferred all his interests to the fine arts department and set out to earn a doctorate in that field.

He began work at the Fogg Museum at Harvard, specializing in 19th century French painting, and while there put up two exhibits that drew national attention. One was entitled "Three Designers for the Contemporary Stage, the other "Connoisseurship", step by step.

The last, which dealt with establishment of authorship identities in the case of various Fogg-owned drawings, was awarded a leading article in art news.

Dorra's PhD thesis is on "The Style of Gauguin's Formative Years." It is almost, but not quite, completed.

Immediately after serving his doctorial directorial apprentice ship at the Fogg, Dorra undertook a year's work and museum administration financed by a scholarship grant from the Metropolitan Museum of Art in New York. He has recently returned from three months study of museums and galleries in Holland, Denmark, Sweden, France and England.

He cherishes no ambitions to be an artist himself and has never studied the technique of painting.

Up at Palm Beach the new director plans to continue the exhibition pro-

gram within the framework already established and hopes to expand increasingly the educational work of the society. Exhibitions will attempt to illustrate important developments of art history, and in each case lectures and film showings will stress the cultural background.

He began work in June on the four major exhibitions the society will present this season of which the first, 18th century masterpieces, will open December 12th.

This show will include eight famous Bouche tapestries made in Beauvais in the mid 18th century, which will be accentuated by fine examples of painting, drawing, and sculpture from the period in question.

Dorra is most enthusiastic about his second show, concerned with pre-Columbian art, which will open January 9. This will contain fabulous objects from ancient Mexico and Peru, selected with a view to their artistic merits and appeal to the modern eye as well as to their position in art history.

A retrospective exhibition of the work of Henri Matisse will open February 6th and the season will close with the Four Arts annual of contemporary paintings and drawings which invites entries from artists all over the country.

Perry Rathbone of dissent some Saint Louis Museum is scheduled to judge the entries for prize awards in this final show. Dorra was born in Alexandria, Egypt and graduated from the *Lycée St. Louis*, Paris, in 1939. He took his bachelor's degree engineering at the University of London in 1944 while doing war work in a British factory.

Two chapters of his doctorate thesis have already been published, one in the Metropolitan bulletin, the other in the *Gazette des Beaux Art*.

# XI

# Florida and Learning More About
# My New Country

WHEN GAUGUIN ARRIVED in Tahiti for the first time, seeing those palm trees, beautiful blue water, and sun-bleached beaches, he must have felt as I did in 1952 as I began my first job in Florida, our own American tropics. I felt that he too must have had hopes, as I did, for a new life in this exotic new country. I couldn't believe how humid Palm Beach was, and yet it was not unbearable, with the ocean breezes refreshing everything. Seeing oranges and lemons hanging from the trees all over town and knowing there were bunches of dates high in the palm trees were, for me, symbols of the abundance of this new country. I loved seeing everyone in short sleeves, and in the evenings flattering white dinner jackets were *de riguer*. The ladies were slim and well-coiffed. They all felt secure enough at their clubs and at private dinners to wear their extraordinary jewels. I had never seen such opulence.

The Society of the Four Arts created a new job for me. I learned in the short month after my arrival in Palm Beach that there were no natives such as Gauguin found, but many New Yorkers and Chicagoans. They wintered in Florida, fleeing the cold of the northern climes, and those snowbirds had a different kind of beauty, a highly polished one. I knew even before leaving New York that my job as Art Director, a title created for me, would be a challenging one. It was exciting to think about planning the exhibitions, getting speakers and musicians, and enlivening the audiences with new ideas, even though I wasn't sure how they would respond to me, a young immigrant, attempting to understand the American mind. My article in the *Metropolitan Museum Bulletin* had just appeared, and Gauguin was still very much with me as I tried to become acclimated to the beautiful new landscape.

It was a balmy December day, perfect Florida weather, on the afternoon that would be my first appearance with the ladies of the Four Arts Council at their "Welcome New Members Tea." The event was written up in *The Palm Beach Post* that morning. In the article, written basically to announce

Clearwater, Florida.

that my first show would be "French Masterpieces of the 18th Century," the reporter accurately reported details of my life up to now and described me as "interesting and international." There was no mention that I was a Jew…merely a suggestion that I was a foreigner. I understood that there was some anti-Semitism in Florida, but so far everyone had been very cordial and welcoming. Some even began to speak French to me upon being introduced. My first gallery talk would be after the preview tea for the members. Since it was the opening of the season at the Four Arts, it would be very well attended by those interested in the subject of French art as well as the socialites in Palm Beach who wanted to be seen.

My schedule for the week was full: talks to give at the schools and continued gallery talks this week wouldn't allow me to go to Clearwater to see Maman and Papa until the next week. They appeared to have settled in nicely, and had friends and a rather active social life. Papa was very pleased with his new surroundings, Mama said when I spoke to her. I could visualize in my mind his enjoying the fresh papaya, oranges, sunshine and attractive people. Even though they had still not become American citizens, they were getting used to new ways of viewing the world and being appreciated by an open-minded, loving American community. I hoped to visit them as often as I could, once I got settled into my new job. Their friends the O'Conners in Clearwater were good solid Americans and introduced Maman to the Unitarian Church where she was warmly welcomed both by members of the congregation and the charismatic Minister who had shown an immediate admiration for her.

DURING MY FIRST VISIT to Clearwater in December, 1952, Maman gave a tea for me to meet some new American friends she especially wanted me to know. I was impressed with their kindness both to Maman and Papa and also to me. Their openly affectionate manner seemed so American to me and their political savvy was impressive. I couldn't help admiring their frankness, and they were not shy about expressing their liberal views albeit somewhat naïvely. We were all interested in the selection of candidates for the upcoming election.

"There is a threat, you know, to America, but I think General Eisenhower can fix it. He at least knows the European scene and has met with European leaders. He is not going to let the Russians push him around." Mrs. O'Conner moved her glasses up further up on her nose as her voice became more impassioned. She turned to Maman with thoughtful affectionate eyes.

"'What do you think, Aimée?"

Maman took a long puff on her cigarette, sat back in her chair and answered, "I think this country always pulls itself out of difficult situations. We'll see if Ike can get the Heartland isolationists to appreciate George Marshall the way he should be. His plan to rebuild Europe is a mammoth one but I believe he is doing it."

Papa was enjoying the exchange and always surprised by Maman's knowledge of English when she peppered her conversation with expressions like the "Heartland isolationists."

"You are right, Aimée, those Midwesterners are being encouraged by Senator McCarthy's anti-Communist crusade. I read recently that the American public fears an encroaching 'Red Menace' more than anything and that it is better to be isolationists rather than to help rebuild Europe."

Mrs. O'Conner looked at him sternly, pursing her lips and narrowing her eyes, before remarking, "Not all Americans are like that. I know Eisenhower is worried about the possibility of Russian power but many of us believe we should stay engaged in Europe in order to keep Russia from becoming stronger, and on the home front we can't cave into the communist conspiracy theory that McCarthy is promoting. He believes erroneously that General Marshall is responsible for bringing communism into the American government. Fear is the weapon he uses so effectively."

"So, who is going to protect America from falling into the same kind of situation that existed when Hitler's power increased daily because he generated so much fear in the people of Germany?" My voice was trembling as I asked that question. The quick response came from Mrs. O'Conner in a clear voice: "Governor Adlai Stevenson of Illinois." She took a sip of her tea and settled into a nearby chair.

"But can he win? He has said he wants to run again for Governor of Illinois and not be a Democratic candidate for President. The Democratic National Convention will be held next month in Illinois and he must be persuaded to run."

Maman sat near her and took out her gold cigarette case as she answered for all of us, "Who can persuade him to run?"

"The boss of the Illinois delegation is Jacob Arvey. He can pull the party bosses of the other states together to 'draft' Stevenson, I think."

I was surprised at how revealing and intimate the conversation had become. They all seemed to trust each other, and it made me happy to know that my parents had adjusted so quickly to their new surroundings and that they had become friends with such intelligent people. The conversation moved on to more general topics including my work at the Four Arts. I was surprised that many of them said they had read about me and my first show featuring the 18th Century masterpieces.

"You must have put in many hours on that show," Papa exclaimed, almost shouting.

"Yes," I replied. "I worked on that show non-stop since my arrival and was very excited about it."

They smiled and encouraged me to continue. "Fortunately, I had already established good rapport with the Duveen and Wildenstein galleries in New York who have generously lent me their Boucher and Fragonard paintings as well as some of the most beautiful drawings by those same artists. My friends, Mr. and Mrs. Robert Lehman also agreed to lend their most beautiful Fragonard, 'The Pillow Fight.' But I have to keep going to amuse that Palm Beach group."

"I had no idea those society ladies were interested in art," Mr. O'Conner said with a smile.

I returned his smile and said, "Oh, there are some. Mrs. Paul Moore is the chairman of the art committee and so easy to work with. She seems to like all my ideas, so we went ahead and planned the next three shows for 1953. The attendance at my first was great, and I hope to attract some of the same people but even more of an audience for the next show that will be very different from the first."

"And what is that to be? We want to come to see it," Mrs. O'Conner declared looking at Maman.

"Fortunately, there were many who supported my idea of a Pre-Columbian show to open on January 9 so that is the plan for the next show to be followed by a rather ambitious exhibition of Matisse's work in February. I must begin working on both as soon as I leave Clearwater. My letters requesting works from private donors as well as from the Peabody Museum at Harvard must go out next week. And then there are the gallery talks to prepare. I love doing those and am surprised and delighted to see that I have a small following. The Matisse show in February is really one I am looking forward to doing and the Arts Committee members at the last meeting were very enthusiastic about it."

"But you must be working all the time, Henri. Do you have any time for a social life? Do you enjoy these people?" Papa had entered the conversation once more.

I gave him what I hoped was a reassuring look. "Life is good, and I am having a wonderful time meeting Americans from all over—particularly those who come from New York and Chicago. They seem to be so sophisticated and worldly. I hope to increase the audiences at the lectures and openings, but it won't be easy. Some of the people are particularly nice to me. They try to speak French to me but with terrible accents. I am afraid the snowbirds love their cocktail parties and are resistant to too much culture, but there are some like the Bings and the Rosenwalds who have lent their works to the Norton Gallery for the upcoming exhibition of French paintings. These part time Floridians have given Palm Beach and Miami a new look. I too am lending my little Signac watercolor to the show."

Papa had been quiet but suddenly put down his cup of tea and, looking straight at me, raising his eyebrows questioned me, "Isn't there still the problem, however, of being a Jew, and isn't there still the not always covert anti-Semitism? Have you experienced that at their clubs where I understand Jews are not allowed?"

"Yes, I have been invited to the Everglades, and I accepted. As I mentioned before, they think I am French so there was no embarrassment when I arrived. The maître d' even spoke to me in French. Perhaps I am a hypocrite not to acknowledge outright that I am a Jew when some unseemly remarks are made. I know most of them think of me as being French or at least European and I don't believe it is necessary to correct them. Do you think I should say, Papa, that I am a Sephardic Jew from Alexandria? You know one reason I didn't correct them is because I really do feel French. We shall see. Maybe next time I will explain."

"No, my son, I don't think you have to explain anything. You are quite right, and I am proud of you. Why stir the pot when stirring isn't necessary?" We looked at each other and smiled and that seemed to be enough to finish the conversation.

Mrs. O'Conner changed the subject rather abruptly by saying "They are very lucky to have you there, and I know this is just the beginning of a very successful career in America. You will not stay in Palm Beach long. You will have other offers soon when they hear what a good job you are doing at the Four Arts.

Director of the Ringling Museum in Sarasota has asked me to come to see their museum when I have a free weekend. He must have read the article about me when I first arrived when I said I was as excited as "a six-year-old at his first circus!"

"Bravo, my son. That was so smart of you to know that Ringling was a circus entrepreneur. I am sure that impressed him."

I stood and began to walk the length of the small room, trying not to show how unsure I felt about my career and my future. "I'm not sure. But I do know that Chick Austin, the current mover and shaker behind the Ringling is very creative and extremely smart. I am told he is a blueblood American and, definitely not Jewish."

# Sixteenth Century World of Art

**BY LLOYD E. OLSEN**

Many Florida visitors and a good share of Florida's art students spent a few days in a 16th century world at the annual art seminar at the Ringling Museum.

The seminars, sponsored by that institution and the Department of Art of Florida State University in Tallahassee, began seven years ago when FSU president Doak S. Campbell and A. Everett Austin, Jr., Director of Ringling Museum, together with members of the Board of Control, sat around a table.

They decided that the two educational institutions, both state owned and operated, should pool their resources to serve the state more effectively.

The first seminar in 1948 survey did most of the long course of the history of art. It established what has become a tradition at the seminars, the invitation of outstanding specialists

Staff and students chat after a lecture. Dr. Henri Dorra, Associate Director of the Ringling Museum; Eloise McGirr, Pensacola; Dr. Sidney Friedburg, Wellesley College; Dr. Wolfgang Lotz, Vassar College; Jane Howard, Jacksonville; and Dr. John Coolidge, Harvard University, evaluate the progress of the seminar.

in the history of art from all over the country.

Since that time, various specialized phases of art and related subjects have been studied annually in a series of two-week, and more recently, one-week intensive study periods under the local conditions existing at the museum. Here art students from Florida State University and guests become acquainted with the larger and one of the most highly selective collections of art in the southeast.

The rigorous program of daily lectures is varied by the showing of movies, the performance of concerts and plays designed to broaden the scope of the study program. Miss Nellie Bond-Dickinson, professor of modern dance at FSU, has brought her group of dancers to the museum on several occasions. Each year the Department of speech from the Tallahassee University has sent players to perform a play closely related to the theme of that year seminar.

The FSU School of Music has contributed a concert annually. Other University department's, English, modern languages, anthropology and political science, have contributed to the programs.

Typical of the visiting speakers who have appeared since the first seminar are: William Zorach, one of the best known American sculptors of our time; Lincoln Kirstein, impresario of the New York City ballet, and Horst W. Jansen, head of the Department of Fine Arts at New York University.

This year's seminar, mannerism, anti classical movement of the 16th century, brought prominent speakers from Harvard, Wellesley, and Vassar College.

The Woodwards arriving in Montevideo.

# XII

# Costa Rica and Uruguay
### MY FIRST FOREIGN ADDRESSES

I DIDN'T KNOW WHAT TO EXPECT when I accepted the job of teaching the children of the America ambassador at that first meeting with Ambassador and Mrs. Woodward in Washington, D.C., but living at the American Embassy in San José turned out to be a wonderful experience in every way. My letters home to my parents were saved and helped me in later years to preserve the memories that I hoped to write about in the future. Mrs. Woodward was the kind of gracious, intelligent woman I admired, and, among other things, I shared both hers and her husband's views and liberal politics. Ambassador Woodward, a career diplomat, was so well informed that I knew I would learn just by being at the dinner table with him. My room at the Embassy residence was spacious and comfortable and looked out on the front lawn of the well-kept garden. The residence was not particularly pretentious, but the downstairs living room and dining room were sufficiently grand to entertain visiting dignitaries and the local officials when necessary. On the other hand, the library was extremely cozy and used for our family gatherings every night over pre-dinner daiquiris to hear the stories of the day from both the children and the three adults that now made up the family.

According to the parents' instructions, there would be a special emphasis on my teaching Bobby, the twelve-year-old, to write, in addition to following the Calvert School curriculum. He had been educated up to now in local schools in different foreign countries where he had never written a composition in English, and I didn't know seventh graders weren't expected to do research papers, using footnotes and annotated bibliographies when necessary. I knew I could teach him these things and to write clearly in English. After all, I had a degree in Philosophy from Vassar. It turned out that I was right. I did teach him, and we both had fun while he learned to be a very good writer. He didn't know that under my tutelage (and with the approval of his parents) he had to write three times more papers than was required by the Calvert

School for graduating from the seventh grade. For example, when we studied Bismarck in the history lessons, I made sure he learned how to write research papers without plagiarizing. Certainly, writing about Bismarck hadn't been expected but he did a wonderful job of reporting on the rise of Bismarck and how he ruled first Prussia, and then succeeded in uniting Germany as a new modern nation. He was a very bright boy, and it was a pleasure to teach him.

Both of us wanted to begin classes at seven in the morning with only a half hour break before lunch. That meant we could have almost all the remaining hours of the day to do what we wanted to do—I could go to the University for classes in Spanish literature and Bobby was free after doing his homework, to play with his Costa Rican friends. Bobby introduced me to a wonderful little fruit called "*mammon*" or "*rambutan*" that was indigenous to Costa Rica and which he somehow found to bring to me. He showed me how to peel one of the little red prickly fruits, separating it from the cluster of golf-ball size *mamones*.

Our day began with a sumptuous breakfast at 6:30. The beautiful rounds of orange papaya and pineapple were something I looked forward to every morning, and the freshly ground Costa Rican coffee was an ecstasy I had never known existed. Fresh orange juice every morning was something I became addicted to for the rest of my life. We began with spelling lessons, then grammar taught in the old school manner as I had learned it in my Fort Worth public-school English classes, that is by diagramming sentences and a thorough study of the parts of speech. The Calvert School teachers' handbook and study guide did not specify those techniques, but diagramming sentences was fun for me and the only way I knew how to teach the structure of the English language. My enthusiasm was catching, and Bobby soon became a whiz at diagramming complex sentences.

His sister Mary who was eleven, went to the regular Costa Rican grammar school. She was somewhat miffed that I spent so much time with Bobby and not with her. I knew I had to fix that. Her Spanish was perfect, and I knew she had a gift for languages, so I suggested that we plan a surprise for her parents' Christmas present. I told her I thought she would be very good at Latin because of her knowledge of Spanish. A friend in New York sent me a good Latin textbook, and we worked secretly on Latin grammar, and presented workbooks in her beautiful, neat handwriting to her parents on Christmas morning. They were pleased and proud of us both.

I had been told before leaving the States that I would be considered a member of the family and therefore invited to almost all the receptions at the Embassy and some of the dinners. If I didn't want to attend, I didn't have to, but usually I did and enjoyed them very much. It was often a good chance to speak Spanish, and I loved that. For me, the most important one I went to was in honor of the pianist, Arthur Rubenstein who was on tour in Latin America. I was pleased I had brought the Ceil Chapman red satin cocktail dress that Daddy and Stanley Marcus had picked out for me for one of my debutante parties. It was perfect and I loved it.

But it was the day after that reception that was even more important to me. Mrs. Woodward had invited me to join her and Arthur Rubenstein for tea. The attractive seventy-three-year-old with his thick white hair was a delight. He kissed my hand when we met and when he said goodbye, as I had learned they do in diplomatic circles. That is something I would always remember. He spoke in a lively engaging manner flashing a beautiful flirtatious smile at both of us. I couldn't help noticing that during the entire time he was with us he kept wringing his beautiful hands. I thought to myself even Arthur Rubenstein must get nervous before a concert, and maybe he was thinking he should be practicing instead of sipping tea at the American Embassy with us. While Mrs. Woodward poured tea, I asked him if he had ever been to Costa Rica before. He replied that he hadn't but that he adored Latin music. "You will hear me play some Latin music tonight. Villa Lobos is one of my favorites."

The Rubenstein concert at the *Teatro Nacional* in San José that night was packed. Cultured "Ticos" knew of Rubenstein and wouldn't have missed his first Costa Rican concert. Mrs. Rubenstein sat in our box with Mr. and Mrs. Woodward, our good friend Florence Lloyd and me, the Cultural Attaché and his wife and the consul and his wife. In the next box over was President elect Echandi with his wife and family. Their box was next to the President's box. It was terribly exciting with all the presidents, vice-presidents, ambassadors, etc....

Just as Mr. Rubenstein had told us at tea, he played Villa Lobos. I had never heard *Rudepoema*, which was one of Rubenstein's signature pieces on that tour, and I'd never forget his vibrancy and passion when he played it that night. The Costa Ricans responded with true Latin enthusiasm. They stood cheering and stomping their feet for some time.

I was invited to almost everything at the Embassy, but attended only those events that I thought would be interesting or those which Mrs. Woodward thought I should attend "for my own edification." Protocol demanded that all the Embassy people stay until the guests of honor left. I found it very amusing at a party for the Naval Attache and his wife, when at a certain point everyone wanted to leave and had stopped drinking except one of the Ticos and his wife who was also being honored, stayed and stayed. They were having a fine time, but they apparently didn't think it was a real party unless there was

Studying Flamenco and classical guitar in Costa Rica was an added delight.

dancing. They began humming loudly and collecting some of us in a conga line around the living room. It was very jolly particularly for the Ticos who eventually saw the exhaustion on the faces of the Embassy staff. Finally, they left around 10:30 and we could all go to bed after a long, tiring day. I knew I had to begin teaching at seven.

The rainy season took a bit of getting used to but at least it was dependable. It rained every afternoon, but it was not a depressing rain as it had been in Poughkeepsie when the sun never came out. In San José it usually began after lunch when I was on my way to the University. It was a hard rain that lasted a couple of hours, stopped and started again. I loved the little black Ford convertible that the Woodwards let me use whenever I wanted. Driving to the University every day and usually stopping off at the home of my new friends, Florence and Joel Lloyd's for a drink or tea afterwards to discuss the day's classes became a habit.

When I read in 1963 of the Irazu volcanic eruption that covered San José in ash, I remembered that picnic in 1958 with other twenty-something year-olds on the rim of the deepest and largest crater in Costa Rica, some 900 ft. deep. The volcano had been inactive for so long we believed it would be inactive forever. The taste of the cold beer we were drinking and the astounding beauty of the site that clear day when we sat on the rim of the volcano and could see both the Caribbean and the Pacific coasts are both still with me. I can still almost hear the voices of those male friends who invited us on the hike and picnic when they began, after a few beers, singing their German songs so energetically that it awakened me from a profound enjoyment of the moment. I didn't know a word of German, but I understood their Hitlarian feeling of superiority, and it was shocking to me. After that day, I never accepted another invitation from those coffee ranchers who had been sent from Germany to work on the coffee "fincas" to learn the Costa Rican art of growing superior coffee beans.

My letters from Costa Rica to my parents were full of the activities, and usually filled with tales of the people I met in the diplomatic corps, some from the university and others through the many friends of the Woodwards, who never lost hope in thinking I would meet Prince Charming.

"June 6, 1957

Dearest Mama and Daddy,

A young French-Costa Rican coffee grower who is one of the wealthiest men in Costa Rica even though he is only 32 began squiring me around. He has taken me to many of the diplomatic functions we were both invited to and occasionally we have had dinner dates and gone dancing. He took me to tour one of his coffee factories and it was there that I realized that even foreign men could be uninteresting. Too bad I was not interested in marrying for money for he could have taken care of me for the rest of my life. However, if I married him, I'd probably have died of boredom and I knew I could never consider living in Costa Rica for the rest of my life.

Last Sunday I went out with him, and when he came to pick me up Alicia, one of the maids, answered the door and Bobby told me the next morning that she ran to the kitchen and said "*Que guapo hombre de la senorita Tony!*" (What a handsome man the senorita Tony has!"). Then she and the cook, and the laundress and the gardener and Bobby all ran to peek out the window to watch him help me into his beautiful Mercedes. They were all so excited. You can imagine all those faces peering out the window. Mrs. Woodward and I laughed heartily at this."

Mrs. Woodward always understood me and knew that eventually I would be bored beyond words by him. That did not prevent their trying to introduce me to young diplomats or other "suitable young men." However, it was clear to them as it became clear to me that I preferred their company and that of the older friends: the Lloyds and the Warners and the people they introduced me to. The Woodwards did everything possible to make San José interesting and pleasant for me. Mrs. Woodward took me to call on the Spanish Ambassador's wife and daughter who is about my age. She (the daughter) knows no one her own age and has been wanting to meet me. When we arrived, I saw a stunning young woman with dark black hair, and beautiful white skin. Her figure was perfect. She was shy but extremely nice, and we became friends to a certain extent. She didn't have much to say and that may be why we never became close friends.

During the next few months we continued to wonder where exactly we would be sent. There was talk of Iceland, which would have been interesting, but Peru even more so. That was what we were all hoping for, but it wasn't until January that we received news of the definite assignment. Bobby became even more unhinged as each new prospect was announced. Disappointment followed elation from one day to the next. Mary on the other hand seemed to be oblivious to it all and spoke like a seasoned diplomat: "It will all be settled one way or another."

"7 Enero, 1958

Dearest Mama and Daddy,

Well, we have received the big news. It is not definitely settled exactly when we are to move, but things should be decided soon. Our next post is Montevideo, Uruguay. It is so exciting and so sudden I can hardly believe it. We are all thrilled. It is supposed to be a very sophisticated country and Montevideo is a comparatively large city. B.A. is just a hop, skip and a jump away. Naturally this will mean I will have a free trip home and will probably go to N.Y. as well as Texas. We are considering driving home via the Pan American highway. Then the Woodwards would drop me off at the nearest place to Fort Worth while they drive up to Washington, D.C. Then we will all fly down to Valparaiso where we will pick up the other car and drive across the Andes to Montevideo. This is not settled either-just talk. Anyway, none of it will happen before the end of February which is election time in Costa Rica...."

When the first of February rolled around the excitement at the Embassy residence about the forthcoming Costa Rican election had reached a pitch. Mrs. Woodward and I drove through San José watching everybody going to the polls. All the cars had one of the three flags of the three parties and everyone was shouting, waving flags, and honking. Then we drove to Cartago (one of the pueblos where the poorer classes live, "the *campesinos*"). They were much quieter, but there were still the same flags waving and the same intensity of feeling. All the people who didn't have cars were picked up in trucks and buses rented by the various parties and then they were hauled off to the polls. Nari, the cook was so excited. She was for Echandi, the arch conservative party because she associated herself with the "*gente bien*" (the upper classes) since she had cooked for so many of them. Her fellow colleagues in the kitchen were all Orlichistas or Rossistas, the parties of what Bobby calls the "plain old *gente.*" We thought that probably Orlich would win but as it turned out the conservative Echandi was elected as the new president of Costa Rica.

Despite the interruption of the elections, the diplomatic social life continued, and I was honored to be included in so many of the parties. Of all, I liked going to the Cultural Attaché's parties the most because the Warners gathered the most interesting people, including the Costa Rican intelligentsia and the cultured internationals. At one of their lively and memorable dinners of twelve for the Central American head of U.S.I.S., I loved speaking four languages in one evening: Italian with the Italian Ambassador, French with several from the French Embassy, and Spanish and English with the others. Kathleen and

Willy Warner were great hosts and became good friends even though they were a little older than me. I knew I would miss them when we left.

The Woodward children were a source of great amusement for me, and I really loved being with them. Bobby was particularly funny. One day I heard the following conversation between the two of them that showed he had indeed learned something from our intensive English grammar classes.

Mary: "I think Barbie and I are going to drop the church choir because there are just too many rehearsals."

Bobby: "Mary, you can't do that. You and Barbie are like the verbs in the choir—without you the whole thing will fall apart, leaving a lot of dangling adjectives and adverbs and prepositional phrases!

At other times he simply made me laugh at unexpected moments. One morning when we were doing the Arithmetic section of class, he suddenly stopped working and stared off into space. I asked "Bobby, what is wrong? Are you okay?"

His response: "Wait just a moment. I'm having a blank. Don't interrupt me. I'm enjoying it." Then after a few seconds he said, "Okay. It's gone now." And he resumed his work.


I LOVED THE SHORT VACATION with Bobby and Mary when we went to Limon on the Caribbean side of Costa Rica. The Caribbean was beautiful and the little town of Limon was covered with palm trees and was kept very clean. It was just what I had imagined the tropics to be like…palm trees all along the beach, mango, banana, almond, and avocado trees everywhere as well as countless other tropical fruit trees.

The park in the center of Limon was acclaimed the most beautiful park in Latin America. It was completely natural and had many strange trees so that it looked like an "organized jungle." There were sloths in the tops of some of the trees and they really merited their name. We were fortunate, however, to see them move ever so slightly.

On that trip Bobby, Mary and I had the Lloyds' house to ourselves, and it was a wonderful little cottage right on the beach. Mary and I went swimming several times a day (before breakfast included), and we were blessed by having wonderful weather the whole time. All of us came back browned and rested.

When I wasn't on the beach or playing games with Mary and Bobby I was reading Thackery's *Vanity Fair*. I finished it and loved it. I was doing a study of 18th century English literature and read Richardson, Stern, Defoe, Swift, Ruskin, Johnson, Smollett, etc. I read Boswell's biography of Dr. Johnson. It was terribly long but I finished it in two weeks.

On Thursday—the 4th of July there was much activity at the embassy… a party for the American children in the afternoon, and a cocktail party for the Embassy staff that night.

Once it was finally out that we were leaving, we were busy with an even more crowded social life. It was sad to be leaving my first foreign address and all the friends I had made, but the idea of going to Uruguay was thrilling, and I was pleased to have the chance to go back to see my parents in Texas between countries.

March 31, 1958
2409 Wyoming Avenue, Washington D.C.

Dear Mrs. Tonetti,

Bob and I were very touched by your thought in sending us flowers. We think that all the good fortune is on our side in having Tony with us— so we should be sending you flowers! She is a wonderfully adaptable person—congenial with all ages. She certainly makes the most of any opportunities—and in San Jose the opportunities were rather limited. She has been a great addition to our family and I already begin to dread the day when she pushes on to greater fields!

We were very disappointed that the drive home didn't materialize as we had been looking forward to meeting the Tonetti family. We will hope for better luck the next time we use the Inter American Highway (which may not be far off, as Bob is determined to be in the first car over the road when it's official opened.)

I suppose that Tony has told you that we are leaving D.C. for the new post on April 16. Vice President and Mrs. Nixon are hard on our heels, arriving in Montevideo April 27—so this barely gives us time to get the beds made. However, the house there is lovely—Nixons and Woodwards can both live there comfortably.

Again, our thanks for the lovely flowers—and the warmest regards to you both.

Sincerely,
Virginia Woodward

The Nixon visit caused a bit of an upheaval but was, as usual, handled well by the Woodwards. Instructions arrived before the Vice-President and his entourage that there should always be a bottle of Jack Daniels in their room. Mrs. Nixon "must have" hard candies to pass out at her visit to the children's hospital, and there were various other demands that were somewhat difficult to take care of in San Jose. The Jack Daniels bourbon was impossible to obtain in Costa Rica even at the "px," so Mrs. Woodward asked that it be brought down on the plane with the Nixons by one of the other state department officials. The hard candies of Costa Rica were not what Mrs. Nixon would expect so those too were brought down from the States and hand delivered to the Embassy residency.

I had no intention of going to meet "Tricky Dick," but at the last minute decided it was going to be such a nice reception that I should go, if only to meet some of the locals. After going through the receiving line once I decided I would experiment with the VP to see if he was paying attention, so I went through again and again. The third time he smiled at me and said, "I know. You are testing me. You've been through this line before." I guess he was paying attention.

That event occurred only a few months after we had arrived in Montevideo, and the Ambassador and Mrs. Woodward were getting settled into their new jobs and new life. They were extremely busy with social engagements every lunch and dinner. Mary had already left for her boarding school in D.C., and it was assumed that I would stay on to teach Bobby another year. After much soul searching, I decided to bring up the issue and the following conversation took place with both his parents.

Tony: "You know, I have been thinking that even though I would love to stay in Montevideo with you, I really think Bobby should be with other children for his own development and welfare. I have taught him for almost two years and have loved it, but it is time I think for both of us to move on."

Mrs. W: "Oh dear, I hate to think of your leaving." She was wringing her hands a bit and smoothing her brow with her fingers which I knew meant a headache was coming on. "But how wise of you and thoughtful to think of Bobby's development. Of course, you are right. We have been so busy since we arrived that I am afraid I have not had time to think of changes for him. He is so happy learning with you, and we are so pleased and comfortable with our arrangements for him with you. But..." and her face suddenly lit up with a new idea, "why don't you stay and be the social secretary here at the Embassy?"

Mr. Woodward, who had been quietly listening and letting us both do the talking, sat up straight and joined in for the first time. "Yes. We'd love to have you stay. You'd be very good at that job and Virginia needs someone right now."

"I am flattered, and I thank you for your confidence in me. But I have already made my decision of what I think is the best for both of us—Bobby and me. I know I would continue to have a wonderful life living here with you." I hesitated and then saw they were both listening attentively "but I really think that I should follow my dream and head for Italy."

No one spoke. Finally, the Ambassador looked at me directly, and said thoughtfully, "But, Tony, don't you think that you should go back to America first and learn shorthand? That will be a great tool for you. Then you will be more equipped to go to Italy."

"No. Definitely not," I said breathlessly. "I tried shorthand in business school a couple of years ago and believe it is harder than learning a foreign language. If I must learn shorthand before I go to Italy, I will never get there."

Mrs. Woodward broke in immediately. "I think Tony is right. She has had a dream of going to Italy before she even came to live with us. She will find her way." She smiled at me and I was moved almost to tears. "Thank you for understanding. I have investigated passage and the school possibilities in Florence. If I show that I am registered at an Italian University I can get a much cheaper fare on the Italian line from Montevideo. I have a Vassar friend and her husband in Rome I can stay with until I get to Florence, and I will be okay." I knew I could stay with Anne and George d'Almeida for a few days but had not yet written them I was coming.

The Ambassador looked worried and reflective, continuing, "But I'm afraid you will have to give up your "special" passport that was only good as long as you are a member of our household. You can of course keep the old one and should. You never know. People at borders are impressed with "special" passports even though they have the word "cancelled" on the cover. We'll see about getting you another regular American passport here. What about your parents? Do they approve of this?"

I had already written to my parents of my plan to leave Montevideo on the next ship to Italy. "They know my plans and I've saved enough money thanks to this job that I am not worried about the future. It is my next adventure and I am anxious to get started with it." I smiled, feeling relieved that I had gotten it all out and they didn't seem to be upset with me. We had a glass of champagne together, and the mood changed to a more celebratory one. When Bobby came into the room and saw us having champagne he said, "I knew Tony would get to Italy one way or another. We're all moving around the world. I guess that's what life is about!"

August 2, 1958
Embassy of the United States of America Montevideo, Uruguay

Dear Mr. and Mrs. Tonetti,

We have just come back from seeing Tony off on the *Conte Grande*—so I thought that you would like to know that she went off as happy as a lark—wreathed in smiles and looking forward to a wonderful time in Italy.

The boat is extremely nice. The third class a bit on the Spartan side—but eminently respectable and not uncomfortable at all. Tony's cabin-mate is an elderly Italian woman who will probably be completely uninteresting—but for the long haul a better bet I should think than a more dashing type might be.

We were all very sad to see Tony go. Her stay with us has been from our point of view a complete success, and we still think we were wonderfully lucky to have found her. Again, I congratulate you on having such a daughter. I hope Mary will turn out as well!

We all miss her dreadfully but I'm sure that she will love Italy and get a great deal out of her stay there.

Bobby went to Buenos Aires on Thursday—and we hope that he will be happy at the boarding school there and will profit from it. We await his first letter eagerly....

My husband joins me in sending you both our most cordial regards—We still have hopes of meeting you sometime!

Sincerely yours,
Virginia C. Woodward

My small cabin in third class on the *Conte Grande* was filled with flowers from the Woodwards, Warners, Lloyds and other friends who were there to see me off. I was particularly touched that they had all taken time off from their busy lives to come down to the dock. As the ship pulled away from the harbor, tears were rolling down my cheek because of both the sadness of leaving these dear friends, and the excitement of beginning the next chapter of my life that would finally be in Italy.

A reception Mary attended with the Woodwards.

Mrs. John F. Kennedy examines Ryder painting at Corcoran Gallery of Art. Left to right: Mr. Herman Warner Williams, Jr., Director of the Corcoran Gallery, Mrs Kennedy, Mrs Edwin D. Graves, Ball Chairman of the Women's Committee of the Corcoran Gallery, and Mr. Henri Dorra, Assistant Director of the Corcoran, 1961.

# XIII

## Moving Onward and Upward in the Museum World

### THE RINGLING MUSEUM,
### THEN ON TO THE CORCORAN GALLERY AND THE
### PHILADELPHIA MUSEUM OF ART

"AT LAST I MEET YOU," Chick Austin glowed with his engaging smile as he reached out to offer a firm handshake. "Welcome to the Ringling. We have much to talk about."

"It is a pleasure to meet you, Mr. Austin. I've admired your work at the Athenaeum and what you have done here at the Ringling. The shows you put on there were amazing."

It was true that Chick was admired and respected by all the major museum directors on the East coast for bringing inspired shows to the Atheneum, and not the least of which was to introduce Picasso to America. He had immediately made me feel so relaxed that I could not help asking naively, "How in the world did you persuade your board to let you have the shows you managed to bring to the museum?"

"Henri, if I may call you that, and please call me Chick. Almost everyone does."

"Certainly. They say one has to know people awfully well in America to call them by their surname." I was trying to be funny and realized he might take that the wrong way. Instead, he smiled while pulling out a chair for me, and then sat on the corner of his beautiful Louis XV desk, slightly swinging his long legs. I was distracted by the shine on the leather of his Gucci loafers and the obviously custom-made English trousers. I noticed he was looking at my suit, probably thinking it was made by the same tailor in London. "You must know that I didn't do it alone. Having Edward Forbes as my mentor and guide was the key to my success there. He always encouraged me to lead the way to making the Atheneum a 'place of pilgrimage for art lovers' and more often than not he was there to back me up with an approval of an expensive new purchase like the Tintoretto I bought without getting prior approval from the board. He trusted my eye for getting the right paintings when I could, and told the Atheneum trustees: 'A good museum director should not follow public taste but lead it, and should buy only the works of the highest quality.'" His tone of voice had reached a new level of drama as if he had to convince me of his beliefs. That wasn't necessary because I had already fallen under the spell of the apocryphal charm of Chick Austin. When he spoke to one, he looked straight into one's eyes and spoke with such assurance one couldn't doubt what he was saying.

We discovered at that first meeting that we had much in common: we had both studied connoisseurship under Paul Sachs at Harvard and treasured his pearls of wisdom. We spent the rest of the afternoon discussing our mutual taste in art and of clothes, our similar strong-willed mothers, and laughing a good deal. Here I was talking to one of Sachs's chief acolytes and having a wonderful time with a man I had heard was remarkable and difficult, but whom I really admired. I hadn't met anyone as articulate since I left Harvard, and he seemed to be trying to convince me that I was not wrong to be impressed.

"I know you are from Alexandria and I find that very exotic. Did you know I spent time on an excavation there when I was at Harvard? I loved it, and it was an important turning point in my growing up. I learned so much with the great antiquities scholar, George Reisner on that excavation in Giza and in Upper Egypt. I'll never forget it." He began striding around the room and stopped in front of me with a start as if coming back from a reverie.

I broke the few moments of silence between us with "My life in Egypt was very different from your stay there I imagine, and also very different from my life here in America." I was flooded with sudden memories that crowded into my mind of my grandmother, great aunt and uncle, and my father and mother. They were all sitting at the dining room table and fans in the corners were whizzing to combat the stifling heat. The servants were serving multiple delectable dishes that caused my mouth to water just thinking about them. "I never want to go back because Egypt is a different place today and there is really no room for people like me there. My life here in Florida has been wonderful, and believe I have a future in museum work."

"Indeed, you do," he said, stroking his chin and hesitating before finishing the sentence. "But I hope you know what you are getting into. Try if you can not to work for a public institution. The political problems are endless. But then, having said that, I would hope that you would come here to the Ringling as Associate Director because I could certainly use someone of your capabilities. When I saw the Pre-Columbian show you organized in Palm Beach I was impressed. I went back again to see what you would do with that Matisse show you organized. That show convinced me that you would be perfect to help me here at the Ringling. That's when I called you to ask you to come see me in Sarasota. I've already figured out your first jobs here which would be to begin organizing our annual art history conference that will be in April. This year I've chosen the title: "Mannerism: The Anti-Classical Movement in the Sixteenth Century."

"But I'm not a Mannerist scholar." Clearly confusion must have shown on my face.

"That doesn't matter. Do you like the idea? I know that is not your chosen field, but I am sure you know the experts in the field and could persuade them to come to Sarasota. I also know that you would be able to fill in with a gallery talk if necessary. Agnes Mongan told me so and I never question her." He gave me another of those beguiling smiles he was famous for, and continued, "We could pay you more than you're getting at the Four Arts and your title would be a step up, *n'est-ce pas?*"

I was bewildered. But my mind was running at full speed as I thought of the wonderful speakers I could get for the conference—beginning with the top in the field, Walter Friedlander at NYU, Wolfgang Lotz from Vassar, and Sydney Freedberg from Wellesley. It would be an amazing coup for Florida, and I was sure they would be delighted to come here because the weather would still be inclement on the East coast.

He came closer and spoke in a quieter tone. "But I should tell you that I don't think I will stay here much longer. I'm getting pretty fed up with the place and all the political problems and difficulty working in a public institution. The Florida controllers are driving me crazy with all their bureaucracy. And I'm anxious to get back to France to start my new museum in Faïence." I was disappointed to hear he thought of leaving what he had started so successfully, but he was not the kind of man who would waste time where he wasn't getting the results he wanted.


THE NEXT FEW MONTHS slid by because once I got to the Ringling there was a series of welcome parties for me due to Chick's wanting to show me off, I think. I had begun work immediately on the conference. The speakers all accepted with alacrity which meant I could really begin to plan the conference program in detail. That was all very exciting, and I really enjoyed the gallery talks I was beginning to give on a weekly basis. The first public lecture was on African Tribal Art in connection with the current exhibition I arranged for the Sergy collection of African sculpture and masks which I had borrowed in its entirety. It received a lot of attention in the press and the attendance at the museum was above anything we had hoped for. Whether the art lovers came out of curiosity about me or because it was the first of its kind, we didn't know, but Chick was very pleased with the reaction of the public. Many African Americans came to the museum who had never been there before. In the gallery talks I emphasized how the art of such moderns as Picasso and Gauguin along with others of the cubist and ultra-impressionistic schools was influenced by the sculpture of the African tribes. Most of the trustees who came to the gallery talks were intelligent art lovers, and asked good questions about the art, particularly the masks. I told them that because the Africans were followers of Voodoo and other mystical religions, their forms of artistic expression emphasized the ritualistic ceremonies. I always ended the talks by relating the exhibition to the moderns. The Sergy collection had clear examples of how African tribal art revealed the same form of expression that Picasso and Gauguin put on canvas when they established first the cubist and later what we call the modern school of painting. Some of the masks were worn in the ceremonies and were destined to frighten away intruders, hence their frightening design. Still others hid the faces of novitiates as they entered upon the inner sanctions of tribal secret societies. The trustees made very flattering comments about my talks both to me and to Chick. They were all from elsewhere: Chicago, Boston, and New York and quite worldly.

Being a bachelor certainly helped me because there were always numerous wealthy divorcees and widows who were included at the opening galas. I was glad to have brought all my Savile Row suits down with me from New York although most of them were too heavy for Florida, and I realized the next purchases from my London tailor would have to be of a lighter material to suit the tropical climate. The evening clothes were still fine though, and that is what I wore mostly with the ties from Charvet. They were much appreciated although I was surprised, they had never heard the name of that famous shop in Paris.

Very soon it became clear to me why Chick was leaving the Museum, and I too began to think of leaving. It was more than difficult and very frustrating to get money out of the Florida control board when we needed it, and everything seemed to be questioned by them, delaying installations considerably. Finally, even though I was at the Ringling for less than a year, I took Hermann Williams's offer at the Corcoran Gallery in D.C. When, out of courtesy, I told Ken Donahue the curator, who had been at the museum long before I came and who never really understood why I had the more senior title at the Ringling and Chick's respect, that I would be leaving at the end of the year, his relief was palpable. His curiosity got the better of him, not resisting the temptation to ask immediately where I was going. I knew there was envy in those words, and I was trying desperately to think how I could ease his discomfort. I decided the truth had to be told and I would bear the consequences. When I told him I would be assuming responsibility as Assistant Director at the Corcoran Gallery in Washington, D.C. his jaw fell. I was sorry for him, and I told him we should both look to the future. I remember saying that he would probably be the one to succeed Chick at the Ringling and that I knew his career would blossom here as I hoped mine also would in D.C. He smiled with relief and we left the museum together.

LIVING IN GEORGETOWN was just right for me. The Corcoran wasn't far away, I loved my job, and there were Harvard friends right around the corner. Being a bachelor in Washington was the best of all possible worlds. The Museum world as I was beginning to know it in D.C. was full of intelligent, cosmopolitan people and very soon I was in that world thanks to the women on the Corcoran Women's board. I had never seen such enthusiastic volunteers who were not only intelligent but were extremely dedicated to helping the Museum. Every event they sponsored was done with taste and the executive ability of a CEO at General Motors. It made my life so much easier because they were a joy to work with and many soon became lifelong friends. Very soon I wasn't limited to organizing art exhibitions. During the next three years I worked with them on numerous exhibitions the first of which was a spectacular Mozart Festival. Then the Dali Ball opened the exhibition of "A collection of Objets d'Art and Jewels designed by Salvator Dali." The honorees were the Ambassador and the Countess de Montrico from Spain who added more than a touch of glamour. The members of the Women's Board were particularly happy when those dignitaries eagerly agreed to come to replace Salvator Dali who had telegraphed at the last minute from his hotel in New York that he would be unable to come. Every year these ambitious and clever ladies produced a ball that they hoped would be better, more lavish in decoration, and with more impressive honorees and guests than the year before. It amused and pleased me that the ladies organizing these balls always solicited my opinion on the décor, guest lists, and menus during the seven years I was at the Corcoran. The exhibitions I worked on began with The American Stage and Living Today in '55, "Visionaries and Dreamers" in '56 to The Family of Man in '58, "Fifteen Painters from Paris" and "The American Muse" in '59 and finally the Ryder Exhibition in 1961 when I had the privilege of showing Jackie Kennedy, the President's lovely wife around the exhibition. It was just before leaving to go to the Philadelphia Museum as Assistant Director. And much to my surprise every year the publicity became even more glowing for my accomplishments. The journalists always liked to write about the glamour of the guest lists. They wrote that the "Night of the Stars" ball and the exhibition that opened that night, "The American Stage" was well attended by literati from New York including Lucinda Ballard and Lee Simonson, the top stage designers in New York. as well as the Washington dignitaries. Lucinda, with her bright red hair and wearing a feather boa was the star of the evening.

It often took more than a year to plan the exhibitions, but I never enjoyed anything more. Both the Washington Star and the Washington Post seemed to be outdoing themselves for praise of the events. I wasn't exactly their 'Golden Boy' but they never missed an opportunity to write nice words about me and my work at the Corcoran. For "Visionaries and Dreamers" one columnist wrote "As guests toured the exhibit rooms one could hear nothing but praise and awe for the genius, Assistant Director Henri Dorra, who was responsible for conceiving, and putting together this exhibition."

But it was for the opening of my most important show "The American Muse" that all the stops were pulled out. *The Sunday Star* wrote on March 30th: "The elaborate installation has been planned by Mr. Henri Dorra, assistant director of the gallery, who was responsible for the stunning presentation of 'The Family of Man' exhibition here several years ago." For that opening exhibition at the gala centennial ball the Women's Committee invited President and Mrs. Eisenhower to be sponsors. We were pleased that 14 Foreign Ministers, members of the NATO Council who had come from around the world to attend the NATO Council meetings came to the ball and the opening of "The American Muse." These foreign guests attended with their wives along with the Permanent Council members and the Ambassadors of the NATO Council meetings, as well as the NATO staff and officials from every country. *The Star* described the exhibition as "a unique study of the growth of American culture, planned by Henri Dorra, Assistant Director." The impressive guest list included important journalists such as Eric Sevareid, Walter Lippmann, and James Resten and their wives. Mr. and Mrs. Alfred Friendly and the Ambassadors from Switzerland, Italy, Austria and Portugal were also there. But the one I was most delighted to meet was the lovely Alicia Markova. Never had I been at such a star-studded event. I was impressed by it all and it must have impressed another Henri, Henri Marceau, Director of the Philadelphia Museum of Art who called soon after the opening of "The American Muse" to ask me to come to Philadelphia. He apparently wanted to have the same "American Muse" exhibition at the Philadelphia Museum and wanted to talk to me about other things.

When I arrived in Philly, Marceau was at the airport. He took me to his club The Franklin Inn, for lunch and then showed me around the impressive museum. After lunch, as we walked into his office at the museum, he closed the door behind him and without further ado said "Dorra, I need you here. Will you leave the Corcoran and come as Assistant Director of our museum? I can offer you more money if that is what you want, but from what I have heard you enjoy working and that is what I will offer you—a chance to create wonderful exhibitions in Philadelphia. I need a good assistant director and we could use another Henri here in Philadelphia. The main liners love the French and they will be delighted to have you here." While I was still a bit apprehensive about the anti-Semitism I heard was in Philly, Marceau convinced me that I would be happy in Philadelphia and insisted that I give notice at the Corcoran immediately.

I thought to myself, Americans are so straight forward. Marceau, even though he sounded French was, I had learned, thoroughly American, born in Richmond. "And it doesn't get any better than that," he told me with great pride. He doesn't beat around the bush. I thought I should tell him I am not really French…only 'du coeur'…that I am an Egyptian Jew." I decided not, at least until I got the lay of the land in Philadelphia. But I did like his effervescence. And I loved the idea of being at this great museum, organizing exhibitions.

*SS Conte Grande.*

# XIV

## En route on the *Conte Grande* and Italy at Last

### ROME AND FLORENCE

I SOON DISCOVERED that I had three cabin mates. The cabin was tiny, but we were almost never there all at the same time. There were two double decker bunks, and one wash basin for the four of us. The two closets were always empty since the nun and the novice wore only their habits and the Italian Signora wore only the clothes on her back. I took advantage and unpacked a few things I could wear in first class and on the excursions when I went on day tours in Brazil and Africa. These filled one of the small closets and the other one remained empty for the entire voyage. One of my cabin mates was an elderly Italian woman whose husband had come to the new world to "strike it rich" and didn't, much to their great disappointment. Having spent their entire savings for absolutely no gain, they were returning penniless to their beloved Naples. The shoulders of this poor Signora were slumped over as she walked, and one could see she was quite depressed. One could almost smell her sadness. The other two were a middle-aged nun and her charge, a beautiful young novice who was almost never out of the sight of her watchful chaperone. There were, however, significant lapses in her guardianship I learned later from one of the ship's officers, Guido Morelli, whose company I immediately began enjoying for the 15-day trip across the south Atlantic.

I was the only *Norte-Americana* on the entire ship. After a few days, the officers must have decided amongst themselves that the handsome Guido was the only one who should be courting me. I saw that the others had stopped inviting me to dance in the first-class ballroom or to have dinner in one of the many dining rooms on the ship. Guido took me all around the ship moving from the first-class dining room, filled with stuffy white-haired seniors to the second where we sat in the bar and danced to the music of the small band there. In third class, I met a charming Italian couple who invited me to join them for dinner whenever I liked and when I wasn't with Guido.

Anna and Marco were about my age and I was pleased to have their friendship. I knew they had just met and fallen in love on the *Conte Grande*. I felt she, in particular, was very much in love but I couldn't help feeling their relationship would last only as long as the crossing to Genoa. I had read about shipboard romances and the Italians certainly had a reputation for being successful lovers. Anna was quite beautiful, naïve and very much a country girl, and I was afraid she would be hurt by this suave Roman who obviously had a way with women. Her eyes sparkled whenever he appeared and he courted her in a surprisingly old-world manner, pulling out her chair before they were seated for the meals, taking her arm when going onto the dance floor and offering her a glass of champagne when they were first seated at the table. He was obviously attracted to her, often showing his affection in public with caresses, to the point of making her blush. But I knew it was none of my business to warn her because she was so happy with him.

Before reaching our destination in Genoa, the *Conte Grande* stopped in Santos, Brazil where Marco, Anna and I descended for the day's sightseeing. Climbing up to the colossal statue of Jesus the Redeemer at the top of Mount Corcovado was the first thing we wanted to see. The statue itself was impressively 98 feet tall and commanded the site overlooking Rio de Janeiro. My two Catholic companions were overwhelmed by the statue to the point that Anna was almost weeping. I, on the other hand, was impressed only by the imposing size and the site rather than by any artistic merit of the sculpture itself. We did have a wonderful time together, and I could see why she had fallen for him. Marco was indeed charismatic. He had suggested we buy picnic supplies to take with us to enjoy at the feet of the colossal statue while looking out at Rio below which was spectacular.

The *Conte Grande* stopped in Dakar for a day before leaving the south Atlantic and heading for Europe. I had never seen such poverty except perhaps in Puntarenas, Costa Rica. It showed in their humble dwellings and the need for replacing the roofs on the natives' huts. Almost no one seemed to wear shoes and there were beggars on every street corner. Hours before arriving at the harbor in Genoa we heard on a loudspeaker announcing that we were to report to the purser's office to retrieve our passports before the final disembarkation. When I tried to retrieve mine I was told, "*Mi dispiace, Signorina* but there is something irregular about your passport, and we will have to call the Consul when we arrive in Genoa to come to the ship to correct it. Meanwhile you will have to stay on the ship in Genoa."

Cristo de Los Andes, Rio de Janeiro, Brazil, August 5, 1958.

Everyone was leaving the ship when we arrived in Genoa, and I was stunned into staying behind until finally I decided I had to take matters into my own hands. I counted to three before staging my most Eleonora Duse scene, complete with sobs and many tears, "You officers pretend to be my friends and court me when we are in the middle of the South Atlantic, and you are far from home. But now that we are back in your homeport you abandon me."

"*Singorina, non piangi.* Don't cry. We beg you. Take your passport. We are not supposed to let you off the ship without getting the consul in Genoa involved but we can't stand to see you cry. Take your passport and go to the nearest Consul to get your passport corrected as soon as you can. It is lacking the stamp on the photo and might be considered a forgery." I grabbed my passport, wiped my tears and hoped no one else would stop me before I could get the matter cleared up. What a way to enter Italy for the first time!

In Rome, the day after I arrived, even without calling, I did what the ship's officers said to do. The waiting room of the Consular section at the Embassy was filled with Italians trying to get visas, and I had to wait for some time before my name was called. The person in charge of passports was an older woman, plump and with several long hairs next to a wart on her chin. I told her my story of having been detained because the usual stamp was missing. She looked me up and down with a skeptical eye and after glancing at the passport returned it abruptly, saying "In Montevideo, like many other Embassies around the world, they do not have the same franking machine that puts the stamp on the picture in the passport. This passport *is* legal as it stands, and you will just have to explain that if you are ever held up again." She smiled falsely and thrust the passport back at me.

Stunned into silence for a moment, I stammered, "You mean it is my responsibility to explain why my passport is not valid? That doesn't seem fair."

"That is the way it is, Miss Tonetti," she smirked. "I am busy now and that is the end of this conversation. You may go."

I quickly left the office before my anger got the better of me. Downstairs in the main waiting room I leaned against the wall and began to recover. It didn't take long for me to remember the Woodwards had given me the name of their friend, Tully Torbert who worked at the Consulate as political counselor to the Ambassador. I called him immediately and when I gave my name to the secretary I was pleased to be transferred right away to a gentle, warm voice. "Hello, Toni. I am so glad you called. Bob Woodward wrote that you would be coming to Rome, and my wife and I have been waiting for you to call us so we could invite you for dinner. Why don't you come up to

174

the office now if you are downstairs?" I couldn't believe how fortunate I was, and the relief was palpable as I hurried towards the elevator to his office.

Mr. Torbert was so unassuming and though his office showed me that he had a very high position, he couldn't have been more down to earth and couldn't have been nicer. He reached out to shake my hand and motioned that we sit in the comfortable chairs next to his desk. He began by asking about the Woodwards since he hadn't seen them for at least a year. I could tell by his enthusiasm when he spoke of them that he had very strong feelings for both of them. After I explained about my meeting with the passport officer he immediately picked up the phone on his desk. I heard him say, "Miss Parks, I am sending down Miss Tonetti's passport. Would you please have the necessary stamp placed on it and she will be down to pick it up in ten minutes. Thank you." He then turned to me, shaking his head, "I can't believe that this has happened to you. It will be fixed; don't give it another thought." He saw how relieved I was, and smiled.

"Now let's move on to a more pleasant subject; my wife and I were hoping to find you before next Saturday. We are having a few people for dinner and would love to have you join us if you are free."

When Miss Parks saw me coming into her office she could hardly contain her displeasure. I noticed that even the wart on her cheek seemed more pronounced in contrast to the color that was mounting in her face. "I disapprove that you went above my head with this issue to Mr. Torbert who is very high up here in the Embassy, but here is your passport with the added stamp."

"Well…Thank heavens I was fortunate enough to have someone I could turn to who could help, and I am sorry for those who might be in my position without anyone to help with this injustice. I am an American citizen and deserving of a passport that works!"

I then took the passport and left her open-mouthed.


"NOW THAT THAT IS SETTLED, all that nuisance about your passport," my beautiful friend Anne d'Almeida began with a voice of authority, "we must get you out of those baggy pants and into something that shows off your figure. I'm taking you to my favorite boutique to get you something beautiful to wear. And put away that black turtleneck. It's spring in Rome," she smiled.

I hadn't realized how dowdy I looked until I saw the clothes in the boutique at the top of the Spanish steps. They were irresistible, and I would have bought everything in the shop if I had had the money because everything I tried on made me feel beautiful, and that was a thrilling new experience.

With Anne's help, I finally decided on two dresses—one for the fancy dinner at the Torberts and the other just for "dinners at the *trattorie* in Trastevere and for your evenings in Florence," Anne insisted. I was already excited to wear them.

Those first two weeks in Rome passed like lightning. I loved the city with all its layers of history and the beautiful monuments and churches, but I didn't have time that week to see even half of them, and thought to myself, even though going to study in Florence was what I looked forward to most of all, I knew I had to return to Rome if only for the captivating beauty of the city. No matter where one looked there was something breathtakingly beautiful. Climbing the Janiculum hill to the d'Almeidas' apartment, which I did often that week, offered new and dazzling vistas of Rome that never ceased to make me glad I was there. While I didn't think anything could be more wonderful than being in Rome I was to think differently the following week when I arrived in Florence.

I really had no knowledge of hotels or *pensioni* in Florence except for the reference to the *Bertolini*, in the novel *Room with a View* where Miss Honeychurch stayed. I so identified with her and realized I was, I think, as inexperienced in life as she was. Alas, that *pensione* no longer existed even a few years after E.M. Forester wrote his novel in 1904. But I found that in 1958 in its place was a similar one on the Arno, which was a good substitute, and that is where I stayed the first few nights in Florence. It was a perfect beginning for my new life in Florence. The first place I wanted to go to was the Brancacci Chapel in Santa Maria del Carmine. I had to see if the Masaccio frescoes I had seen in Art 105 at Vassar were as beautiful as I had imagined. I was not disappointed. Even in the darkness of winter they were spectacularly colorful.

Uncle Eric, who adored Florence, had written to his friend Bruno Bearzi about my coming, and he was one of the first people I contacted. I knew he was a restorer on works in the Uffizi but didn't know how important he was in the art world of Florence, and that he had also restored the Ghiberti doors on the Baptistery, and other important landmarks in Florence. He and his family became my Florentine family and welcomed me for lunch every Friday. Neni Bearzi was about my age; she was also a student, and we became fast friends. When I told Signor Bearzi I needed an inexpensive place to live he recommended a *pensione* on the Borgo Pinto near the *Centro per Stranieri* where I had enrolled. Some of the restoration sculptors who worked for him were staying there, and he quickly arranged for me to be there too. It was indeed very inexpensive, and a little shabby, but I had nothing to compare it with, and I loved being with those Greek sculptors at meals which we shared at a large round table. When my protective, demanding and imperious friend Alex Mylonas, the brother of my Vassar roommate came to visit me he was horrified by my surroundings and let me know right away.

"You can't stay here! I will find another place for you to live. Florence is too special for you to live in this Spartan—I should say slovenly—environment!"

Alex always made me see things I had never seen before. Then, looking around as if for the first time I saw the stains on the antimacassered living room chairs, the water marks of previous rains on the wallpaper, the dust balls everywhere, and the chipped dinner plates on the dining room table. I even smelled for the first time the garlic that permeated the room.

I was taken aback by his sudden remark, but I knew that he knew everything about Florence, past and present. So I let him help me move the very next week. To celebrate, he took me that night to Sabatini's and introduced me to the local Florentine specialties followed by a dessert which included his instructions for cutting a whole orange without using one's fingers, only a knife and fork. "You must learn this, Mary, because then when Italians see you cutting it carefully and methodically, section, by section, they will know you are not American." That was typical of his curious remarks that I often didn't understand.

The beautiful uphill winding street, the Costa San Giorgio, was on the other side of the Arno where Alex had found me a lovely apartment with a fabulous view of Florence that included the Duomo, the Baptistery, the green and white striped Giotto campanile, the Palazzo Vecchio and the gorgeous orange tile rooftops of the city. The owner of the apartment, Marina Ivanov-Rinov, agreed to giving me a room at a very reasonable price, and the use of the kitchen and the living room. We got along well and she was a great help in teaching me even more vocabulary words, and the places to go nearby for the necessary things: the *paneficio* for the best bread, the *latteria* for milk and eggs, the *macelleria* for the best meat at good prices, the *fruttivendolo* for the fruit and vegetables that we bought every day. We descended the Costa San Giorgio on her Lambretta, the motor scooter, a preferred means of getting around because it could go between cars, around buses, etc. Dangerous maybe, but exhilarating! The walk to school across the *ponte vecchio* every morning was at a time when all the vendors were raising their shutters, putting out their beautiful fruits and vegetables and the beginning of a lively day in that glorious city. I got to know Florence very well because walking was my favorite thing to do. I wanted to see everything: all the 450 churches, all the palazzi—whether new or old, tumbling into ruins with paint peeling off the paintings or newly restored, and of course all the museums.

I finished my exams at the university and did very well, much to my surprise. I received a 27 out of 30, which was the next highest mark they gave. Just after my oral exam I was talking to some of the American students who always seem to know everything newsworthy. One young man standing next to me suddenly said to no one in particular, "At times like this I wish I were a girl!"

"Why?" I asked him.

"Didn't you see that announcement on the bulletin board? There is a wonderful job offer to live with a Venetian doctor's family in Saint Mark's Square, teaching the children English, then to spend January and February skiing in Cortina, a month at the Lido and then a month in their palace in the Veneto region.

It sounded wonderful, and even though I wasn't really interested in this kind of job, I thought perhaps it would be a great opportunity to reach my goal of speaking good Italian by living with a Venetian family. I wrote to them immediately, remembering what Ursula, my Corning German friend, had said to me, "You don't have to take the job, but go meet them and find out what it is." And I reminded myself that I had been looking for an excuse to go to Venice.

I was totally unprepared for the unbelievable experience of Venice as I walked out of the train station. The beautiful Grand Canal was irresistibly right before my eyes and I understood immediately why so many people with romantic souls are drawn to this city. As I looked at the swarthy skinned gondoliers I saw in their handsome faces the same pride and energy that made Venice the world's leading seaport of the 13th, 14th and 15th centuries. I gave the Guarnieris' address to the first gondolier I saw, and was soon experiencing one of the most romantic trips of my life: being rowed down the Grand Canal, past glorious palazzi on both sides of me, hearing the sounds of voices that I had never known, shouting, singing and laughing. I felt I could have been in the 18th century rather than in 1958.

My hosts greeted me at their apartment that struck me as perfectly Italian—comfortable yet tastefully furnished with dark antiques and, I assumed, portraits of ancestors. It was right next to the bell tower in Saint Mark's square, another reminder of where I was and the good luck that had come my way. Dr. Guarnieri immediately offered me a glass of Campari. We then sat down to a splendid but simple meal with the best pasta I had ever tasted, *bigoli in salsa* which was cooked *al dente* and topped with a sweet and sour sauce made of small, tender pieces of sardines and a good dose of vinegar. I had never seen the thick spaghetti called *bigoli*, a Venetian specialty, and was surprised that each of us was served a beautiful small mound of it as a first course, to be followed by the main course of fish or meat along with a side dish, a *contorno* of a perfectly prepared vegetable. After lunch, we continued to speak (always in Italian) about the job in detail.

The Signora Guarnieri was a lovely blonde Venetian woman who appeared to be only a few years older than me. Her lively personality was charming, but it was her husband, Doctor Mario Guarnieri whose sense of humor kept us laughing all through lunch and whose unassuming manner was most appealing. He said during the interview, "You might think me a very rough man as I am not an intellectual. I don't know that you will be interested in meeting our friends as they are not interested in history or art history...I think you have received a better education than I have and you are perhaps more intelligent than my friends but you are certainly welcome to join any of our parties and to be with us when we have company if you chose to do so. But of course, you will make friends here in Venice and are free to go out as often as you like in the evening."

I liked his unpretentious manner and his humility but I knew, from my spies in Florence that, in spite of what he said about himself, he was from a very good bourgeois family, a doctor of law, and that he had definitely received a very good education. I liked also how much he loved his Venetian heritage and his traditional, comfortable life, and he certainly responded when I said I wanted to see everything in Venice.

The Guarnieris' agreed to everything I suggested about the job including free time to explore Venice and the salary, which was far more than I had expected. "You are free to go out any evening and you will have every morning and part of the afternoon free to study or go to classes or museums when in Venice, and when we go to Cortina you will spend half a day skiing or skating with the children. Moreover, it must be understood that you are to speak only English with our children at all times." They also said I could entertain my friends in their apartment. My duties would consist of walking the children to school in the morning, picking them up at noon, having tea with them in the afternoon and always speaking English to them. Both Caterina, who was ten, and her brother, Keki (Francesco) only seven, had already been taught English and their accents were English rather than American; they both were beautiful to look at and well mannered. Caterina was particularly charming and had the delicate face of a Botticelli. While the entire family assessed me, I was making up my mind too.

These were nice people and I was sure it was a good idea at least for the time being. When Dr. Guarnieri offered me the job, hoping I "would enjoy Venice and the time with them," I told them I wanted to finish my courses, stay in Florence until the end of the semester, and was planning to go to Switzerland for two weeks at Christmas but that I would be delighted to come to live with them in early January before they left for Cortina. I liked the idea of driving through the Dolomites with them from Venice to Cortina which would be another new adventure. They had assured me there would be room for me as they always took two cars: one filled with people and the other with luggage.

Another good stroke of luck in Venice, aside from the job offer, was my meeting a friend of Marina's, my Russian-American roommate in Florence. That friend was an Armenian woman, a 61-year-old American painter who had lived in Venice for years and was as bright, alert, and intelligent a woman as I had ever met. She told me about having lived in Leningrad during the revolution and of the horrendous tales of her escape with her family during those years just after the revolution. We had tea together the day after I arrived in Venice and she took me to dinner the next night, introducing me to some of the local painters and American Fulbright students. She was sure that her Venetian and American friends "would take care of me" and I felt comforted by that. She was a great friend of Peggy Guggenheim and also of Gold and Fizdale who lived in one of our houses at Snedens, and whom I remembered with such pleasure when I was 16. I thought it was fortuitous that I now had two such distinctly different groups of people to know in Venice—the establishment natives of Venice with whom I lived and the artists, collectors, and students who were so different from my host family but whom I identified with and admired.

After returning to Florence with the job firmly settled, I wrote to my parents: "What a beautiful, perfect life I am leading. It is so wonderful to be able to do and see so many things I have always imagined." One of my Florentine friends said to me when I told her about the new job and my going to live in Venice, "I think you lead the most perfect life one can lead!" It did seem so.

In contrast to that euphoric period of my life, my parents in Texas were having to make difficult financial decisions, which I learned from my father's letter waiting for me at the apartment on the Costa San Giorgio when I returned from Venice. In it, he told me that he was going to have to sell the most beautiful house at Snedens Landing, the "Ding Dong" because of the stress of the education bills from Princeton and Choate. They had received an offer too good to turn down. As I read the news in his long letter the tears rolled down my cheek and I sat down immediately to write the following:

"I just received your letter tonight which contained the news of the 'Ding Dong.' Naturally when I read it I couldn't help feeling a little sharp pain run through me but I am sure that you, Daddy, feel the pain much more than me at having to sell that lovely house. Did you ever read the

My Fullbright friend, Perry, Venice, 1959.

Chekov play, *The Cherry Orchard*? Roughly, it is the story of a family who, for generations, had lived in the same house and who had, up until the last generation, enjoyed all the pleasures of a wealthy aristocratic Russian family. The play deals specifically with this last generation who categorically refused to give up the family estate even though they needed the money. They had been offered a great deal by one of their lackeys who had become rich enough to buy the estate and lovely cherry orchard. These Chekov characters are so much involved with the idea of what their name and the house meant to them that the end of the play follows in a natural and tragic way showing they were completely incapable of coping with the reality of having to sell... I don't mean to imply that you have been inept in the management of the properties at Snedens or that it is a 'tragic situation' but rather that the selling of the 'Ding Dong' is a symbol of so many beautiful things we can't hold onto forever. If selling the 'Ding Dong' means that you will have less stress in your life then selling is what you should do, as difficult and painful as this is for you."

After finishing the letter, I looked out at the skyline of Florence, and felt strangely relieved and happy. This was now my home and the beauty of this city has become a part of my life. My mother's advice when I first arrived in Europe came to mind suddenly, that I must see something beautiful every day and do something I could not do in America. Florence had already begun with new experiences and my mood lightened as I remembered that I had made a date to have an aperitivo with one of my professors after classes the next day at noon.

Count Carlo Rusconi was a tall Florentine aristocrat who took my arm as we walked to the *Piazza della Signoria*. He spoke such beautiful Italian I wanted to imitate his every grammatical construction. He seated me at the café so that I could admire all at once, without turning my head, the crenelated fortress-like Palazzo Vecchio, the beautiful copy of Michelangeo's David in the arched Loggia and the hustle and bustle of Florentines scurrying to their luncheon dates. Then, smiling, he asked me what I would like to drink, and I responded with the first thing that came into my mind, "*A cappuccino, prego.*"

"*Veramente?* A cappuccino at this hour? Don't you want an *aperitivo?*"

I could feel my embarrassment creeping across my face in a flush. I managed to stumble out in Italian, "What are you going to have? I'll have the same."

He turned to the waiter and said, "*Due Punt e mes.*"

It was the most sophisticated drink I had ever encountered. Deliciously sweet and slightly bitter. It took only a few minutes to feel the alcohol take over my empty stomach and go to my head. There was a twist of lemon peel that I managed to nibble between sips. I began to relax and finally the Italian language came quite fluently to my lips as the professor gracefully led the conversation from the fanaticism of Savonarola, to Michelangelo, to restaurants in Florence. He wanted me to know all of his favorites. I told him I hardly knew any. He also named some people he thought I should meet in Cortina, and whom he would write to, especially an attractive young woman almost my age, Toni Maraini.

Before I knew it, we had moved into lunch, with his ordering everything for me and making sure I was at ease, and all the while teaching me something new. He was as cultured as Florence itself. I thought of how my mother would have approved of this new friendship. I realized it wasn't just the food that I loved about Italy. It was the people I was meeting who shared my love of the ubiquitous beauty seen on a daily basis, and who appreciated my passion for learning everything about where I was. There would be several more encounters in Florence like this one before I left for Zermatt and my new life in Venice. I couldn't imagine any other place in the world that would be as exciting as where I found myself in 1959.

Franklin Inn Club founded in 1902, was a social venue for published authors and illustrators and soon became a gathering place for novelists, poets, scholars, actors, playwrights, and journalists.

# XV
# Philadelphia and its Downside
OLD PREJUDICES STILL ALIVE AND NEW REALIZATIONS

HENRI GABRIEL MARCEAU, the Director of the Philadelphia Museum, met me at the airport, and took me again to his old club, The Franklin Inn, introducing me to everyone as we entered the dining room, with complimentary remarks about me to each one he greeted.

"Dorra here will be a great addition to our staff. He is a smart Harvard educated Art Historian, knows his way around the world, and he is much more French than I am," he chuckled. He straightened his bow tie and continued towards a table marked "Reserved Dr. Marceau." The red leather, comfortable chairs that we passed on our way to the dining room were all filled with rather corpulent, well-dressed men reading. They looked up from their newspapers to greet Marceau and to check me out. I also noticed the Persian carpets were very good ones, albeit somewhat worn. They had lost some of their color but added a genteel look to the main rooms. The dark wood-beamed ceiling also contributed to the feeling of coziness that Ben Franklin must have enjoyed at the club in his day.

When we were seated, he lowered his voice and said, "You must be a member of this club, Dorra, and I'll put your name up for membership." His voice became even lower as he looked sternly at me over his glasses: "I know you will come here often, and bring the people you need to. The food isn't exactly what you would get at Maxim's, but I am sure it will compare well with your clubs in D.C." He was right. It wasn't in the remotest way like the food at Maxim's, although I was getting used to the American luncheon style of no wine, and beginning with a salad course and then moving on to the entrée usually of a chicken pot pie or a piece of tasteless beef with a brown sauce and mashed potatoes.

"Well, Dorra, we are all anticipating your showing of 'The American Muse' here in our museum. I am sure it will be as well received as it was in D.C. That will be your second installation. But your first will be a small show on some French paintings in a private collection here in Philadelphia. We will go on from there. Remember there are Mainliners who will be attending the opening night. Many of them are potential donors and you will have to make a fuss over them. They will probably be coming to your gallery talks too." He was getting more excited, and that excitement was catching. As we walked out of the club, he took my arm, saying, "You know I think you are going to be a great hit here in Philly. The donors love Frenchmen." I smiled and thought to myself, 'perhaps Philadelphia wouldn't be so bad.'

At the reception after my first gallery talk, I noticed a svelte, attractive woman, sheathed in black was approaching me. She held out her hand for me to shake it, and said, "My name is Charlotte Bruckner. I enjoyed your talk very much, and was delighted to hear you speak with such authority on American art particularly since I noticed that your accent is not American but an English one. Are you British?" She smiled and her arched eyebrows became even more prominent as she asked this last question. I was still not used to women shaking hands the way they do here in America and I was somewhat startled by her direct personal questions that I knew no European woman would ever ask.

"No, I am not British; but that is a long story. I am glad you liked the talk because it has become a very important quest of mine, to understand the American mind. That is what I tried to do in the next talk I will be giving on my latest book, *The American Muse.*"

"How interesting. I shall look forward to hearing that." She then did something I thought very unusual. Putting down her glass of wine, she clutched her handbag. The tone of her voice became low and silky. "I would love to hear more about your views on American art." Then with her lips curving into a soft smile, she continued, "Why don't we have a drink together next week and you can inform me. I work at the Chicago office of Harcourt Brace, but I still have work to do here in Philadelphia and don't leave until Thursday."

I was stunned. Here was an American young woman asking me to have a drink with her. Of course, I said yes. Why not? And then thinking of my manners, I quickly added, "But why don't I take you to dinner instead?" I managed to get out the invitation without stuttering.

She nodded, "I'd love to. If you're currently into things American why don't we be consistent?" She tilted her head to show a beautiful profile and continued, "How about the City Tavern in the old city on 2nd Avenue?

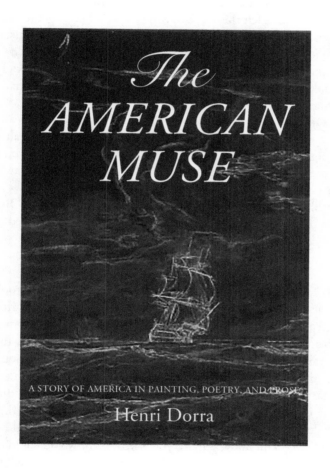

Do you know it? It's one of the oldest in the city and has decent food…not particularly French, which I think you must be partial to, but they pride themselves on the fact that Benjamin Franklin was supposed to have dined there, and it is one of the best in Philadelphia."

"I don't know many restaurants here, so that sounds fine. I'll make a reservation for 8:00, and meet you at the restaurant, okay?" Things were moving so fast, but I felt this was someone I would like to get to know. I took out my diary and wrote down her name next to Tuesday's date just as she was turning to leave. "Till next Tuesday!" I confirmed.

Looking over her shoulder as she moved away, "Yes. Till next Tuesday… and I'll look forward to hearing more of your views on American art and the American mind."

Still somewhat bewildered, I was taken off guard by Marceau who had suddenly appeared out of nowhere. "Well, Dorra, I see you have already made progress in meeting an attractive young woman. Not bad. But I am sure there will be more, so don't get attached so fast. Who was she? I never saw her before here in the museum."

Mumbling in an inarticulate way I managed to answer him, "Just a young woman in publishing who is from Chicago apparently. She loved my talk, it seems."


THE GALLERY TALKS that Marceau insisted I take charge of took up most of my time in the next few months, but that didn't keep me from having an active social life which he seemed to enjoy organizing for me. I wasn't used to being out every evening with people who didn't appear to share my views or values, but I think I was beginning to learn more about America and becoming more familiar with the American way of doing things. I had already learned at Harvard about martinis and wouldn't make that mistake again, but there were other things I needed to learn. One of the curators, Peter McConnico, was a friendly young man about my age and he had said earlier that day, "You know, Henri, you asked me how you could learn more about how the American mind works and I think you should read Mary Worth. You'll learn a lot by reading the comics."

Maybe he was right but at any rate I looked forward to seeing Charlotte and couldn't get her out of my mind, and her forward invitation to have a drink. That had never happened to me before. She was unusual. And attractive. And I thought, so American.

ONCE WE SETTLED at our table in the back room of the restaurant which I was assured would be quiet, I ordered champagne. She looked at me intently and asked suddenly "So how did you get started on American Art? I thought French art would be your specialty. Or are you the 20th century de Tocqueville explaining our country from a French perspective?"

"Before we get into that subject and others I think we should order." The waiter offered some suggestions not on the menu and we both decided that the fresh dover sole would be the best. Closing the menu, I ordered it for both of us, along with fresh asparagus, a bottle of Sancerre and a Grand Marnier soufflé for dessert. Charlotte looked at me, nodding in agreement, and raised her glass to a toast, "To our future friendship. Now do tell me about yourself. How long have you been here in America?"

Once again, she had taken control of the conversation and out of courtesy, I felt I had to answer. I told her I had been very fortunate in living first in Cambridge at Harvard, then New York working at the Metropolitan Museum, then in Florida, and most recently in Washington before coming to Philly. "They are all so different and I must say I felt most at home in D.C. for it was there that I made the most friends."

"Is that how you judge the cities? By the friends you make?"

"Not really," I managed to smile at her, and continued. "But I must say the people I met in D.C. were most congenial and perhaps that was because they were all connected to Europe in some way. I don't know that I will find the same here in Philadelphia. Marceau has been extremely nice in introducing me to everyone and they have all been very cordial, but I think they find me very strange."

"I doubt they think you strange. A little exotic perhaps because you are, after all, a foreigner. They usually like Frenchmen though," she said laughing.

"Philadelphians strike me as being much more American than in New York and D.C. because of the people I met."

"Whatever that means," she said with a querulous look.

I answered right away. "It is said that there are no classes in America as there are in Europe, and those are very difficult to move out of once you are established in them. But I have found, particularly in Philadelphia, that those classes are very well defined and it's money that defines them."

She was sipping her champagne and seemed prepared to accept the brief silence that followed, before I interrupted it with my own direct question to her. It seemed to me that she was getting more of my views than I was getting hers. Perhaps I shouldn't have been so outspoken. Time for a change in the conversation. "Forgive me for intruding. You mentioned that you wrote your PhD on Boucher. Are you still involved with Art History and writing about

18th century French Art?"

"No, I am no longer doing any writing on French art or any art history, for that matter." She paused and seemed to have read my mind. "I don't know what I want to do. My current job leaves me unfulfilled but then I do have to earn my living." Her sadness permeated the room, and I was very much affected by her sudden change of mood.

"What then would you like to do with your life if you could do anything," I managed to ask.

"Well, I would like to live the way you appear to. Without a care, traveling back and forth to Europe, and writing when you feel like it. However, that is certainly not in the cards for me, as they say, since I have had to work for everything I have during my entire adult life. Nothing was handed to me the way it seems to have been with you." The bitterness in her voice was so palpable it made me sad and hesitant to speak. Yet I couldn't help responding, "You know so little about me and what I have experienced in the past few years that I wonder how you can assume my life has been easier than yours."

It must have been the champagne that loosened my tongue. I was not used to telling strangers anything personal and certainly had never confessed that my life had been anything but perfect. But somehow her sadness made me want to tell her about my own. I felt a kindred soul, but I refrained. There was a significant silence before I finally broke it and spoke again, "I have tickets for a beautiful concert by the Philadelphia Symphony tomorrow night, some nice Brahms. Would you like to go with me?"

She took a bite of the soufflé before answering, "I already have a ticket but we could certainly have dinner together before if you'd like. I'd like that." We finished our soufflés and the Sancerre while keeping up a steady, lively conversation. Unfortunately, we stayed away from personal topics by a mutual yet non-expressed agreement, always returning to the subject of de Tocqueville and American art. I had wanted to know more about her life, why she seemed so bitter and somewhat sad, and yet I didn't want to pry.

"Do you really believe that de Tocqueville's view of American art, and specifically his view that Americans will always want the useful and insist that the beautiful be useful is a characteristic of American art and of American taste?" In a new found burst of excitement about the subject, she had raised her voice, "Do you even like American art if that is the case?"

"It fascinates me and is so like the American mind as I know it. I have observed, and this is a good trait, that Americans are much more practical, and pragmatic than Europeans, don't you agree? For Americans, everything must work."

"I really haven't met many Europeans and never had this conversation with anyone before, but I think you might be right. If that is true, that Americans love the useful and what works, I guess I am very American."

"But you don't seem very American to me yet. You have indicated that you are fatalistic, almost cynical and that is not very American. Americans are so optimistic and positive. You are different and don't really fit the image I have of most American women." I regretted saying all that, but it was too late. Her reaction was perfect. She slipped her hand under my own which was resting on the table, and said simply, "I think you understand me."

"I'm not sure of that," I said, looking into her eyes and then I squeezed her hand before continuing, "Shall we go? It is getting late."

She postponed her departure for a few days and we had several more evenings together before she returned to Chicago and even a long walk and picnic in the country when I took a day off. It was a splendid spring day and I had found a wonderful walk in a forest not far away from the center of Philadelphia. The trees were large, and the forest was dense. The picnic tables were empty, so we settled ourselves at one, and opened the bottle of Beaujolais which turned out to be the perfect choice for the woodsy afternoon. I was enjoying myself but noticed that, unlike me, she didn't seem to enjoy the beauty of the spot as I did. That was a very revealing day. She was even sadder than usual while we were repacking the picnic basket and leaving the countryside to return to the city. "Are you all right?" I asked, gently putting my arm around her waist.

"As all right as usual," she answered. "I always find nature a little depressing. I don't know why. It reminds me of how insignificant I am and how out of touch with the world I am."

I didn't know quite how to answer this, so I didn't. Then she remarked, "Do you think me strange? I suppose I am a little neurotic…" she gave a little laugh, moving her hand to her throat in a nervous way. "It's from having wanted so much all my life and never quite being satisfied with what I have. I am twenty-nine years old and have accomplished nothing."

"No. I am sure that is not true. You are not strange, just unusual and quite depressed if I may be utterly honest, and I don't know why. You are an extremely intelligent and lovely woman who should not be so unhappy." I dared to ask the question I had almost asked several times before when on several occasions she had looked particularly melancholy and distant. "You have so much to offer and I don't think you should feel so sad. Have you thought of seeing someone…professionally, I mean?"

We were walking briskly towards the car when she turned suddenly. "Yes. I have thought analysis might help. I would love to see a good professional, but I really can't afford it on my salary."

We had reached the car and I held her in my arms while she sobbed uncontrollably. I was almost moved to tears myself, never having seen a woman cry so intensely.

FOR THE NEXT FEW MONTHS, I went every other weekend to Chicago to see Charlotte or she came to Philadelphia. We were enjoying each other's company, getting to know each other, and even the silences in our conversations were mutually acceptable. There were times when I felt, however, that her smiles were insincere. It was as if they were too constant, and would never fade, and had been applied with adhesive tape. Although there were often serious conversations about her moods we both tried to stay away from those subjects that seemed to produce tears more often than not. Occasionally she would talk about her childhood and particularly her Polish mother, whom she said never really understood her.

It was after several months that she seemed particularly relaxed with me and volunteered out of the blue, "I don't see myself as a wife." She crossed and re-crossed her legs unaware each time that her skirt hitched higher to show her perfectly formed knees and muscular thighs before she would stand suddenly facing me to smooth and lower her skirt, and reestablish herself in an upright sitting position. "I would cut a poor figure, I'm afraid. My mother said to me once, 'You are far too self-centered to be anyone's wife.' I didn't weep when she said that because I sensed it was a true statement that I had already accepted."

I took her hand and kissed it. She then threw back her head which was covered with soft black waves, cut close to show her perfectly shaped head. Her long, lean body was slightly arched as she looked at me, and gently laughed. "I don't pity myself, you know. I am quite used to the fate I have been given, to be alone."

Her fingers were softly curled around a handkerchief in her lap which she suddenly dropped and reached for my hand. I smiled at her and she smiled back – that was a rarity I knew did not come easily or often. But I was always thrilled when that smile was produced, showing perfect white teeth between full bright red lips. "You have a beautiful smile and it should be seen more often," I said.

"Then it would no longer be special." Her dark blue eyes sparkled with pleasure, and she allowed herself a little laugh. "You do have a way of making me smile, even laugh."

But it didn't last, her lighter mood. Instantly the darker mood returned and we were quiet together for a few minutes.

"Do you think you could be made happier by not being so alone?" I ventured.

"Not particularly," she answered looking down at the twisted handkerchief in her lap. "I am used to my own company and used to being depressed most of the time."

"You mentioned a few weeks ago when we were first together for the picnic outside Philadelphia that you thought an analyst might help but you couldn't afford it. We have become much closer since then and I have come to care for you a great deal. It saddens me to see you so unhappy. Let me help you." I saw there were tears in her eyes and regretted having continued the conversation to the point of making her cry. "If you really want to see an analyst and can find one in Chicago you like, I'll pay for it."

"That makes me happy to hear you say that. Yes, I would like that very much." For the rest of that year, 1961 and the first part of 1962 Charlotte was working with a good analyst. We continued to see each other either regularly in Chicago or in Philadelphia and she seemed to be getting better, less depressed, and not so distant, but still quite ill at ease. While for me, she had become the most important person in my life, and I liked having someone to care for. I had become more relaxed and never really thought about my own day to day life. I was only thinking about how to make Charlotte happier.

One morning I saw all the curators going into Marceau's office. I became aware at that moment that I had not been asked to that meeting, nor for that matter to any meeting called by the Director. I realized that my career at the Museum had taken a strange turn. Marceau had also stopped inviting me to join him at the Opera, theatre and dinners. I didn't know why he seemed to be avoiding me, even excluding me. One night at the theatre I went up to speak to him and saw that he had deliberately turned his back away from me. I tried again a few nights later at the Symphony. The same thing happened. I realized it was intentional.

He had been speaking with one of the mainline donors of the Museum in a whisper, so I hadn't heard what they were saying but I did hear her say the word "Jew." They had been talking about me, I gathered, because they were suddenly silent when I approached. These affronts, together with my being excluded from the acquisition and exhibition meetings, were signals I had ignored. There were no requests for me to write catalogues and the only responsibilities I was given were the gallery talks. I needed to talk to someone and decided to speak to Peter McConnico, whom I considered my closest and only friend among the colleagues at the museum. I asked him to come to my office that afternoon. After the usual inquiries and friendly non-committal remarks, I told him I was quite bothered by the fact that Marceau had no longer involved me at the important acquisition and exhibition committee meetings. When he recruited me, he made it very clear that this would be part of my job. I asked Peter if he too had observed this recent exclusion.

Peter, squirming a bit in his seat, uncrossed his legs, pushed his glasses further up on his nose, and looking straight at me said, "Henri, I have wanted to tell you this for some time because I like and admire you. I know you are not being used to full capacity here in Philadelphia and I am afraid I know why and should clue you in although it is somewhat brash of me. Did you recently have a conversation with Mrs. Murphy, that large, rather demanding donor at the Museum?"

Then I remembered a previous conversation I had had with her in which she had rather pompously and even pedantically stated, "Mr. Dorra, in Alexandria, I am told there are three groups of people. The Muslims, the Copts and the third…those others, the Jews. I know you are from that great city and which group did your family identify with?" Needless to say, I had never disguised the fact that I was a Jew but I had never been asked this question directly. I was, of course, flustered but managed to express myself rather articulately for the first time on this subject.

I answered her as politely as I could, "You see, Mrs. Murphy, while I am in fact Jewish, I consider myself primarily French because that is where I was educated, where I have spent most of my life so far, and my parents, although not born in France certainly are French *du coeur*, if you know what I mean." I had smiled at her hoping to turn the tone of the conversation to a lighter one. She remained stony-faced and, before turning to leave abruptly, said simply, "I see."

Peter said that he thought there must have been something like that because Marceau had spoken to him privately, asking if he knew "Dorra was a Jew, and not really French." I interrupted, and how did you respond to that question?"

"Of course," I quickly responded, he is both."

I stood and walked slowly over to my desk where I managed to say, "Well, Peter, I am glad to have had this conversation and it certainly explains the sudden transition in my relationship with our director and the diminishing of my responsibilities. I had mistakenly excused these recent exclusions by thinking that it was the way things were done at this museum. The Director does everything here. I hadn't reached a worried state, but the sudden change, and this conversation, have caused me to do some serious thinking about my career in the museum field. If being Jewish is going to affect my career here I need to think more *seriously* about a change."

"I am not sure of this, but I believe you will continue to get jobs as assistant director in American museums, if you so choose, but you will never be Director." His eyes met mine and reflected the kind of sympathy I had not seen before in this country. "The reason for this I am ashamed to say is because you are Jewish."

I stared at him in amazement for a few seconds without responding and saw an honesty in his face that reminded me of what I believed about the American male: they have a genuine consideration of others, an unusual frankness, albeit often naïve, that I've never identified with most European men. I felt grateful for his honesty. No one had ever said this kind of thing to me.

"Yes. My situation here is not a comfortable one and I must tell you that I have taken steps to further my career elsewhere. I hope, however, that you are not correct about my future in the museum world because I am a Jew, albeit a non-practicing one. I have been offered a job as Executive Vice-President of the Art Association of Indianapolis and in charge of all artistic responsibilities at the Herron Museum of Art there. I've never been to the mid-west, but I am going for a second interview this week. I do hope that this kind of prejudice is not going to follow me to Indianapolis. They were enthusiastic about my coming and seem so positive out there. I like that."

After Peter left my office, I picked up the phone to call Charlotte.

"Charlotte, I have decided to leave Philadelphia and I think I will take that job in Indianapolis. It may not be perfect, but I really think I don't belong here in Philly. Things have gotten worse."

She was silent for a few moments before responding, "Do you really think it will be better there?"

"It's closer to Chicago, you know...only about a two-and-a-half-hour drive."

I broke what seemed like an endless silence from the other end of the line. It was ominous and I didn't understand it. Finally, I offered, "I'll call you when I leave for my final interview in Indy next week," and I hung up the phone.

The Guarnieris' apartment next to the clock, on the right in St. Mark's square in Venice where Mary lived for a while.

# XVI

## Venice, Cortina and Feltre,
## then on to Rome and La Dolce Vita
## and Big Decisions

WHEN I ARRIVED at the Guarnieris' apartment in Piazza San Marco with my right foot in a walking boot the expression of alarm on all their faces was evident. Before they could say anything, I smiled and tried to give them a reassuring look, "Don't worry. I had a not too serious accident on the slopes but I'm better now. The doctor in Zermatt said I could ski in a week as nothing was broken, just torn tendons and it really doesn't hurt when I wear my ski boots. In fact, I don't have to wear the walking boot after tomorrow because it will have been a week since I started wearing it."

Dr. Guarnieri looked skeptical. "That's good because we were hoping you would ski with the children in Cortina next week. We hope to leave Venice in three days." I reassured him that I would be ready and was looking forward to the Cortina slopes.

Venice was covered in fog in December, giving it even more an aura of mystery and out of another century. It was a pleasure to walk the children to their schools nearby, and then with my detailed *Touring Club Italiano* guidebook I spent the morning hours of the next week roaming the streets of Venice, exploring the beautiful churches and stopping for a cappuccino in an unfamiliar piazza. Few people were in the streets, and certainly no tourists, just regular Venetians doing their marketing and living their regular lives. I felt I was protected by anonymity with the hood of my raincoat pulled down almost over my face, until it began raining seriously, and then I ducked into the nearest church—always finding an unexpected new treasure, according to my fabulous detailed guidebook.

It was a serendipitous discovery in the Church of Santo Stefano to find one of Tintoretto's versions of the Last Supper, unlike any other because of the angle the painter chose to show us and also because of the physical dynamism of the apostles, so characteristic of the Mannerist style. The apostles were all actively doing something, except for one who appeared to be napping next to Christ. I was immediately drawn into the scene where some of the apostles moved about the table or engaged in conversation. One was trying to engage a dog with a plate of food, and a child was shown prominently in the foreground lounging on the steps while playing with a small animal. Although the church was dark, one couldn't help being drawn to the luminous green, blue and rose satin robes. I had seen many variations of this famous Bible story but this one drew me into the scene more than others because of the striking dynamism of the figures, including Christ in profile at the corner of the table, shown leaning into the apostles. The quasi horizontal table reaches back to a female figure whom I was surprised to see almost lurking in the background with her bosom showing above a low-cut dress. This too was unique because in other Last Suppers few women are shown. The *Santo Stefano Last Supper* is one that most tourists don't get to see because they are in such a hurry, and because the more famous version of the same subject is in the Basilica di San Giorgio also here in Venice.

Sometimes in the afternoons I took the Guarnieri children to explore parts of the city that were unknown to them, and we made a game of getting lost in Venice, running over bridges and skipping into a new campo that appeared unexpectedly, and which was unfamiliar to them. It was exciting for them and for me always finding new frescoes, paintings, and churches. Visiting the churches soon came to an end, however, because the parents felt they were damp and unhealthy for the children. I regretted this editing of our exploring, but we continued our discoveries in the unknown parts of the city. The church interiors I had to visit alone when the children were in school.

JUST AFTER ARRIVING in Cortina I was pleased to meet Toni Maraini, a lovely young redhead whom my friend and former Professor Carlo Rusconi asked me to look up. We skied together every afternoon across country, stopping occasionally to chat. It was relaxing, beautiful, and the way I preferred to ski. It was never nervous making and I saw so much more. We occasionally stopped just to admire the vistas, or the drifts of snow glistening in the sunlight on the heavily laden branches of the pine trees. One day Toni stopped suddenly turning back to look at me with an enthusiastic smile, "I know what you should do. You must come with me to a very interesting literary salon hosted by two charming older white Russian ladies in a magnificent chateau. We meet every Monday night to discuss some of the attendees' poetry and short stories. The people are from everywhere in Europe and most entertaining."

That turned out to be true. It was a superb antidote to the vacuous conversations that took place every day at noon at the Hotel de la Poste where the minor nobility convened for after ski aperitivi and gossip. It was there in hushed voices, with Campari at our lips, that we learned the latest about who was sleeping with Count so and so's wife, and what was going on at the villas next door when the husbands were away. Between sips of champagne and flirtatious smiles, the wealthy newcomers from Milan and Turin were regaling the grass widows of their latest success in the business world, and new relationships were beginning. The loudest buzz was caused by the scandalous behavior of a Venetian friend of the Guarnieris who, in her husband's absence was being flagrantly courted by a Roman prince. I was mildly shocked but the Guarnieris assured me that marriages had been saved for centuries due to this lasting Italian custom, "unlike in America where there are divorces at the drop of a hat."

Anyone who was available and willing was subject to the possibility of an extra-marital affair during the high season at Cortina. I listened with interest to the often-repetitive conversations because it was another way to improve my Italian. It didn't much matter what the content of the soap opera conversations was because I was listening on another level, to the grammar construction and the vocabulary. Furthermore Dr. Guarnieri informed me with much delight that the Venetian woman causing the great stir was jealous of me because of my beaver coat which was apparently a symbol of inordinate wealth in Italy. She told Signora Guarnieri that they shouldn't be "so nice" to me, and that I should be treated as a servant, not as a member of the family. The Guarnieris were amused by her childishness and told me to just ignore her. What made it even harder and more confusing for me was that her husband had begun to make overtures to me, asking if I would meet him for a drink in a remote section of Venice. My responses were firmly negative.

In direct contrast to the vacuous après ski meetings at the Hotel de la Poste, I very much enjoyed the stimulating conversations of the intellectuals at the weekly gatherings of the Russian sisters.

Spring finally came, followed by a sweltering summer which meant the family would be moving to the Lido, as they did every June. One of the Venetian customs that has been carried on up to the present was that the first families continued to be "in prima fila", on the first row with their cabanas at the Lido beach. Every day at the stroke of noon an army of servants, wearing

The Guggenheim palazzo on the Grand Canal.

white gloves, took the ferry from Venice across the lagoon to the Lido with tureens of piping hot pasta to be served on the beach, along with the rest of the hot meal. I felt once again that I had been thrown back to times past where the luxuries of a Patrician life were taken for granted. The contemporary Venetians had no idea how remarkable this struck outsiders. Eating steaming hot pasta on the beach served to us in our bathing suits by maids with white gloves struck me as the height of luxury...and decadence.

At the end of summer, the program for most of the Guarnieri friends and certainly for our family was to leave Venice and, even though I was interested in seeing as much of Italy as I could, and to learn about the customs of the natives, I didn't like to the idea of leaving Venice where my social life had picked up considerably. I was invited to parties in very different Venetian circles given by Peggy Guggenheim, Countess Gozzi of the Fortuny fabrics business, and students still remaining in Venice during the summer months. The parties at the Guggenheim palazzo on the Grand Canal were the most impressive, always attended by the leading artists of Italy and other "*personaggi,*" characters often dressed in fanciful costumes. One party stayed in my memory for a long time. There weren't many women present because the hostess didn't like sharing any spotlight with other women. The Guggenheim daughter, Pegeen, appeared in a sleeveless white dress which was not particularly remarkable in itself but one couldn't miss the stark white bandages on her wrists. She had once again tried to kill herself. This immediately got the attention of most of the attendees at the party. I was curious about her life; she seemed to have everything and yet there was an aura of sadness around her that I found interesting and made me sympathetic towards her. The talk at the party was mostly about the art at the biennale that year: who had been selected from America, who from Italy, and the general resentment of those artists not asked to participate.

I felt privileged to have been invited and was stunned when the Guarnieris told me I should not be going out as much as I had been, and particularly to those gatherings frequented by "questionable" people. Naturally I was beginning to resent this attempt at controlling my social life, but we were to take off for Feltre within the week, so I bit my tongue and decided not to protest.

I didn't realize that when we went to Feltre, the paternal grandmother would be reigning supreme. Her two sons brought their families and entire entourages from Venice to the palace. The servants of each household helped in the kitchen, and serving at meals, in addition to being in charge of cleaning that particular part of the palace which their family occupied. I had known Dr. Guarnieri's younger brother and his English wife in Venice but hadn't seen much of them until we were all living under the same roof in Feltre. It was hard for the grandmother to accept the fact that I was treated as a member of the family and not a servant. Being allowed to have meals with the entire family was almost too much for her. I noticed early on that everyone had white rolls placed at their places except for me. Mine were brown. After several days, I turned to our server and said gently *sotto voce* that I too would like to try the white bread. She looked startled, turned to the grandmother with an inquiring look. but before anyone could say anything Caterina addressed our server, "Never mind, I would like to try the dark bread." She quickly reached over and took my bread replacing it with hers. It had been a subtle attempt on the part of the grandmother to distinguish me as not quite a member of the family. The Doctor and his wife had noticed this distinction, were embarrassed by it but chose to ignore it. They, and their children Keki and Caterina continued to treat me with the utmost affection and respect but the grandmother continued to make it perfectly clear how she felt about my position so that my life in *villeggiatura* at the palazzo no longer felt comfortable. Even if that were not the case, it was not my idea of fun, particularly when I longed to be enjoying the more exciting, and glamorous life in Venice.

To make matters worse, the younger brother of Dr. Guarnieri had a serious crush on me causing me to literally run from him through the vast halls of the palace. Dr. and Mrs. Guarnieri found this very amusing and did nothing to stop his pursuing me. It was the last straw before I spoke one evening saying that I had decided to leave them and return to Rome. I didn't explain why but I think they understood all the reasons for my leaving. It was true that this family treated me better than the other families in Venice treated their au pairs, and that was why I stayed as long as I did. Never was I made to feel I was an employee, and therefore inferior. There was mutual respect between us even though there were differences of opinions. I think they viewed me more as a foreign friend who had come to live with them on a temporary basis and one whom they could trust implicitly with their children, whom we all adored.

THE TRAIN FROM VENICE to Rome took just over three hours giving me a chance to move from one world to another and to begin a new life. It never occurred to me to be frightened traveling alone in Italy, in fact this was part of my whole new experience, and being free to go and do exactly what I wanted to do. Perhaps this fearlessness was due to my American naiveté and my love of adventure. The excitement of living in Rome in 1960 was palpable. Preparations were underway for the 1960 Olympics to be held there the following summer. My timing was perfect. I didn't realize at the time how serendipitous it was that the bookkeeper for the Rome Bureau of Time Life was going on leave, and a bookkeeper was needed immediately. Although I was hired as a "stringer", I agreed ingenuously to also fill in as the temporary bookkeeper while the regular one was on leave. This proved to be the most difficult part of the job because I was never very good at numbers. It did however get my foot in the door and led to a permanent position in the Rome bureau during the Olympics in addition to being in charge of the soft pages, "the Art, Fashion and the Movies." It was heaven to be back in Rome at this very exciting time of La Dolce Vita. Fellini captured beautifully the pervasive spirit in his monumental movie with the same name. Rome was electrified with confusion and excitement by the forthcoming Olympics together with the festive atmosphere of La Dolce Vita. One morning on the front page of *Corriere della Sera* a picture appeared of a street with two traffic signs pointing in opposite directions both saying "One Way." Everyone wanted to come to Rome, and those of us who were working there felt we were in the best of all possible worlds. Just walking along the Via Veneto was a thrill because you never knew who you would see. I often saw Sofia Loren who greeted me warmly in passing, which caused heads to turn to see who she was greeting so enthusiastically.

I loved my job at Time Life (Teemay-Leefay as the Italians called it) and aside from the interviewing I had the additional pleasure of attending the parties and receptions for all the movie dignitaries. My Time bosses were married and preferred to stay at home unless it was "really fun" and then I was to call them. I was getting to know the minor movie divas and other Italian film people as well as those from *United Press, Associated Press, Newsweek* and some of the European journalists. Everyone knew of, and respected Life Magazine in those days, and being identified with it gave me a good entrée with the other journalists attending the Olympics.

I was meeting everyone through my work at Time Life but having my friends, the d'Almeidas there to help me was a great boon. Very soon after my arrival Anne d'Almeida helped me find a charming little apartment up on the Janiculum hill close to them and to the American Academy. The unfurnished apartment was soon filled with the necessities and was very comfortable and convenient. It was near the bus stop that took me down the hill, through Trastevere and dropped me on the Corso near the Via Condotti where I walked over to the Spanish steps and up to the Time Life office on the Via Sardegna. I always stopped at my favorite bar for breakfast—a *cornetto* and a cappuccino. Early morning in Rome was as bustling as later in the day but

Mary at Time Life Bureau, Rome, 1960.

with different kinds of people—the garbage collectors, the traffic officers, and the workers setting up their fruit and vegetable stands, and opening their shops for the morning shoppers. They were all beginning their day while the tourists and dolce vita lovers were still in bed. I loved the energy of the Romans that filled the morning air as they were off and running. At that time of day, about 8:30 and comfortably cool, I found an excitement in the atmosphere as if something wonderful was going to happen.

I soon became familiar enough with Rome that it seemed to be like a small town filled with friendly people and easy to move around in. I didn't own or need a car because there were the convenient buses and taxis if I needed them. Being at Time Life added a certain cachet to my life and opened doors to make my life a particularly glamorous one. My small salary allowed me to live comfortably but not extravagantly, while my most cherished luxury was the Elizabeth Arden salon at the bottom of the Spanish steps where I went for my beehive hairdo and upkeep thereof. On the side I was offered different writing and translating jobs that allowed me to keep my wardrobe up to the latest fashion. I almost never had dinner alone either because of visitors from the States or my Italian escorts who introduced me to the various wonderful restaurants all over the city. Walking around Rome was still one of my favorite things to do, and the long lunch break allowed me to indulge in this adventurous pastime. I never tired of visiting the Roman Forum, and if it became too hot to picnic there I would often retreat to a newly discovered church to find its treasures and collect my thoughts. Strolling through the Borghese gardens was another favorite way to spend the lunch hours, thinking of Henry James and his wanderings through the park watching the school children at play and smiling at their boisterous laughter.

WRITING SPEECHES and the press releases for Princess Marcella Borghese was another way to make ends meet with additional income, and I enjoyed working with her. Prince and Princess Marcella Borghese, both delightful, asked me to come back to New York with them immediately and to be a part of her cosmetics company that was a new subsidiary of Revlon. Although I enjoyed the work I declined the offer to leave Time Life immediately for a permanent job writing for her company in the States. I told them I would look them up whenever I returned to New York but that it wouldn't be right away. They were disappointed when I turned them down, but my life in Rome was just too perfect for the time being and I was a little leery of becoming too committed to the Borgheses before looking at other options once I returned to the States.

Good things seem to come in bunches. The most flattering was the offer to be head of Time Life advertising for all of Italy. Ralph Davidson had come to Rome to interview me, and I was definitely interested. But when I asked if I could take the job and stay in Rome, he said firmly, "No, moving to Milan would be necessary. That's where the advertising money is." To be honest, in retrospect I knew it would be a serious career move and that was something I wasn't sure I wanted at that particular time in my life. Davidson, who offered me the job, was persuasive and said they wanted a woman at the head of advertising in Italy, and that he thought I would be perfect for the job even though I was only 27. I loved challenges, and this would definitely be one, never having had any interest in or experience in advertising. Writing was one thing, but the business world was something else, Thinking about this possible career change caused me to think again about possibly returning to New York, and to begin a more serious life, one that was not merely designed around having a good time. I had often wondered if I could make a drastic change to the business world where I would be making a lot of money, as many of my friends were doing in America. I had never given much thought to that subject since I always had enough to live on and enough freelance writing jobs kept coming my way so that I was never destitute. Being where I was, and having enough time to enjoy life to the fullest had always been more important to me than making money. These values had motivated my taking the jobs in Costa Rica, Uruguay and so far in Italy. An odd sadness overcame me from time to time and caused me to make the next important decision: to forget about recent job offers that would keep me in Europe. I recognized the sadness as homesickness for America. Along with that feeling, some words of one of my Time Life bosses came glaringly back to me, "When you begin to be irritated by the very things that interested or amused you about the Italians, it is time to leave." And I knew that time had come for me as it had for her. The new challenge, of returning to New York and finding a job that would lead to a career in the business world was beginning to clearly take over my thoughts. After all, that is what people did in America: "make money." I had never been interested in that, but now I recognized this was what I should do next. Harry Doyle, President of the Princess Marcella Borghese Company said he would help me once I returned to New York, and I felt encouraged just remembering this.

AROUND FIVE DAYS after I booked my passage back to New York, I received a strange postcard from the Department of Citizenship at the Roman Commune. It said, "Report immediately to this office." I knew it must be

Mary with friends at the Trevi fountain, 1960.

another Italian mistake in the vast bureaucracy of the Italian government, but I did as I was told, taking the post card with me. After presenting the card at the first station I encountered I was told to go "through that door." It opened onto another room with a group of officials sitting at slightly more impressive desks, one of whom pointed to another door and said, "Through that door, *prego*." That door opened onto a beautiful room filled with Italian paintings in the Veronese style covering the walls. I noticed an Italian official pecking at a typewriter with two fingers who greeted me with "*Il passaporto, prego*" without even looking up from his work. When I gave him my American passport he stopped typing, looked up at me and said in Italian "passports can be forged. Perhaps you are not really an American citizen." My mouth fell open in shock, but I managed to respond in an almost bus driver's vernacular, "*Ma come, non sono Americana*!!" A few more questions ensued to which I answered more calmly, realizing that this was a serious situation and no time for hysterics. When he heard me speak he complimented my Italian and asked how come I spoke Italian so well and that my name was Tonetti—an Italian name.

"You must be Italian," Then after a brief pause, "You have been very happy here in Italy haven't you?"

I couldn't imagine where this conversation was going and responded, "What does that have to do with anything, whether I have been happy here or not. Of course, I have."

"*Dunque, Signorina, Il governo Italiano ha bisogno di Lei.* The Italian government needs you. We can make you an Italian citizen in a few days. You are very well situated here to be of help to us. Espionage can be fascinating," he added with a slight smile.

I was beginning to feel faint, and I was afraid they had already started working on making me an Italian citizen. I had to think fast. Knowing that Italians always respond well to sexual innuendos, and not wanting to hurt his feelings, I treated it as a sort of romantic proposal and chose my words carefully. "I am very flattered, Signore, but I cannot accept your offer. I have to return to America because...*c'e la Mama*. She is very ill, and I must take care of her." This lie came tripping off my tongue with great sincerity, and it was as effective as I had hoped it would be. The Signore folded the papers in front of him, which obviously had to do with me and said with feeling, that of course he understood. "One must always take care of one's parents first." After being ushered out of the office politely but precipitously, I breathed a sigh of relief, and knew my imagination had saved me once again.

The last month in Rome was full of going away parties and tearful goodbyes. The thought occurred to me fleetingly that maybe I had made a mistake, and dreaded giving up my job, my apartment, my friends, and a life that could only be described as perfect. I was frightened for the first time by going into the next phase of my life. But it was clear to me that it was time to go home. I was stepping again into the unknown although I was returning to what had always been home. I was twenty-seven years old, with no job and no plan, and my confidence, though rarely shaken, once again took a dive. What would I do? I needed to find out who I wanted to be and how I should start to be that person. The only thing I had figured out that was definite was that I should return to my country. I called my friend, Anne d'Almeida and announced, "I'm returning to America but might be back here sooner than you think. Rome feels more like home to me and I do feel more Italian than American right now. *Vedremo.*"

Tuesday, March 12, 1963

THE INDIANAPOLIS NEWS

# Herron Official is Many-Faceted Man

### BY EVIE BIRGE

Henri Dorra the executive vice-president of the Art Association of Indianapolis, has black hair and what the French call "marron" (chestnut) eyes.

As those who have heard him lecture at the Herron on Gauguins's life and works, or Seurat's mathematical theories, can testify, he speaks English with an accent reminiscent of Charles Boyer.

Equally at home in English, French and Italian, Dorra also picked up a little Arabic in his childhood, which was spent in Egypt and France.

"Like Indianapolis, the town of LeMans is well known for its automobile races", said Dorra, who drives a "British racing green" Jaguar.

In anticipation of Egyptian independence, Aubrey was educated in both French and Egyptian schools until he was 13. Then he wasa sent to a school, *Lycée St. Louis*, in Paris. Later he studied engineering at the University of London.

Here, he lives in a house full of books, modern furniture in his own small collection of modern drawings and paintings. He is unmarried.

Dorra discovered the fine arts at the age of 24. In 1948, while working for a graduate degree in engineering at Harvard, he took two art courses in summer school.

Classical art and medieval architecture proved so exciting that, to his family consternation, he discarded his sliding rule and plunged headlong into the field of art. Six years later he received his PhD from Harvard. His field of specialization was modern art.

While working for his degree, Dora I'm here at the Metropolitan Museum of Art in New York as a student fellow, Learning the museums operation. Later the tour European museums.

Before coming to Indianapolis, he was an assistant director of the Corcoran Gallery of Art in Washington DC, and more recently, of the Philadelphia Museum of Art.

After four months here he says he likes his work and the people with whom he works.

"I find it very exciting," he said with his characteristic directness and vigor, "That the leaders of industry in Indianapolis realize that a city's cultural institutions are among its most important assets.

"I chose Indianapolis from a number of opportunities because of the excellent reputation of the Herron School of Art.

"I Believe that a museum should be a free university where are all who come can obtain information and find enjoyment, and a source of stimulation for future artists."

Among the exhibitions which Dr. Doraa organized while at the Corcoran was one called "The American Muse," in which American paintings were displayed with literary quotations reflecting similar trends.

In 1961, this material was published in theexxe book under the same title. The reader who dips into the handsome volume, available at both the State Library and the end nap at Indianapolis Public Library, will linger over pictures and text, and find himself charmed by their juxtaposition.

For example, besides the color plate of a George Caleb Bingham's famous painting, "Fur Traders Descending the Missou-

Henri Dorra, new executive vice-president of the Art Association of Indianapolis, at his desk in the new addition to the Herron School of Art.

ri," is the following quotation from "Huckleberry Flinn": It was a monstrous big River down there, sometimes a mile and a half wide... not a sound anywhere's... The first thing to see, looking away over the water, was a kind of dull line, that was the woods on t'other side; you couldn't make nothing else out; then a pale place in the sky; then more paleness spreading around; and the river softened up a way off, and warn't black anymore, but gray."

The book is full of such parallels.

Dorra's major work, "George Seurat," written in collaboration with John Dewald, is a critical study of the French painter. A scholarly, expensive ($37.50) book written partly in French, it may be perused in the reference library of the Herron Museum.

Use of this library, incidentally, is not restricted to members of the Art Association.

Dorra now is working on two books, he finds time to write only on vacations. One is the life of Gauguin; the other a study of the relationship of art and science through the ages.

"The latter appeals to both sides of my split personality," he explained." Artists have traditionally been very much interested in science. Both artists and scientists, after all, are concerned with interpreting the universe."

# XVII
# Indianapolis and Seeing a New America
## PLUS ÇA CHANGE

CHARLOTTE APPEARED in Indianapolis a week after I arrived in the fall of 1962. Before I saw her descend the stairs from the plane, there were three other young women in camel hair coats. Charlotte's, however, was tightly belted to show off her slim waist and shapely legs. She wore a brown and white Hermes scarf that was neatly folded around her neck. I was pleased to see that she was carrying the brown alligator handbag that I had brought her from Paris last Christmas. I thought she looked quietly elegant.

She said she wanted to help me find a place to live and although I was surprised she had made the trip without telling me she would be here, I was grateful she had come to help me. I felt suddenly warm all over just seeing her, and even though I had never kissed a woman in public before I couldn't help rushing to embrace her. I pulled her close to me and kissed her. The kiss was a long and passionate one, and we were oblivious to the stares of those around us. She laughed softly, and I realized how much I had missed her. Although we talked on the phone almost every evening, we hadn't seen each other for two weeks. We were walking to the baggage claim arm in arm when she abruptly stopped, smiled, and said in a clipped business-like tone, "I do hope we can get started immediately to see some realtors. That's why I came out here. I want to find the perfect house for you."

I had set up appointments with the realtor who would show me some houses for sale and for rent, and Charlotte was eager to see them all. It was a process I dreaded, but I wanted to make a decision as soon as possible In fact, after seeing only three houses, with her arms folded in front of her in a determined way, she told the realtor "I think this one will be perfect for the various events he will host for the museum. His paintings will look great in these rooms with nice high ceilings, and there is ample room for the dinners and receptions he will organize as the new Vice-President of the Herron Art Association and Art School." With her chin jutting out, her head held high and the tone of her voice almost imperious, I had never seen her so commanding. I was embarrassed that she volunteered all that information about me to the realtor whom she had just met. Besides, I wasn't quite sure I wanted to buy a house just yet. I was thinking of renting. The realtor was quick to jump in. "You won't find anything unfurnished for rent that would be right for you, I am quite sure of that."

The realtor looked pleased that Charlotte had nodded in agreement, and before I knew it, I had bought a beautiful three-bedroom Normandy-style house in a great location. I hadn't given much thought to "location" when in Philadelphia, and I paid the price for that when trying to sell it a year and a half later. I didn't want to make that mistake again. One of these bedrooms could be used as a study where I would spend most of my time when I wasn't at the Museum or teaching at the Herron School of Art. We stood in front of the large fireplace in the living room and I looked around at the well-proportioned room and noticed that the windows were placed so that enough space was left for pictures to be hung on the walls. One large window opposite the fireplace offered a view of the superb garden in front of the house.

Once we had finished the arrangements for buying the house, Charlotte said she wanted to return to the hotel to rest a little before dinner, so I dropped her off at the hotel and went back to the office where Ralph Constable, an important trustee had come to my office unannounced. He was dressed in a tailored pinstripe suit which was unusual for the Midwest at that hour. In addition to the sweat that he kept wiping from his brow, his bald head was glossy, and his glasses gleamed with another shine, making him look at the same time both pretentious and a bit comical. He immediately presented me with some papers that he wanted me to sign. "You don't need to worry, Dr. Dorra, this is just a routine affidavit of works I have given to the Museum."

I looked over the papers carefully and saw that his gifts had been made the previous year and the date had been changed to this year.

"But I can't sign this. I wasn't here a year ago when you gave these drawings to the Museum."

"Oh, that really doesn't matter," he smiled, and shifted his weight from one foot to the other. "Because you are currently in charge of the acquisitions, your signature is all that is necessary."

"I am sorry, Mr. Constable, but I really think my signature would have been necessary last year when you gave your gifts to the Museum. To change the date would be illegal."

An awkward silence followed. His face was beginning to turn crimson, and he turned away abruptly saying, "I regret that you feel that way. You are not off to a very good start; I must tell you. I'm an important part of this Museum and you will regret having taken this position. I can assure you of that."

"But, Mr. Constable, surely you can understand that I cannot sign my name to something that happened before I came to Indianapolis. Maybe you should ask Wilber Peat who was director at the time to sign it. He was here then, not I." My voice had suddenly become a little louder.

Without bothering to answer me he simply turned, and before leaving the room he tossed over his shoulder as an afterthought, "Oh, and you needn't bother to tell anyone about this exchange today, Dr. Dorra. It can be just between us." I wished him a good day and added, "Of course, Mr. Constable. We all want what is best for the museum. Hopefully together we will be able to persuade other city leaders of industry like you that Indianapolis needs a good museum as one of its primary cultural assets." He looked surprised at this remark but continued to walk away from me without commenting.

WHEN I JOINED CHARLOTTE that evening at St. Elmo's Steak House for that first dinner together in two weeks she was more reserved than she had been in the morning. The unpretentious restaurant had a wonderful reputation and enjoyed a remarkable wine list, the best in Indianapolis. It was my favorite restaurant there and reminded me of why I loved the Midwest… like the people of that city, so unassuming, yet everything was handled with style and a love of life. I wanted the evening to be special because we hadn't yet had a meal together in Indy and also because I was grateful she had come to help me find a house. I told her she had been so knowledgeable this morning about choosing the right house for me here, and that I was very pleased and happy to have her here with me. I saw that she was rubbing her forehead and looked tired.

"Are you tired, my dear?"

"Yes, I must say I am. But let's not spoil a nice evening. Tell me how your day went. I want to hear everything."

"Let's have a drink and celebrate my buying the house. Then I will tell you about some of the important things that have happened since I got here."

"Already you have important things happening? All good I hope."

"Well, I may have perhaps antagonized one of the most important trustees by refusing to sign an affidavit of his gift that had been given a year ago."

"You mean he wanted you to predate the gift. But that is illegal." Her eyes narrowed, and she continued to speak intensely and with conviction. "He should never have asked you to change the date of his gift for income tax purposes."

"Yes. But his tone was almost threatening as he assured me that he would make life difficult for me at the museum since I wouldn't go along with him by signing the paper. I think he is the most powerful among the trustees."

"I wouldn't worry about him. You've already made some good friends here and they won't let anything happen to you or your career."

"The trustees are apparently disagreeing rather heatedly about where the Museum should be, and I really can't do what I was brought here to do until they finalize their decision. Bob McCarthy, who like me, has just arrived on the scene, feels stymied until they decide whether to go out to Butler University or expand the Museum at a downtown location."

"Have you expressed an opinion to anyone about this?"

"No. I have been careful not to. I don't want to antagonize any of them."

"Where do the trustees who have the most money stand on this issue?" She asked this with a certain vehemence that surprised me.

"There is money on both sides, and one side or the other would most certainly not honor pledges if their side doesn't win their location choice. Mr. Herman Krannert, a successful and highly respected businessman has been courted by a group of powerful trustees to be chairman of the board. They call themselves 'the Museum Alliance.' Bob says that it is known that Krannert is not particularly interested in expanding the Museum, but he is interested in pleasing his wife. She apparently loves art and has urged her husband to help build a new beautiful museum in downtown Indianapolis."

"Then I don't see a problem. If you haven't taken sides you should at least voice your opinion because your job will perhaps depend on their decision, and it seems the most powerful trustees want the Museum downtown...or at least their wives do." She smiled as she added that last bit.

"I know. And Mr. Eli Lily, another powerful trustee also wants the Museum to be expanded downtown. But there are others including Mr. Harold Edwards who wanted to take advantage of the offer at Butler University to move the Museum to their campus on the outskirts of the city, and a movement to make this happen has already been started. I should go out to see the campus to be fair to both sides but I haven't had the time to do so yet."

We continued to talk about the museum's problems until I saw that she was losing interest in the whole matter and I really couldn't blame her. I knew she had said she was tired at the beginning of the evening, but I didn't know if she was telling the truth and just didn't want to spend the rest of the evening with me now that she had accomplished her "mission" in finding me a house. She didn't object when I suggested that we should call it an evening since she was so tired.

Charlotte and I continued to make plans to see each other every other weekend when I would drive to Chicago or she would come to Indianapolis. As the months went by our relationship continued much the same despite the distance between us. At least I thought it was the same. But in January when we had made a date for me to come to Chicago for the weekend things came to a head, showing me that I had not understood that a change had indeed taken place in our relationship.

Because the trustees were still in heated disagreement about the location of the museum and since both sides had representatives lobbying for their respective position, Mr. Edwards, one of the trustees who was also on the board of Butler University approached me. He asked if I would come with him out to see the Butler campus and where they proposed to put the Museum. He also insisted, "It would be financially irresponsible not to move the Museum to the University campus."

Mr. Edwards added that he had arranged with the chancellor to meet me and said we would go on Friday the 20th. "I have already asked our new development director, and he's on board as is the chancellor. But I'd like you to be there too." I gulped and asked if there could be another date. He shook his head and said no; that date was chosen by the Butler chancellor. "He's a very busy man, you know, and we really can't change the date. It was the same day as I had planned to go to Chicago and I had no choice but to call Charlotte and cancel our date. She was furious because she had already bought expensive tickets for the theatre and had made hard to get reservations at two restaurants for the weekend.

"But Charlotte, surely you can understand my position. I must go, and that is the date the trustee arranged for us to be there. I can come next weekend."

"No. I have made other plans for the next weekend." There was an edge to her voice that I hardly recognized.

"I am sorry you feel that way and sorry to disappoint you, but I have no option," I weakly volunteered.

A silence followed that was longer than usual when she was at odds with something I said.

"And there is something I wanted to talk to you about that really can't wait."

"Can't you tell me now what is on your mind?"

"Well. I really wanted it to be in person because it is so important." She hesitated for what seemed an interminable length of time before saying, "At my last meeting with Dr. Adler he told me I had become much stronger, healthier and less sad since I had first come to him. But then he told me something that surprised me."

I swallowed and waited for her to continue, almost afraid of what she was going to say.

"He asked me if I didn't think I would be even healthier and happier if you were not in my life."

My mouth fell open, not thinking I had heard correctly. "And do you agree with him?" I was almost stuttering, so afraid of how she would answer.

"I do."

I didn't respond right away but she continued as if my response was unnecessary. Her voice took on a different tone, a more assertive one.

"I have to tell you that I think he was right. You and I must stop seeing each other. You have your career in Indianapolis ahead of you and although I am very grateful for the year and a half of treatment you paid for me it is just too difficult for me to continue this relationship when we have so many miles between us and there are so many other differences between us. And..." She hesitated. "I guess I will always resent the economic disparity between us. Everything seems so easy for you and I have had to work so hard for the little that I have."

I had almost stopped listening to her and hadn't seen it coming that she would break off our relationship so suddenly. I was still stunned by her words, "I do" and wondered if she was being completely honest with me. Were there other reasons why she wanted to stop seeing me? I asked if there was anything else, she wanted to add or was that it?

"You can't really believe that you know me and believe my life has always been easy if you ignore what I have told you about the difficulties I have been through in leaving France, the hardships I faced in England during the war when I worked at night in a factory in order to go to school during the day, and then what I experienced as a Jew at Harvard and after the war." I saw that my hands and the phone I was holding were wet with sweat. I couldn't quite believe I had revealed all that about myself. I had never mentioned all those hardships to anyone, and it had suddenly come out without my realizing it.

"*Merde*, Charlotte! There must be something else. Have you met someone?"

"True. I have ignored all of that in your past. I just know that today you live well, and I was drawn to that life which is so much more comfortable than the way I live now in Chicago. And right now your job demands so much of your time. Frankly, Henri, I have concluded that your job is more important to you than I am. I really can't be second fiddle and have begun to see someone else here in Chicago."

I realized she had thought it all out carefully. I was in a state of numbness. That night I thought hard about it all, reviewing our times together, and trying to remember if there had been any happy times together or if it had all been just a matter of my seeing someone whom I could take care of. It was obvious that I was attracted to Charlotte because I needed to take care of someone and particularly of someone who needed me. By dawn I realized she didn't care for me as much as I wanted to care for her, and I should move on with my career in Indianapolis if that was what was in the cards for me. And perhaps I should be more concerned about my own happiness in the future rather than someone else's. Throwing myself into my work was what I should do, and that would be the way I would spend my remaining time in Indy.

WHEN I WAS FIRST ASKED to take the job in Indianapolis, I knew I was brought on to help change the Museum and make it a cultural center for the entire Midwest. It was a pleasure to work with both Bob McCarthy and my new friend Evans Woolens, who was asked by the board to evaluate the two proposed sites for the new museum. All three of us got along well from the beginning, and there was an immediate feeling of mutual respect. We always laughed a lot together and had until recently been amused that the board didn't seem to agree on much of anything. They had been arguing about the location of the Museum since I arrived in the Fall of 1962, and they were still dithering as we got into the spring of '63. Bob and I were well aware of their heated disagreements at the board meetings, but it became difficult for us to be amused at their lack of agreement because neither he nor I could go forward with planning or with fundraising until we knew where the Museum would be.

In order to be better prepared to fundraise, Bob studied the minutes of the board meetings going back to 1958. We met regularly, usually over a beer after work, and Evans often joined us in what usually turned out to be a jovial gathering of good friends. Bob kept us informed about the Board's disagreements. At our most recent meeting of the three of us he volunteered, "You know, Henri, the arguments were so heated before we were hired that several of the board members resigned in protest."

"I know and that is why Mr. Edwards, the trustee who wants the Museum to be at Butler University, with all expenses paid, invited us to go to see the Butler campus. He wants us on his side and not on the side of the powerful

Mr. Krannert who is the new President of the Museum board."

Bob's eyebrows were arched as he continued to fill me in on some of the details of the board minutes.

"Back in 1960 Mr. Krannert said he would be President and give a large sum of money only if fourteen others would pledge 'large amounts' before the annual meeting of the Art Association."

I shook my head and finally admitted, "That was two years before we arrived and not much has changed has it? I've never seen such jockeying for power nor such elaborate intrigue going on behind the scenes. I certainly want to steer clear of that, but I know we have to go to Butler to appear at least somewhat impartial."

"You are right, Henri, and even our friend Evans Woolens who is always the optimist agrees that our jobs are not secure and certainly at least half the money will not be forthcoming no matter where the location of the Museum is finally determined. Frankly, and this is just between us, I have begun to think of leaving. I don't like the mood, the infighting and the lack of decisions."

"Bob, as much as I would like to stay here, I completely agree, and I too have started to look around. I had high hopes for the Museum, and I like the people here."

By the time we finished our beers, the mood had changed from a jovial one of good fellowship to a more serious and depressing one. I walked briskly to my little green Jaguar with a heavy heart. Things seemed to be tumbling down all around me, first Charlotte's blunt and sudden news, and now I was seeing more clearly that there might be no future for me at the museum in Indianapolis. It would take years for the Indianapolis Museum of Art to open its doors at the Oldfield estate which the Lilys pledged to give for the new Museum, and I was losing my patience. I felt suddenly tired and discouraged.

When I arrived at home there was mail which I looked through, and saw immediately a letter from the Art Department at the University of California in Los Angeles. I tore open the envelope and reading quickly I saw that there was an enthusiastic offer to be the Interim Director of the UCLA Art Gallery and a position to teach in the Department of History of Art. But they wanted me to come as soon as possible and that would mean I would have to sell the new house. I couldn't believe I just bought a house and now I would need to sell it. Hopefully I could get out of it this time without a loss. But that letter gave me the lift I needed to act. The next day I called to accept the position at that prestigious University.

Visitors at the Indianapolis Museum of Art enjoy the gardens of the former Lily Estate at Newfields.

Diana Vreeland, 1960. Photo courtesy of Library of Congress

# XVIII

# Back to New York with *Harper's Bazaar*, Diana Vreeland and Revlon

FROM THE WORLD OF BUSINESS
TO EXPLORING THE WORLD OF CONSCIOUSNESS RAISING
AS WE DID IN THE 60S

THE DAY AFTER I RETURNED to New York I called Harry Doyle, the President of the Princess Marcella Borghese company whom I had met in Italy. I was delighted although surprised that he seemed glad I called, and asked me to come to the Revlon office at 666 Fifth Avenue to meet "someone who could be very helpful." Lorrie Eyerly, a petite and dynamic businesswoman had an engaging smile that would often burst into a belly laugh. As the Director of Fashion Publicity and Promotion she was one of only three women executives at Revlon even though it was a business designed to appeal to women. I liked her right away although I was intimidated by her brusque manner. The first thing I noticed about her was how well coiffed she was, and I was to learn later that the time she spent at the hairdresser's she considered most important. At that first meeting we got to know a lot about each other. On the one hand Lorrie was tough, yet as I came to know her I learned she was a generous, kind and gentle friend. She had worked her way up Seventh Avenue to one of the top jobs at Revlon, always learning and not always making friends, but always acquiring admirers. At that first interview after Harry Doyle left us alone in her well-appointed office at the top of the 666 building on Fifth Avenue between puffs on the long cigarette holder she held between two fingers, she wanted to know about my life in Latin America, the year and a half in Italy and even a bit about Vassar. At the end of that hour she said rather emphatically, "I would love to have you work here at Revlon as the Assistant director of Fashion Publicity and Promotion but," and she hesitated briefly. "You don't know anything. Get a job working with Diana Vreeland. Learn as much as you can about fashion from her, then we will talk." She stood, extended her hand to shake mine and turned towards the door to show me out of her office. "Keep in touch," she added with a smile. It was an abrupt dismissal but I understood how busy she was and didn't have all day to spend with me. It was not hurtful.

It wasn't too difficult for me to get an entrée to *Harper's Bazaar*, and I didn't realize until much later how fortunate I was with my connections. A friend of my family's, Didi Lowndes who was about the most fashionable person I knew, didn't hesitate to say "Oh I know Diana, and Carmel Snow too. I'll give them a call and ask that they interview you as soon as possible."

Before I knew it I received a phone call from the personnel office of *Harper's Bazaar* asking me to come in and meet the two most powerful women in fashion at the time. I wore my best black dress and a sparkling necklace of green beads and rhinestones which I had bought in Rome just before leaving. Mrs. Vreeland commented on it, "Your necklace is stunning. Did you get it in Italy?" I found she was so easy to talk to that I hardly noticed we had spent at least forty minutes talking about life in Rome, foreign languages and everything else. I could have stayed forever. Then, since I was having a fascinating time with this woman, and so totally relaxed I even forgot I was being interviewed for a job, I asked her in all my naivete, "Mrs. Vreeland, do you take fashion seriously?"

She looked at me with a questioning look, as if that were a trick question. She must have realized that it was just my sincere interest in her as a person, and also that I was obviously new to the world of fashion, and totally ingenuous, she answered slowly and quietly, "Yes. I do. It's another way of recording history, and," she added, almost as an honest afterthought, "I've always been mad about clothes! You can't have been born in Paris and not be."

All at once I blushed, realizing how stupid my question was and how gracious she was to answer the way she did. She knew I would understand that answer having put fashion in a historical context, and I suddenly did. I never looked at clothes or fashion trends again in the same way. She had already begun to teach me.

I noticed the black snood she wore over her slicked back hair. She sat up tall in a straight back chair, and her office was filled with pictures of fashion models wearing stunning clothes the likes of which I had never seen. There were also photographs of her with all sorts of people I didn't recognize and some I knew were famous in their various fields. It was a world I had no notion of, and I felt as foreign in it as I had when I first stepped off the boat in Genoa. But if it meant the first step into that new world I was excited to be making it.

"I wish we had something more important for you but the only job in the editorial department I can offer you now is that of Assistant Accessories Editor, and you won't be paid very much as you probably know."

"I think that sounds wonderful. I'll do my best not to let you down," I responded.

"I know you won't let me down if you give me your ideas. Don't get lost in the back of the office and do go with the fashion editors on their shoots and let me know if you have ideas for locations. I will want to hear from you."

I could hardly wait that afternoon to call Lorrie Eyerly to tell her the good news that I was hired by Diana Vreeland who seemed to like me. My immediate boss was a timid, trim woman who came from Women's Wear Daily and who was terrified of Mrs. Vreeland, to the point of never coming in on Fridays when Mrs. Vreeland met with all the fashion editors for the weekly wrap up to hear what they had found in the market. It usually involved her rantings, tears on the part of the editors whom she called "fashion-less" and insults the likes of which I had never imagined. No wonder my boss never came in on Fridays and always sent me to show what she had found. Since I was not responsible for my immediate boss's "finds" I wasn't afraid, and treated the meetings as "research" by listening carefully to what Mrs. Vreeland didn't like about the new finds. One of the editors, Polly Bell, befriended me and often invited me to come on location with Suzy Parker and Richard Avedon for her fashion shoots. She was dramatic, had fabulous taste which Mrs. Vreeland recognized and, like me, was unafraid. She worshipped Mrs. Vreeland.

When I was not busy in our accessories office I began to organize the jewelry in the closet so that all the jet was in one drawer, the pearls in another, the rhinestones in another, etc. It would make things much easier when the fashion editors came rushing in to rummage through the drawers looking for specific kinds of jewelry for their shoots. One of these editors who was known inside the office and outside in the real world as a very "difficult person" to work with came into our office to look for certain pieces for her shoot for that afternoon. When she saw the drawers so neatly organized for a change she showed her displeasure by dumping all the drawers onto the floor in a heap. Two days of my work was there on the floor in front of us! Everyone in the adjoining office shook their heads in astonishment when I asked, "Why did you do that?" She responded simply and with a sardonic smile, "because I wanted to," and turned on her high Ferragamo heels, flouncing out of the office. I began picking up the jewelry and sorting it out piece by piece. Temper tantrums were not unusual as I reported to Lorrie at one of our weekly meetings late in December.

"I think you have learned enough there during these past eight months. You can now come to Revlon as my assistant. I know you will be a great help to me, and I will teach you what you will need to know. We'll get that started."

"Oh my God. I can't believe this. I have been putting up with these women for what seems an eternity, and I can hardly wait to come to Revlon."

"And you have been a good sport during the whole trial period. I've seen that." She patted my hand and added, "Now it's time for a drink to celebrate your liberation."

Things moved rapidly after that. I was called into the Revlon personnel department three days after seeing Lorrie. The job was officially offered to me with such an increase in salary I could hardly believe it. I told Polly Bell about my leaving, and she was happy for me. She was the only person I would really miss at *Harper's Bazaar* other than Mrs. Vreeland whom I hadn't yet told I would be leaving. When I called her to say I wanted to meet with her as soon as her schedule would permit, I was surprised that she asked me to come to her Fifth Avenue apartment for tea to discuss whatever was on my mind. That was an invitation I never expected and which I accepted with alacrity. Never had I seen such STYLE! There were banquettes covered in Roman stripe silk. The rest of the living room was completely red. "Red is the great clarifier-bright and revealing. No house painter gets it quite right, I've found. It should be as vibrant as the red caps on children in Renaissance paintings." Her curious and unique *bibelots* were on every table top, in silver, gold, ivory and ebony. As she would say so often "I was mad about red!" We were drinking a delicious Chinese tea from small red porcelain cups when she suddenly asked, "So my dear, what do you want to tell me?" She took a drag from her long silver cigarette holder and faced me with those piercing eyes.

"Well, I hate to leave you and *Harper's Bazaar*, but I have been offered a wonderful job that I can't turn down. It is with Revlon as Assistant Director of Fashion Publicity and Promotion and I am to start in two weeks." It all came out breathlessly and when I had finished she squeezed my hand and said "Good for you. I knew you were not destined to stay long in the back office of *Harper's Bazaar*, and on Monday you will read in the *Times* why I am not displeased that you are leaving the magazine." I was so relieved that she wasn't angry with me, and although very curious, I didn't ask further what she meant.

In the *New York Times* the following Monday I read that Diana Vreeland was leaving *Harper's Bazaar* to become Fashion Editor at *Vogue Magazine*. The fashion world in New York was aghast. She had been the fashion mainstay of Bazaar since 1936, and now she was moving to her leading competitor.

Lorrie Eyerly made sure I knew not only the cosmetics part of Revlon business but the hair and deodorant divisions as well. As part of my training I went to meetings with the sales force, and I also worked a couple of days at the Revlon counter at Lord and Taylor selling the new colors, treatment products and "getting a feel" for what women wanted in the way of beauty products.

At the first meeting I attended with the sales representatives, Mr. Revson berated his sales force reps loudly and in no uncertain terms. "There is SUN in California and why are there are NO Revlon sun screen products in the drug and department stores? I don't know whose fault that is, but you are all to blame." Charles Revson was a force. I remember a story Mrs. Vreeland told me about her connection with him in the very early days. She had taken the last of her very special European nail varnish down to him at the suggestion of her New York manicurist because "he could possibly copy it." Revson did in fact, from studying her varnish, develop one which dried faster than anyone had ever used in America, and one that had great color and didn't chip. When I first met Charles Revson he apparently knew I had worked with Mrs. Vreeland. I told him how much she respected the business he had built. He smiled and said, "She's a force to be reckoned with, isn't she?"

I replied, "Yes. She is someone I admire very much. And she was glad I came to work here at Revlon."

Writing for beauty magazines and supplements was more difficult than writing about Hegel and Kant for my Philosophy classes at Vassar, but I learned. My first assigned article ran several pages and brought many compliments from Lorrie: "Change the color of your makeup when you change your wig." Then the most difficult assignment was a press release on Revlon's newest deodorant. And so it continued.

Lorrie taught me, step by step, how to make the presentations to department stores for the spring and fall colors of nail polish and lipsticks, coordinating the color with the latest fashions of the season to create the newest fashion look. There was a total new look to be presented including the newest skirt length, shoulder pads (or not), eye shadow, eye liner, gloves, hair color (and how to achieve it), jewelry, and of course the newest "Million Dollar Red" or "Jungle Peach" or whatever new color Revlon was promoting.

Meanwhile aside from learning the beauty business, things in my personal life were happening. When my father heard I had accepted the job at *Harper's Bazaar* at such a low salary he was dumb-founded. He thought I had lost my mind. Is that all I could get, with a Vassar education, and all the languages I had under my belt? I explained it was like an apprentice job working for the most important woman in fashion today, and I wanted to learn about it. Apparently I was convincing because we never spoke about it again.

IT TURNED OUT my father had colon cancer, and that was one of the biggest shocks I ever had. I loved him so much and couldn't bear the thought of losing him. But I did. I had asked for a brief leave of absence from *Harper's Bazaar* in order to go back to Fort Worth to be with my father whose health was deteriorating quickly. We had some wonderful conversations about life, philosophy, leaving childhood and taking on responsibilities as adults, and marriage. He wondered if I were ever going to get married. I told him not to worry about that and that I was only twenty-eight. I told him I wanted a marriage that was as good as his, and that I could wait if I had to, in order to find the right person to spend the rest of my life with. He seemed relieved if not convinced. He didn't live long enough to know that my next job paid four times as much as I had been getting at *Harper's Bazaar* and that I wouldn't have gotten it had I not apprenticed with Diana Vreeland.

Each day in New York at that time brought new experiences, lessons in how to live, and what was important. New York was a petri dish for those who wanted to learn about life, and I was learning more about myself, discovering what I wanted, and certainly what I didn't want my life to be. It was at this time that I had fallen in love again. This time, like my grandmother, with a sculptor. He was unconventional and he introduced me to things like peyote, Timothy Leary, and Subud. Subud has been described as a religion by some, others call it a cult and others an education, or as the followers of Subud called it "a spiritual dancing." It was at least a movement that began and was restricted to Indonesia until the 1950s when it spread to America. When Oliver first talked to me so enthusiastically about "consciousness raising" and Timothy Leary, he said, "Aldous Huxley wrote about it, and I think you will find Subud as fascinating as I do. There's a meeting house on 14th Street. But first, let's go to the cocktail party for Timothy Leary that I've been invited to."

It was in the early sixties that I was first introduced to Subud and told about the wonders of Bapek, the founder of Subud. Their meeting houses were spreading in Britain and America, primarily in California and New York, including the one on 14th Street in New York that Oliver took me to, and where I went for the following two months before I decided to move to California. It was because of Oliver's belief in and enthusiasm for Subud that I, a supposedly intelligent person, religiously attended twice a week these strange meetings where the participants surrendered themselves to the "flow of light," trying to "feel in touch with the Holy Spirit" by spontaneous movements, shouting and singing. Eventually, after a three-month trial period they would be assisted by "helpers" who had already been "opened" and they would themselves be "opened" by Bapek to the joys of the "spiritual exercise," the latihan.

The problem for me, and there was one from the onset, was that in order to be a member of this spiritual group one had to surrender oneself completely, and "follow what happens from within." One had to be "free from thinking, free from passion, and from desire." At one of my first meetings the woman next to me (we were segregated from the men) would suddenly be so free she would jump up and down, clap, whoop, whistle, skip, and then begin laughing or crying. Early on, I had my doubts about joining this freedom-loving group that based itself on surrendering completely to a "cleansing" in order to "be completely at one with one's higher, deeper self." Although this was in the early sixties, I guess I still had one foot in the fifties and I, like my closest female friends, no matter how "liberated" we were, was still dominated by the pervasive male culture, and influenced by the current male we happened to be involved with at the time. It was not the way most young women felt but a few of us disdained convention, didn't want to be married right away, and wanted the freedom to operate at our own speed, unencumbered by marriage and the life prescribed by the conventions of the time. I knew I wanted to travel and see the world on my own, and not be tied down as a housewife. I had to find out who I was before that happened.

But I had fallen in love again. Oliver had given me an engagement ring and I was excited at the idea of becoming the wife of this free-thinking man and living in California. At the same time I knew I was acting impulsively in leaving my job at Revlon, my friends in New York and moving to California. We both thought it a good idea to at least live in the same state before we married, and I managed through my contacts in working for Revlon to get a job in L.A. with the May Company as their Director of Special Events, even before giving notice at Revlon.

Oliver and I talked about how it would be when I moved to L.A. "I really would like to have my own apartment," I declared.

"Of course, and we will each have our own space. That is important to me too. You must understand that you will always be second in my life. My sculpture will always take first place." I remember thinking that this might be a problem, but as long as there were no other women competing for his affection, I could live with being second fiddle to his sculpture.

I moved to California having completely understood that I was still going to have to support myself and that meant having a secure job and salary. I didn't mind that because I also was still somewhat interested in exploring the world of business as a new adventure.

The job of Special Events director meant opening new Los Angeles May Company stores complete with the releasing of homing pigeons, arranging fashion shows, book signing events for the book department, setting up demonstrations for the housewares department, and being on call for all other departments at the May Company to help improve their sales. I was learning a lot, overworked, and underpaid in a world I learned was not very interesting to me.

Meanwhile I was also learning that my fiancé and I really were on different wave lengths and that it was not going to be a marriage made in heaven. After about eight months we decided mutually that we were not a good fit, and I gave him back his ring. Another decision was made at the same time. I gave notice at the May Company and enrolled in the Italian department at UCLA for the Master's degree program. I would have a small salary as a Teaching Assistant in Italian and make extra money on the side working for Mattel where they paid me handsomely for various writing projects. Things were changing at a breathtaking speed. Sitting at my desk in the new apartment, looking out over the skyline of Los Angeles I smiled to myself thinking, I am still free, and this new California world is open to me with even newer opportunities for writing and learning in the exciting classes at UCLA.

Royce Hall where Mary had most of her graduate school classes in Italian and where she taught that language.

The catalog Henri worked on with his seminar students.

# XIX
# Los Angeles and UCLA as a Foreigner

AFTER ARRIVING IN LOS ANGELES and finding my rental car, I drove along the coast to the apartment I had rented, sight unseen, at the Barrington Plaza in Westwood near the University. I knew the drive would take longer than on the inland highways, but this way I could see the Pacific Ocean for the first time. I couldn't resist the temptation to park, take off my shoes and walk a bit on the beach. It was glorious! I could see the mountains behind me, hear the roaring of the ocean, and feel the shudders of delight as I remembered spreading my toes in the strip of golden sand along the beach at Agami, west of Alexandria, as a child. I was doing the same, here, in Santa Monica.

Why did I remember that city? I was never an Egyptian, even though I was born there. It was as foreign to me as Los Angeles. I knew I would never be a Californian even though I felt strangely at home in Los Angeles—more than I had ever felt any place else in America. I was a foreigner here, just as my parents and I were foreigners in Alexandria.

The good memories of my sometimes happy childhood came flooding back thanks to the smell of the salt air, and sight of the graceful wrap of the beach around the waterfront here in California, just like at the Alexandrian harbor. It all seemed familiar and a good omen.

The only thing missing was the Pharos lighthouse, that Seventh Wonder of the World. I couldn't help smiling at the thought of my being in this magical city so far away from Egypt yet so like the memory I have carried with me of my birth place. Particularly, the memory of my father giving me my first sip of beer from his glass when I was around 8, was so vivid I could once again taste the cool frothy malt that left a tingling sensation on my tongue. These were happy memories of my father, but I also remembered the growing distance between us, how he appeared less and less in my teenage life, and as I grew older how we grew apart, and we even came to distrust each other for years until we were reunited in New York.

Here on the Santa Monica beach, my whole body was comfortable and relaxed for the first time in many years, and I looked forward to my job at U.C.L.A. I breathed the warm fresh California beach air easily, and was grateful for it. My asthma attacks as a child brought both my parents closer to me, and when those attacks happened I would sleep in Father's room, and he in Mother's next to it. When my breathing got bad, they would both sit on the edge of my bed, waiting to make what could be a fateful decision: Father was ready to give me an injection of the only effective medication, Evatmine—a substance that could quell the attack in minutes just as it could kill, and as rapidly. They waited for things to get worse, so as to take the biggest chance when there was no alternative. They were full of love on those nights. When things looked bad, they would ask me to take another breath, a good strong one, as if it were a personal favor. Then they would glow with happiness when the drug had had its effect, and the air flowed freely. We would all kiss before going to sleep.

Arriving at the penthouse apartment in Westwood, the sunlight was so strong that I knew I would have to cover my collection of pastels, drawings, and watercolors with towels to protect them from the strong California sun streaming in through the many windows. The Redon, "Germination," my pride and joy, I particularly wanted to keep protected from the sunlight since it was a fragile black and white charcoal drawing. The face in the center of the sunflower is barely visible and the whole symbolizes fertility and new beginnings. It would have the place of honor in my new home and perhaps offer inspiration for another book that was already beginning to "germinate." I could not pass up the opportunity to buy this Redon when I saw it in New York only the previous year.

The expansive views of the Los Angeles skyline all the way to the Pacific from my wrap-around balcony certainly enhanced the setting, making it a perfect place for cocktail parties that I would be hosting for the museum. From the first time I walked into the apartment I could envision guests, drinks in hand, discussing art while the waves crashed behind them, and the sound of the ocean giving us a quiet soundtrack.


WALKING INTO THE SMALL ROOM for my first graduate seminar, I was surprised and thrilled to see those bright faces all of whom appeared eager to work. There were eight of them.

Odilon Redon, *Germination*, (c. 1890-96), Museum of Modern Art, N.Y., formerly in the Dorra collection.

*Te faruru (Here We Make Love)*, Paul Gauguin, 1893–94,
Museum of Modern Art, N.Y.

"This seminar will be about the important 19th century movements leading up to the birth of 20th century art. There will be an exhibition at the end of the year showing your work in this class that will be called 'Years of Ferment: The Birth of Twentieth Century Art,' and I would like each of you to help with the research." I spoke clearly, but with enthusiasm as I thought about the project. "There are eight of you and eight movements to be covered. Rather than assigning a particular section to each of you I would like you to choose one that is of particular interest to you."

I paused, then took from my battered leather briefcase a red Los Angeles Angels baseball cap filled with eight pieces of paper, each with the name of a period leading up to 20th century art. There were a few giggles when I held up the cap, but I didn't let this bother me, and continued on.

"I have written on separate slips of paper the eight different influential movements we will be studying and have put them in this hat which will be passed around. Please pick one." I hesitated a moment and looked around to see their reactions. Their expressions were mixed but all were smiling. I smiled back at them.

"This is going to be fun for you, I hope. If you don't like what you draw you can put it back in the hat and choose another. We'll let the ladies go first if you three gentlemen don't mind." The first four sitting next to me were the older women from the Los Angeles area who were working on advanced degrees: Mrs. Josef von Sternberg, Mrs. Pietro Castelnuovo-Tedesco, Mrs. Dolores Yonker and Mrs. Jack Sisk. They each picked a slip of paper from the hat and read aloud the subject they would be researching: Art Nouveau, Romantic Symbolism, Expressionism and Fauvism.

"Are you all pleased with your selection?" I asked.

There were nods of agreement and all answered enthusiastically almost in unison. Mrs. Castelnuovo-Tedesco was the first one to venture a comment. "This should be fun. I've always wanted to know more about Romantic Symbolism and have read Mallarme and some of the other French Symbolist writers, but don't know much about the Symbolist painters."

When Mrs. Von Sternberg raised her hand, she spoke in a soft hesitant voice. "I drew Expressionism. Other than Munch I don't know who is to be covered in this section."

I jumped in before any further objections from her. "I think Munch is important enough to be discussed in an entirely different section which we'll call 'Transition to Expressionism from Cubism'. But you should focus on the Viennese Gustav Klimt and the Swiss Ferdinand Hodler who are both worth studying."

"Will you really be able to borrow a Klee for the show?"

I was pleased she already knew a little about her subject and responded immediately, "Yes. In fact there are several I know I can borrow from the National Gallery in D.C. and from private collections. Some will be works on paper rather than oils but they will show your research of the movement nicely."

She seemed relieved. I knew these California students were used to their professors being relaxed in the classroom—often even smoking in seminars, so I tried moving towards them and sat on the edge of my desk for the next responders.

"Mrs. Sisk and Mrs. Yonkers, are you happy with your choices?"

"Fauvism is something I have always been fascinated by but didn't know it was such an important influence on 20th century art," Mrs. Yonkers volunteered. "That is what I chose and I'm very happy with that."

I turned to the last of the older students, Mrs. Sisk. "And you, Mrs. Sisk, What did you get?"

"I am equally happy with the influence of the Art Nouveau artists."

"Very well. We will begin with your research as that movement is the oldest and a very important one. Mr. Tarr, what did you draw from the hat? Are you pleased?"

He was one of the young male students in the Seminar who hadn't yet spoken much. He cleared his throat and then spoke in a disturbed voice. "I got the pre-Expressionism movement Cubism and am not too happy about that because I have done a lot of research on Expressionism and wanted to focus on that period. But you have let Mrs. Von Sternberg have it."

I saw that he was upset and quickly said that there was that other period to be researched for the text I would be adding called "Transition to Expressionism from Cubism," which would focus on Munch primarily. "Mr. Tarr, you know about the 'affair Munch,' I am sure. It was the beginning of a modern art movement in Germany."

"Maybe. Wasn't that when the leading artists' association, the *Berliner Kunstler Verein* organized the avant-garde show when Munch was invited to participate? There were such violent reactions that the show had to be closed only a week after its opening."

"Bravo, Mr. Tarr. And you know then that the closing produced even more violent reactions which culminated in the formation of a group eventually known as the *Berlin Secession*. You will see that this period of transition has a number of very exciting artists and I am sure you will enjoy working on them."

He nodded, seeming placated, so the remaining students continued to take one of the last papers out of the hat. The next one to choose was a rather shy young woman who had hardly spoken, Miss Martha Spiva. "Oh, it looks like I get 'Pont Aven and the Nabis' which I know nothing about."

"You will enjoy them and I'm sure you already know some of the artists associated with this period between 1886 and 1899. Bernard might be the best known, but there are also other great artists like Paul Serusier, a great admirer of Gauguin. Serusier took him to a nearby woods and literally dictated to the young painter as he sat down to paint: 'How do you see those trees? They are yellow. Well, put down yellow. And that shadow is rather blue. So render it with pure ultramarine. Those leaves red? Use vermillion.'"

We were all getting excited, and I stood up to walk while I spoke. I couldn't help interjecting: "Serusier took Gauguin's ideas back to Paris to show his avant-garde comrades at the *Academie Julian* where they were all studying, and a group was formed including Maurice Denis, Pierre Bonnard, Edouard Vuillard and Ker-Xavier Roussel. You must have heard of this group calling themselves the Nabis, after the Hebrew word for prophet and you'll enjoy working on them."

"Yes. Dr. Dorra, I think I will, and I love Serusier."

Miss Jeanne Teilhet, a stylish woman dressed in soft grey spoke up in a pleasantly accented French voice, "Well. There are only two of us left, Dr. Dorra. Are there two slips of paper in the hat?"

"Yes. Why don't you draw one of them, Mademoiselle?"

"I drew Cubism which of course means Picasso doesn't it? That is fine with me."

"And you will do a superb job, I know. I assume you are French, which will be very helpful because there are some wonderful articles in French on the subject of Cubism and Picasso in particular. And of course, there are the French poets Mallarme and Rimbaud whom you are no doubt familiar with and who so influenced the Cubist painters."

She nodded and smiled pleasantly.

"And I will be the last, said Mr. Barry Darret, with a very engaging grin on his face. He drew the last paper from the hat, reading "the Origins of Cubism 1907-1918." I suppose that means I will come before Miss Teilhet and her work on Picasso. Who exactly do you include in the originators of Cubism, Professor Dorra?"

"You must begin with the banquet given by Picasso in the early years, that is in 1908 honoring Henri (le Douanier) Rousseau. Those in attendance were the ones who contributed the most to the birth of Cubism, the most revolutionary and far-reaching artistic development of our century. The two most important were of course Pablo Picasso and Georges Braque. But you will find that Guillaume Apollinaire, an early chronicler of Cubism, along with the critic Andre Salmon and the poet Max Jacob, were also present and very influential. The inimitable Gertrude Stein came with others who collected works by Picasso and Matisse and you must include Maurice de Vlaminck who, although he is generally thought of as a member of the Fauves, is given credit for having discovered one of the major historic sources of Cubism, that is 'Negro art.' It will be up to you to research this important influence on the Cubist artists."

Miss Teilhet raised her hand and asked almost plaintively, "And am I to cover all of Picasso's periods or just his Cubist period?"

I returned to sit behind my desk and took a sip of water before answering her. "I think you will have to explain a little how Picasso went from his early phase of a rather loose, impressionist technique into the 'blue period' and the 'rose'. Hopefully I can borrow a really nice example of one of Picasso's rose period portraits from the Solomon Trust in Boston. But it's up to you and your research to tell Picasso's story and his influences on 20th century art."

The students were writing in their notebooks, jotting down every word I shared, and clearly already beginning to plan their own work. The sound of their pencils on the paper meant we were off to a good start.

I was making a list of the most important works I could get a hold of to make "Years of Ferment" a really important exhibition, and I knew my friends in New York, D.C, and Philadelphia would help me. Thinking of Philadelphia reminded me of the first time I met Charlotte and my mind drifted suddenly back to her. I had not thought of her at least for a day because of the excitement of my new job and the preparation of my classes that were so engrossing. I think I had already begun to heal.


LOS ANGELES was a bit like Palm Beach in that it was very social. As a new bachelor, I was immediately invited by members of the Arts Council and the Museum board to everything going on in LA: the art exhibitions at all the museums, openings of shows in the galleries, fundraising galas, dinners for visiting dignitaries and cocktail parties given by the local "in crowd." It was very festive, but tiring. My work day usually started early since I had to call the East Coast to begin assembling the works for the first exhibition, and I usually didn't get home until seven or eight when I would begin preparing the next day's lectures.

There were also meetings I had to attend with the ladies of the Arts Council. They had already begun preparing for the upcoming fundraiser, the Thieves Market, a grand affair to be held in the May Company parking lot. Apparently this board was terrific at gathering all sorts of treasures to be sold in different booths—everything from designer ballgowns to records, books, kitchen equipment, full sets of china, linens, silver and everything else. They were very good at evaluating each item and hoped to make a lot of money for the museum. As a foreigner, I had never been to anything like this and had to assume that they knew what they were doing. I was told it had been a very successful event for several years, and the *crème de la crème* of Beverly Hills always came to buy each other's donated items. These American ladies were most impressive, I soon learned.

Mary and Henri, early courtship in Los Angeles.

# XX

# New Beginnings in Los Angeles
# and Two Worlds Come Together

BEING BACK IN THE ACADEMIC WORLD, teaching Italian and speaking that beautiful language every day with my colleagues in the Italian Department at UCLA was the way I wanted to live. It was so comfortable and so much fun at the same time. I particularly enjoyed the Boccaccio seminar where we all laughed out loud at Boccaccio's off-color stories and the seriousness of our professor as he guided us through each seduction of young nuns and naïve damsels in distress. But it was the teaching of Italian grammar and the enthusiasm of my students that really made me happy.

Many of the students in my three beginning Italian classes had Italian last names like me. They were interested in learning to speak the language, and I told them the first thing they must do is to pronounce their names correctly. I said their names with a particular flair, and they smiled and imitated me. We were all having fun. "Your grade for this semester will be based on three things. *Prima di tutto*, we will have quizzes every week and those grades will be averaged and make up 1/3 of your final grade." When I said quizzes every week, I heard deep sighs but continued on explaining why I did that (not to torture them but to help!), "I do this so that you won't try to cram everything into the final week of the semester before the final exam. To learn a language you must repeat new words to keep expanding your vocabulary and use the new expressions every day. Then secondly, the attendance in class is another third. I don't want anyone skipping class because if you do you will soon get behind. We will be moving very quickly and if you miss even one class you will find it hard to catch up. This rule is for your own protection. The last third of your grade will be the final exam. If you flunk it you still have the other two thirds to help you pass the course."

"But *Signorina*, the other sections don't have to have weekly quizzes."

"I don't care what the others are doing. My goal is to have you all at least pass and to have fun doing it. And we will have fun, I smiled. *Capito?*"

There were some mumblings in the back of the room, and I addressed the husky football players who were speaking to each other, "Do you gentlemen have something you want to share with the rest of us?"

"*No Signorina.*"

"Well I have something to share with you," I smiled. The small phonograph that I had brought to class that morning was turned on and began to play the Italian version of "Downtown," the hit song of that year. As soon as they heard "*Ciao,*" the first line, they all started laughing, even the football players. "Downtown" had been changed in the Italian version to "*Ciao Ciao,*" and they loved it.

I had regular sessions every Monday at four for those who wanted extra coaching or those whom I suggested might want to come. The football players dragged slowly into the classroom at that hour every Monday afternoon where I fortified them with milk and cookies and the week's newest grammar.

Senior members of the department had prepared the exams and neither the students nor the various Teaching Assistants could see the finished product until they walked into the exam. A few days after that final exam, I was called into the office of the professor in charge of TAs. I was shocked when the professor asked me quite directly, and immediately after I was told to sit down: "Signorina Tonetti, I think it is impossible but did you and your students have access to the exam before it was taken last week?"

"Why no. We certainly didn't see the exam before it was handed to the students from the sealed envelope by you, Signora." My face was turning red because I knew what she was implying and yet I knew we were totally innocent.

"Your students did far better on the exam than any of the others and we in the department couldn't understand why their exams were almost perfect." I saw her hand shaking as she said this. She was, I think, as uncomfortable as I was.

"All I can say is that I worked hard with all of them. Particularly the ones who needed additional reviewing. We had quizzes every week so that I knew they were all caught up with the latest grammar and vocabulary. I wanted them all to pass so I added an additional review section on Monday afternoons and many of them took advantage of it." I stopped suddenly, realizing that my voice had become louder and more intense as I went on. "It paid off I think... And we did have fun." I saw that the professor had begun to relax a bit and that was a comfort.

"Well, I guess we have to accept that. Your added classes must have made the difference and you are to be congratulated."

"Thank you, *Signora.*" And I walked out of her office with very mixed emotions. They had thought we cheated the system which offended me.

And yet I was pleased to have exonerated myself and my students. I ran my fingers through my hair, smoothed my skirt and tried to look composed after undergoing an interview that was upsetting to the head of the TA's as well as to myself.

TEACHING AGAIN made me realize how much I had missed it. However, when Mattel contacted me asking if I would come down to El Segundo (wherever that was) for a possible new freelance job, I accepted more out of curiosity than anything else. The words of my friend Ursula at Corning Glass in New York came to me: "You don't have to accept the job but at least find out what is involved."

That first meeting at the Mattel office with Mr. Steve Lowrey, the head of product development was unlike anything I had ever been to. As he led me to a private office I noticed several small cubicles where other people about my age all were working hard at typewriters. I could see some of them staring at dolls propped up on their desks as we passed into a private office. "We all use first names here at Mattel. Please call me Steve." He offered me a chair, and after sitting behind a desk, he pulled out from a drawer a funny looking chimpanzee with a ridiculous smile on his face. In contrast to the smiling chimpanzee, Steve's face was serious as he thrust the doll at me saying, "We'd like you to create the personality of this doll by giving us 20 lines, 11 of which he will say when a string is pulled. This is like our other very successful new doll, 'Chatty Cathy.' Can you do it?"

I looked at the chimpanzee who was dressed in a red vest and sporting a bow tie looking for all the world like my idea of a successful politician. "Of course," I laughed. Immediately several lines popped into my head and I thought, "How hard can this be?" We worked out the details in the next half hour and I went back to my apartment with a new assignment I was excited about. Even though I had a paper to write on Petrarch for one of my Italian classes, I sat down at the typewriter as soon as I got home and looking at the chimp sitting next to the typewriter, I began to laugh and to write. He seemed to speak to me. "Let's go to the zoo and see the people." "When I grow up I want to be a politician." "Have you got a banana for me today? I'll share it with you." The lines came tumbling out. Before I knew it there were twenty statements. It was hard to shift back to my graduate school assignments on Petrarch and Dante after that, but I did.

The secretaries in the Italian department were very excited when Mattel would call looking for me and insisting they had to speak to me immediately. I was annoyed at the audacity that they would have the secretary interrupt my

Tatters, one of the Mattel dolls Mary created the personality for when her string was pulled.

class with the urgent message, "Mattel must speak to you right away."

"Please call them back and tell them I will speak to them when my class is finished."

The urgent message I found out was that they wanted me to come down to talk about a new assignment: Barbie was going to become an actress. And they needed to know what kind of literature they should put in the new theatre box. I gave them three ideas to choose from, which they did. The final choice meant that I was to write plays based on stories they all knew: Little Red Riding Hood, Cinderella, King Arthur (and Queen Guinevere) and Aladdin and the Wonderful Lamp. That assignment kept me busy the following summer when I was also teaching a summer school session of two beginning Italian classes. I looked at my messy desk at home and smiled at how ludicrous it was that I was writing about Petrarch and Dante and at the same time about Little Red Riding Hood and King Arthur.

MEANWHILE, I had met a very attractive man through Anna and Henry Seldis quite by chance. The Seldises had invited me to attend the Thieves Market, a benefit for the UCLA Art Museum where all kinds of high-end designer clothes were sold. I really didn't want to take the time to go when I had preparation to do for my classes the next day but it would have been rude not to accept. Unfortunately it wasn't until an hour after I had arrived at the site (the May Company parking lot) that I found my friends. A heated discussion in Italian ensued about where we were supposed to have met that night each giving a different location.

I was completely oblivious to anyone standing nearby when Anna suddenly turned to me and said, "You haven't met Dr. Henri Dorra here."

She smiled at me and then at him, "He is the director of the UCLA Art Museum."

I immediately turned to look at him for the first time, seeing a handsome man dressed in a well-tailored dark blue suit and soft brown eyes that struck me as rather sad. I noticed his dark wavy hair and his beautiful silk tie as our eyes met, and he gave me a warm smile to which I responded rather formally, "How do you do?"

We didn't shake hands as he did not offer me his. There was a long silence that was a bit awkward for me until regaining my composure I said, "Sorry we got carried away about not finding each other when we first arrived. And I am so sorry we were speaking in Italian. Do you know any Italian, and did you understand the conversation we were having?"

"*Perfettamente*," he responded with a big smile. Then almost without a pause he said, "I would like to improve my knowledge of Italian opera and I have been told there are some wonderful records that have been donated. Would you help me find them?"

This struck me as a lovely way to begin a relationship although a bit forward, and I didn't hesitate to respond. "Of course," I answered. Anna was nodding in approval as we walked forward. We spent the next hour together talking as we wandered from booth to booth, looking for Italian operas. After we had found a wonderful booth with practically every opera ever recorded, I looked at my watch and to my surprise it was eleven o'clock. I knew I had an eight o'clock class the next morning, so I turned to face this new friend, and said, "I'm sorry but I have to leave now because I have an early class tomorrow morning."

"Will you have dinner with me next Friday?" I noticed that a charming black curl had fallen on his forehead which he brushed back as he spoke.

"I'd love to," I smiled.

He took out his little black leather engagement book and wrote down my address. "Great. I'll pick you up at seven."

He was so poised, looking and behaving the way I imagined every European gentleman must look and behave, even though my experience with "European gentlemen" was somewhat limited. I was astonished at how easy it had been to talk to this absolute stranger whom I knew practically nothing about. He closed his little engagement book, shoving it into his jacket pocket while we both smiled at each other for no apparent reason. Then he accompanied me to my car. I was pleased I had had it washed that afternoon so that even though it was an old car it was a clean one and showed someone cared for it. *"A bientôt"* were his last words as I climbed into my little Chevy.

*"A vendredi!"* I responded.

ON OUR FIRST DATE, later that week, he took me to the Bistro, a very good restaurant in Beverly Hills that was the "in" place that year. I had never noticed cars particularly. They were, for me, just a means for getting from one place to another. But I saw his shiny little racing green Jaguar in my driveway, and I was stunned. As I settled into the luxurious leather seat and noticed the polished wooden dashboard I couldn't help remarking "How beautiful your car is!"

"Thank you," he beamed as if I were complimenting him instead of his car. "I take very good care of it, and I hope to take good care of a wife someday." His face was turned towards me and there was the beginning of a smile. Was he testing me?

Not knowing what to say, there was silence for the next few seconds which seemed interminable. I wondered if I should jump out of the car which had just started to move or just pretend I hadn't heard what he said. I chose the latter. It was the most forward thing any man had ever said on a first date, and I wasn't sure I liked it. I certainly had not thought of him in terms of marriage. How unconventional and odd of him, I thought, but said nothing. As the evening progressed and we were enjoying the exquisite filet of sole and Sancerre, I learned much more about the handsome new stranger with the beautiful voice and slightly English accent. I found the dark hair against an olive skin attractive and when he smiled the dimples became deeper in his cheeks.

"I wasn't embarrassed, just surprised. And a little panicked." I added, "because you were so direct in saying you would take good care of a wife someday. Frankly I have avoided thinking seriously about marriage since the ending of an engagement and a serious relationship was still quite fresh in my mind." I couldn't believe I was so honest in revealing that information to an almost stranger on our first date.

"I understand," he quickly interrupted. "I too have just ended a long relationship which was very painful. Apparently, I completely misunderstood her so it was quite a blow when she said it would be best if we didn't see each other again. I guess I'm not very good at judging people." The sad expression on his face didn't remain long. "But I know now it was a good thing that she ended our relationship and I feel free again," he smiled, looking straight into my eyes. I looked away knowing that I was blushing.

ON OUR SECOND DATE, Henri gave me a copy of *The American Muse*, his latest book that was a history of America through prose, poetry and paintings. "I wanted you to have this. Although I don't know you very well you do remind me of Mary Cassatt and particularly of what Henry James wrote about American women. You probably know this quote: 'Conscious of so few things in the world, these unprecedented creatures [American Women] were least of all conscious of deficiencies and dangers."

How could he have known that Henry James was my favorite writer? He was the first man to compare me to those fresh Jamesian heroines and I was enormously pleased. I blushed again, knowing that he was offering a supreme compliment.

He continued in the same vein: "Mary Cassatt always felt she had one foot in Europe. You too seem to have that characteristic and yet your other foot is firmly planted in America. Don't be insulted when you read that

Jamesian quote in my book about American women being 'unaware of life' and its dangers."

He smiled, adding, "I must say your positive attitude about life is infectious. It is also very American and so charming."

We were entering the restaurant, but I felt I had to respond to at least one of his remarks. "What you say is true about my having one foot in Europe. I even told my parents after a year in Vassar that I was a 'throwback' to my French grandfather and that I related to him more than to any of my other ancestors. When I first went to Europe I felt I had already been there. I was so at home. And after living three years in Italy I now realize how comfortable I was in that country even though I was a foreigner."

"I too have had that feeling of being a foreigner here in America. I do love living here and am trying to fit in. Perhaps you can help me become more American?"

I looked at him and saw he was serious. "Oh no. You mustn't try to do that. That is part of your charm—being as European as you are." Again, I felt my cheeks flushing, and felt more and more like the naive ingenue from the pages of Henry James.

When he walked me to the door and said goodnight, he said how much he had enjoyed the evening, and taking me in his arms he kissed me for the first time.

After that date, we saw each other every evening for the next two months before he left for Europe.

I wrote my mother about him in May of 1964:

> I have been with Henri Dorra almost every evening since he will be in Europe most of the summer. He is coming back in late July. Although he asked me to go to Europe with him, I thanked him and said I couldn't do that. However, he did give me a round trip ticket to New York and wants me to join him there after my exams for a few days before he goes to Europe and before I must begin working as head copywriter at Mattel. I don't know whether I shall use the ticket or not. I must say I am very tempted and think I shall probably go. I told him I couldn't accept such a present and he said, "Why not? It is just like going to the beach." It seems extravagant to me and New York is a little further away, and it costs a little more than to go to the beach. But I don't think in this day and age there really is too much difference if one has the money and the time.

I didn't go. However, my Mother was the only one I wrote to about my feelings for Henri. In one of those letters to her I wrote:

*Young Girl at a Window*, Mary Cassatt, 1883-1885, Corcoran Gallery of Art.

The most general appearance of the American (of those days) in Europe [was]that of being almost incredibly unaware of life—as the European order expressed life.... Conscious of so few things in the world, these unprecedented creatures [American women] were least of all conscious of deficiencies and dangers; so that, the grace of youth and innocence and freshness aiding, their negatives were converted and became in certain relations lively positives and values.

—HENRY JAMES, *Critical Prefaces, 1907*

I am very anxious to have you meet him, and I do hope you will be able to come out here the latter part of the summer when he will be back from his visit with his mother in Paris. He has become very important to me, and that feeling is different from anything I have known before. It is perhaps very good that he will be away for a couple of months. I can then get a new perspective when I see him again. Right now, he just seems more extraordinary than any man I have ever known: the best of all the men I have been serious about. We shall see.

I haven't really told you much about him and it is rather complicated—his background. He is 40 and an American citizen although he was born in Alexandria, Egypt of French parents. He speaks English with a beautiful English accent, as well as French and Italian. He was educated in France, England and America (Harvard) and has a degree in Engineering as well as a doctorate in Art History. He is a Sephardic Jew which is, in my opinion, very rare and marvelous. He is rather short and has thick wavy dark hair. As you know his mother lives alone in Paris since his father died some time ago when they lived together in Florida after having been separated during the war. It seems they have quite a lot of money but not too much. He has a good sense of humor and very good taste. Furthermore, he thinks I am the most important person in the world. He is in no way cruel or mean or self-centered which is something I've not encountered in many of the other men I have known. I don't want to jump to conclusions or rush into anything and am trying to be as levelheaded and rational as I can be. There may be fantasies connected to him the way I've always had with everyone else I have had feelings for, but I don't think so. This is one of the differences I feel, and it is important.

When Henri returned from Europe at the end of the month, I met him at the airport and right there in the parking lot he brought out from his briefcase a beautiful garnet necklace. "I saw this in an antique shop in London and I bought it immediately because it reminded me of you."

"Oh, I can't accept this. It's too much." I stumbled.

"Well, I'll just have to keep it until you will accept it. I bought it for you." He looked hurt.

"In that case," I gently took the box from his hands, "I guess I should accept and wear the necklace tonight. I have never had anything so beautiful."

He took me in his arms, and we were both beaming with delight. It was a sudden realization knowing that I really loved this man. I knew with certainty that my future with him would be what I had always dreamed of having and that I would never be bored in his company.

The more he told me about his life, the more I loved and admired him for overcoming so many difficulties. He was so open with me about where he had come from, the way they lived in Alexandria which was so foreign to me and yet so exotic and appealing. I loved his stories about his mother and his grandmother who had had such an influence on him as he was growing up. Listening to him was like reading a novel with the ups and downs of his life both before, during, and after the war. He had been truly engaged in a world scenario while I, on the other hand, living the sheltered life in Texas and enjoying the carefree life of Martha's Vineyard summers, had been protected from the horrors and degradations of World War II that affected so many.

We saw each other every day after that last meeting, and he proposed to me two months later. Elaborate plans for a wedding at the waterfall at Snedens were made to include friends from all over the country. Sitting next to each other in the living room of his apartment we looked out at the sparkling lights of the Los Angeles skyline, and he explained almost breathlessly, "You are what I love most about my new country and I am so glad I found you. The openness, and yes the naiveté, combined with your inquisitive mind, love of adventure, and your remarkably positive outlook are all so American, and that is what you thoroughly are, and I am not." He took my hand and held it before finishing his sentence. "But I believe that even our differences will make a wonderful future for us. As we continue to discover even more about each other our lives will be a remarkable adventure for both of us." He chuckled before continuing, "You see I am even becoming more positive and American due to your influence. It's a big step for a 40-year old bachelor, but I am anxious to begin this most important adventure with you."

I squeezed his arm and responded, "I too am finally ready to go on this adventure because it will be with you. I used to think that marriage would be a closing of possibilities for new adventures, a relinquishing of freedom as I thought of it, and a closing of the book, so to speak. But now that I know you, I know that our marriage will be the opening of a wonderful new life full of new adventures as I had always dreamed of. You have lived such a full life beginning in exotic Alexandria, then growing up with a wonderful French education in Paris, and finally experiencing the full thrust of the War in England, and I, on the other hand, was only on the periphery of all that and safe in Texas before I began to experience the big world around me. Living and working in Latin American and Italy helped me grow up and become the person I am today—a little better equipped to be your wife and share with you those new adventures instead of living them alone. I never thought I would say that, but it is true. I am ready to join you."

Henri and Mary on their honeymoon en route to Capri, 1965.

# EPILOGUE

Henri Dorra and Mary Tonetti were married on June 26, 1965, at the pergola her grandparents built on the shores of the Hudson River. It was a "*Fete Champetre*" bringing together some of their friends from the previous decades from all four continents. The couple spent their wedding night at the Stanhope Hotel in New York City in anticipation of an early departure for their honeymoon beginning in Paris, driving through southern France, Italy and ending in Capri. They stopped again in Paris before returning to the U.S. where they both began teaching their classes at the University of California in Santa Barbara.

Before arriving at 1 avenue Hoche to meet her mother-in-law for the first time Mary was warned by her husband: "If she's not nice to you we will leave immediately." This sounded ominous to Mary but when the beautiful glass door on the ground floor of the classic *hotel particulier* apartment was opened by a petite, smiling Aimée Dorra, it was the beginning of a beautiful, loving relationship. Her first words were, "Welcome, my dear, I am so relieved. You never know what they will bring home at his age!" Shortly after, they sat in the antique-filled living room with three beautiful Persian carpets stacked on top of one another in each room where Aimée declared in her best Sargeant major tone that they must come back to Paris often, and that the apartment with everything in it was now theirs. Furthermore, she herself was moving at the end of the week to Lausanne, Switzerland where she could live more easily without traffic and noise, and where her emphysema would be more easily tolerated. Mary was left *bouche bée* by this fairy tale announcement of the apartment gift which they continued to enjoy for the next thirty years.

It was in 1969, four years after the marriage that their first baby, Amy Lawrence Dorra was born. For Mary, it was the happiest moment of her life while it took one whole year until Henri would ask, "How did you know it

253

would be such a joy to have this baby in our lives?" Amy joined her parents for the annual trip to Paris where Henri continued his research on the next book published in 1973, a highly respected art history textbook, *Art in Perspective* that continues to this day to be compared favorably to Janson's *History of Art*.

When Helen Hyde Dorra was born in 1972 that did not stop the burgeoning Dorra family from returning to Paris for a year, or a partial year, for the next thirty years. Henri received a Guggenheim fellowship to work on symbolist art theories in Paris where both Henri and Mary continued their research and writing as well as the enjoyment of family and friends and "the good life" in Paris. Ultimately *Symbolist Art Theories* was published in 1994, a summation of Henri's findings on the links between symbolist artistic and literary aesthetics.

The Dorra girls came to love the French people and the French way of life as much as their parents did. (They had no choice!) One of Henri's characteristic remarks on the subject of French food should be recorded. When Mary was organizing a conference in Santa Barbara: "Ethnic Influences on American Cuisine," one of her many events for the American Institute of Wine and Food, Henri told her quite seriously, "I think I know what ethnic food is. It's everything that isn't French." Later their friend Julia Child with whom Mary cooked for many years, laughed when she heard this, "Henri is sooo French."

Shortly after the Dorras met the Childs at a luncheon given in their honor Julia said, "We decided that if people like the Dorras lived in Santa Barbara we would be happy to live here too." The Dorras and Childs dined together at least once a week in Santa Barbara, and they continued to laugh, cook, and share their mutual love of life when in Cambridge or at the Childs' home in the south of France. This relationship continued until the deaths of Paul, Henri, and finally Julia.

Everyone grew up or at least got older as the years flew by. Henri continued to teach at UCSB and he published until his retirement. Some of his students thought he was the best teacher they had ever had even though he was also known to be the most demanding. After Amy and Helen left for their universities (Brown and the University of California at Berkeley, respectively) both Mary and Henri continued to write and publish. Through her connections as the chairman of the Santa Barbara chapter of the American Institute of Wine and Food, Mary began to write travel stories for *Gourmet Magazine* and contributed to the *New York Times* and other publications (*Travel and Leisure*, *Elle Décor*, the *Los Angeles Times* among others) articles on famous gardens, food and fashion. At one point in the nineteen eighties Henri told her, "People will take you a lot more seriously if you write a book instead of all these articles." That remark was the impetus for her first book, *Beautiful American Vegetable Gardens* published by Clarkson Potter, a subsidiary of Random House. When it was finished and in the publisher's hands Mary was exhausted with the writing of last-minute captions and the great relief and satisfaction of having a book published. It was at night when Mary was about to go to sleep that Henri said, "Well, I'm not letting you sleep until you tell me the title of the next book." She was exhausted but knew he was serious and without missing a beat she responded, "Beautiful American Rose Gardens." He then answered, "That's good. You must write it. Now go to sleep." That book sold over 5,000 copies in the first six months.

Fortunately, Henri's magnum opus, *The Symbolism of Paul Gauguin Erotica, Exotica, and the Great Dilemmas of Man,* was finished before he died in 2002, and his words of encouragement resonated often with his wife, pushing Mary on to write two more books, one of which is this one.

Photo courtesy of Baron Spafford

# BIO

MARY TONETTI DORRA (Mrs. Henri Dorra), who has lived in Santa Barbara for over 40 years, grew up in Fort Worth, Texas, graduated from the Hockaday School in Dallas and from Vassar College in 1956. She lived in Italy for three years where she studied at the University of Florence and then worked as a research-reporter in the Rome bureau of Time-Life. Upon returning to this country she attended graduate school at UCLA, obtaining a master's degree in Italian. She taught Italian at UCLA, then at the University of California, Santa Barbara in 1965 and, before her return to writing, devoted herself to husband, children and garden in Santa Barbara and to community service. The Dorras lived part time in Paris since their marriage in 1965.

Since 1980 Mary has lectured extensively throughout the United States. She has written travel articles for *Gourmet Magazine* and the *New York Times* as well as garden articles for *HG, House Beautiful, Elle Décor*, the *Los Angeles Times Magazine* and *Travel and Leisure*.

An article "Colonial Kitchen Gardens: A National Legacy" appearing in the April 1993 issue of *Gourmet Magazine* was the genesis for her first book, *Beautiful American Vegetable Gardens*. Her second book, *Beautiful American Rose Gardens*, also published by Clarkson Potter is now in its third printing.

KIRKUS reviewed her third book, *Demeter's Choice a Portrait of my Grandmother as a Young Artist*: "An aspiring female sculptor pursues art lessons at home and abroad, carves a place in history and finds love along the way in this well-written historical novel...an elegant tale of a female trailblazer whose remarkable story deserves a wide audience."

Mary remains active in Santa Barbara life, writing and serving on the Granada Performing Arts, Opera Santa Barbara, and Camerata Pacifica boards.

# ACKNOWLEDGMENTS

I AM VERY GRATEFUL to my friends and fellow authors, Anitra Sheen and Lily King, who offered invaluable advice and encouragement along the way. And to those in the Solvang Writers' Group—Cynthia Appel, Rebecca August, Judith Chumlea-Cohan, Janie Gustafson, Kim Hernandez, David Holden, Lenore Hughes, Hector Javkin, the late Barbra Minar, Sandy Nathan, Karen Newsom, Tina Stambaugh, Trudy Way, and Sharon Whatley—who often steered me away from pitfalls. And special thanks to friends Dr. Ray Launier and his wife Nicole who listened to chapters read aloud and to Dr. Larry Feinberg who fact checked some of the art history and offered valuable comments. Kandy Luria Budgor was also of invaluable help along the way.

This book would not have seen the light of day without my editor, Robert Krut to whom I am extremely grateful.

Karen Sketch did more for me than design this book. She supported and steered the book to its final pages.

A number of people helped with the research: in Florida, Katie Edwards, former Director of Communications at the Society of the Four Arts in Palm Beach, Debbie Walk, former archivist at the Ringling Museum of Art in Sarasota and in Washington, D.C. Leah Richardson, former Public Services and Instruction Librarian Special Collections Research Center George Washington University Libraries which holds all archives of the Corcoran Gallery, Evan N. Miller, Archivist at Indianapolis Museum of Art at Newfields, Indianapolis, Indiana, and Dean M. Rogers, Special Collections Assistant Vassar College Library.

My daughter Dr. Helen Dorra and Anitra Sheen deserve special recognition as careful line editors of this book.

CPSIA information can be obtained
at www.ICGtesting.com
Printed in the USA
FSHW012045251021
85738FS